July 26, 1986

To the Potters —

Enjoy! Enjoy! As
I have in creating it!

Love,
Jim

The Scottish Highland Games in America

The Scottish Highland Games in America

Emily Ann Donaldson

PELICAN PUBLISHING COMPANY
GRETNA 1986

Library of Congress Cataloging-in-Publication Data

Donaldson, Emily Ann.
  The Scottish Highland Games in America.

  Includes index.
  1. Highland games—United States—History.
2. Highland games—United States—Directories. I. Title.
GV722.5.H54D66 1986   .793'.025'73   85–28479
ISBN 0–88289–474–9

Photographs by Ginny Vroblesky except where indicated
Artwork by Stewart Duval

Manufactured in the United States of America
Published by Pelican Publishing Company, Inc.
1101 Monroe Street, Gretna, Louisiana 70053

To John and Nellie
who made me Scottish
and gave me John

To Jeff and Maude
who made me Southern
and gave me Emily

And, mostly, to John and Emily,
my loving parents

Contents

Acknowledgments

By rights, this should be a chapter unto itself. I knew *very* little about the Games when I started my research to write a book on the subject. Perhaps that's just as well; I may have forsaken the idea if I knew then what I know now! How well I remember those Jacksonville (Florida) Games in 1980. A friend "told on me," saying that I was writing a book on the Games. To my dismay, I was taken from tent to tent and the news was revealed. I expected questions pertaining to my authority to write such a work. Instead, I was given encouragement, praise, and offers of support. By the end of that day my mind was set on accomplishing this goal.

How far I've come! I began at the Jacksonville Games something that I have enjoyed thoroughly and that has proved to be of tremendous value in getting a "feel" for the Games: mingling with the crowds and striking up casual conversations with my fellow onlookers. During the heavy events competition that day, I began talking with a likely looking prospect—a brawny, redheaded young man—and asked him why he came to the Games. He replied with aplomb, "Because I'm a Sassenach!" Not wishing to appear any the less, I let the subject go. I eventually learned that he was (innocently, I trust) calling himself by a term used by Scots when speaking with contempt of an Englishman! I hope I have at least learned to speak the language.

Because I knew so little, I had to depend on the expertise and the generosity of those who knew their subjects best. I have spent hours on end with some of these kind folks. At times I must have frustrated some of them, but they were as patient as I was persistent. People have opened their homes to me, done interviews by tape, telephone, and in person, written long and flowing epistles—all unbegrudgingly. They have helped unfold the story of our Games. They have had a part not only in the making of the history of the Games, but in the recording of it.

With so many folks contributing so much, my greatest fear is that I will unwittingly overlook someone who has helped. I hope not; all have been important. To all the individuals and Games who have completed questionnaires and answered my letter and telephone inquiries, thank you! There are too many of you to list separately, but you know who you are.

I must, however, specify some folks who have gone the extra mile and have helped me an extra measure.

Chapter 1—David Webster gave me a quick affirmative when I asked him to write an opening chapter for this book. He also supplied the photographs for this chapter. He has been in the Games world for many years and his inclusion here helps to cement the efforts of our countries.

Chapter 2—Dr. Gerald Redmond (more on him later), Don Bond, Dr. Renny McLeod, Herbert MacLeod, Professor Rowland Berthoff, the St. Andrew's Society of Philadelphia, and Hugh Morton (photographs). Donald Francis MacDonald has literally given me a blow-by-blow account of the founding of the Grandfather Mountain Games. To him I owe a debt of gratitude.

Chapter 3—Ed McComas (more on him later, too), Fred Vaughan, Gordon Varnedoe, and Pete Hoyt.

Chapter 4—Roddy MacDonald, Maclean Macleod, John Bosworth, Jim Ling, Calvin and Chris Biggar, Bill Merriman, Sandy Jones, the late Duncan McCaskill, Sr., Malcolm MacCrimmon, and Tom Wiethers.

Chapter 5—Christie Freestone, Marguerite Reid, Janet MacLachlan, Cathy Hynd, Hugh Bigney, Vera Miller Patterson (photograph), and Ann Langston (photograph).

Chapter 6—John Turner and Paul Brockman.

Chapter 7—Dr. Gib McLaughlin and John Shropshire.

Chapter 8—To all who have answered queries and added me to your mailing lists, multitudinous thanks.

Thanks for permission to quote from Dr. Redmond's books go to Associated University Presses of Cranbury, New Jersey, and from Francis Collinson's book to Routledge & Kegan Paul Ltd., London.

If it had not been for the Baltimore St. Andrew's Society and the particular help of Art Hamilton and Al Schudel, I never would have gone to the Santa Rosa Games. Through a grant from that group, my photographer and I were able to go to California so I could do research on and attend our oldest Games. Thanks to them for believing in me from the beginning. Thanks to Leonard C. "Chuck" Bearman, who "discovered" me at the 1980 Tidewater Games and encouraged me to come to the board meetings of the Virginia Scottish Games so I could see what goes on behind the scenes. What a help that was! Thanks to my sister-in-law, Faith Donaldson, for her hard work on the Games map in chapter 8. Stewart Duval designed the dedication page and other artwork you see throughout this book. Thanks, friend. Kit Wienert, who knew nothing about the Games except what I constantly babbled to him, read and critiqued much of my manuscript before I submitted it to Pelican Publishing Company the first time. Thanks for your wisdom and your forbearance. Polly Theriot, my editor, also knew nothing about the Games before she worked on this book. Her understanding of the subject and—more fondly—me is remarkable. Thanks to her wisdom and care, this book is cleaner, more precise, and much more readable—and those are difficult words for an author.

Gerry Redmond has supplied not only a wealth of information, but friendship and moral support. My kindred spirit, he loved and wrote about the Games before I even knew about them. Thanks to his meticulous work on the early U.S. history of the Games, my work in that area had a solid foundation from which to start. My dear friend Jo Lagatutta is one of the few other people I know who will, like myself, push herself beyond reasonable limits to get a job done. She typed most of this manuscript twice! Her husband Jim helped run the house and their two daughters so that she could type into the wee hours of the morning. Many a night I sat by her side, proofreading as she typed. I don't know many folks who will overextend themselves for you, but Jo will and I'm glad she's my friend. My friend Ginny Vroblesky traveled to nearly all of the Games with me, taking photographs for this book. Let me assure you that it takes creative effort after a while to see the same event from a different angle (said appropriately). She laughed with me, cried with me—she knows me inside and out. She is more than a friend/photographer; she is a sister. Last, but foremost, this book would never have even been thought of had it not been for Ed McComas. He subtly mentioned it, subtly loaned me his Scottish books on the Games, and subtly got me interested, then hooked. He has been an objective source of much information, a sounding board, and true friend, as have been his wife, Anne, and their sons. I feel honored that they have included me as part of their family. I thank them all for putting up with hours of Scottish Games talk and for sharing the joys and heartaches I've dumped on them for the past five years. To Ed goes my fondest thank you.

The Scottish Highland Games in America

Part 1
HISTORY OF THE
SCOTTISH HIGHLAND GAMES

Introduction to Part 1

When most Americans today hear the word "games," they immediately think of the Olympic Games, or at least some type of mammoth sporting event. But more and more Americans are learning about and becoming fans of the Scottish Highland Games, a unique festivity encompassing much more than sports: it encompasses a tradition.

Although the roots of the Scottish Highland Games are over 900 years old, the Games as we know them today represent a continuing tradition of over 200 years. Not bad, considering that Scotland is a small country whose sons and daughters are scattered in British-settled areas across the globe. In that scattering, they took with them a love of their country and their heritage that, for many, could not be destroyed. This love was passed on to succeeding generations and, though it may then have been diffused, it remained strong—strong enough that in the 1980s it still stirs those whose hearts are in the Highlands, whether they have actually been there or not.

The tradition that we Scots enjoy today was not blithely passed from one generation to another. It was fought for, wept for, subjected to all manner of adversity for—but never relinquished. The result is evidenced in the components of the Games today. There is a boldness and a preciseness and an aura of perfection seldom exhibited in other ethnic displays. And there exudes a sense of pride and joy from all participants, competitors and non-competitors alike, also seldom experienced by other groups. These feelings are there because the Scots believe in what they represent; the legacy was attained too dearly to do otherwise.

The Scots work hard at having fun. None of the events competed at the Games allow walk-on participation. Contestants study hard and spend long hours of practice time preparing to compete at the Games. Tradition demands it. The dances, the athletic events, the pipe tunes, even the patterns and colors of the kilts tell the story of Scotland's sons and daughters. When you witness these events, you are witnessing a representation of a way of life.

Today the Scottish Highland Games are thriving in Scotland, Canada, and the United States, as well as a few other locations. The Games of each of the "big three" countries have their own style, and each individual Games has its own flavor. The Scottish experience is different everywhere; if it were not, we would not feel the thrill of exalting native Scots dignitaries at our Games or the wonder of attending a gathering in the mother country as we do. But there is a common bond that unites us all. I once heard it described very well: the phenomenon that draws us together at the sound of the pipes, the tossing of the caber, or the dancing over the swords occurs because these are experiences that "shake up our genes."

The attraction of the Games predates the *Roots* phenomenon— the interest in family history that awakened in the U.S. in the late 1970s—as they have been going strong for many years. It is true, though, that the recent surge of interest in genealogy has made more and more people realize that their Scottish heritage is a rich and romantic one. But this book is not a study of the sociological foundation of the Games. Rather, it is intended to show that the Games are here to stay. They have survived despite governmental prohibitions, wars, depressions, and simple lack of interest.

There are over 80 Scottish Highland Games in the United States today, varying in degree and range from small events attracting local people to grand-scale international happenings drawing over 30,000 spectators and competitors.

I attended twenty-five different Scottish Highland Games in

the United States in preparation for writing this book. This was important to my research, since the Games do reflect their varying geographical areas. However, I found that the people of the Games are alike in that they share a deep love of their Scottish heritage and give generously of their time and talents to perpetuate this colorful and exciting tradition.

This book is not mine; it is ours. It belongs to all of us who share a love of the history and traditions of Scotland. Indeed, I have had the joy of studying the background of the Games in depth, which has resulted in my feeling a deeper sense of appreciation and pride as I witness and partake of the Games. And I now feel more akin to people competing in 100-degree temperatures in 100-percent-wool kilts; proud parents and teachers escorting young dancers around the country to watch the Highland fling for the umpteenth time; businessmen who are also professional Scottish Games athletes and spend their weekends throwing heavy implements for six or seven hours, often without even a short midday break; and massed bands of more than 100 pipers and drummers covering a field and sending a chill up the spine and a tear down the cheek.

I hope you will feel it, too.

1

The Games in Scotland

DAVID WEBSTER

"If we dwell too much on the past, we neglect the present; if we ignore the past, we rob the future."

I don't know if those are the exact words the old crone said as we huddled around the peat fire when I was a boy, but I think I have grasped the essence of her homespun philosophy.

We live in an age of transition, but it has always been thus; perhaps Adam said the same thing to Eve. However, one thing is very different today: the speed of change has accelerated at a previously unknown rate. In those boyhood days when I went to the forest to gather wood for the fire and sat around the hearth at night listening to tales of old Scotia, I could never have imagined that one day I would travel not only to the great Highland gatherings, but all over the world to gatherings attended by royalty, heads of state, and other civic dignitaries in such places as the Orient, Africa, and the far-off Antipodes in the company of Scotland's greatest Games stars.

David Webster of Irvine, Scotland, is an internationally known authority on and promoter of the Scottish Highland Games. He organized the World Heavy Events Championships and has also organized and served as commentator for Games in Scotland, the United States, Canada, Sweden, Japan, and Australia. He has written hundreds of articles and more than twenty books pertaining to sports and history and has lectured extensively on the subject in Europe. Professionally, he is a regional director of leisure, recreation, and tourism for the Scottish government.

9

It was during my early years in the northeast of Scotland, where the Games are interwoven into the social fabric of rural life, that the gatherings took their strongest roots. Looking back, although many things have changed dramatically, the great traditions and practices of Scottish Highland Games have largely been kept intact. The activities have spread far from the mountains and glens, but they have kept the character and charisma that have thrilled countless Scots over the centuries.

In outlining the development of the Games, I have used an anecdotal, not an academic, approach for the early period, since it is now almost impossible to separate fact from fiction. By doing so, I may unwittingly confound scholars looking for material that can be indisputably authenticated. I cannot give such assurance for early material, but I can honestly say that I have spent a lifetime searching for information from a very wide range of sources and have gone to great lengths to find original material and check facts whenever possible. In addition, I have, along with some of the giants of the Games, helped to shape the more recent history, and I have tried to be meticulous in recording incidents, facts, and figures.

HISTORICAL ROOTS

So where did it all begin? Even the most demanding of historical purists will admit that Scottish gatherings are hundreds of years old. The laws enacted after the 1745 Rebellion (see text of the Act of Proscription) were specifically aimed at stamping out Scottish traditions in dress and recreation that could be linked, however remotely, with the arts of war. There can be no doubt that manly physical sports were an ideal preparation for the close combat of earlier times, as opposed to the push-button warfare of today. Even the bagpipe was considered a weapon of war; the inspiring effect of the pipes in the battles of the western front in World War I supports the validity of this view.

There are early glimpses of Highland Games and gatherings. We cannot accept the often fanciful stories of Games in Druid times as wholly accurate, but they seem to be based on documented Druid celebrations: fertility rites, religious festivals, and harvest thanksgivings. The Ceres Games in Fife, Scotland, claim to be the oldest continuous Games, dating from 1314. They were first held to celebrate the safe return of 600 of the district's bowmen from the Battle of Bannockburn, in which Robert the Bruce gained independence for Scotland by defeating Edward II's army. The Ceres Games have been held ever since, except during the periods of the Act of Proscription (1746–1782) and the two world wars.

Although Ceres boasts the longest continuous connection with Highland Games, the prestigious Braemar Gathering claims to have older roots, dating back to King Malcolm III of Scotland, who came to the throne in 1057 and was killed in 1093. The influence of Malcolm Canmore is seen in every aspect of the Scottish Highland Games. The spectacular sword dance in the dancing competitions is said to have originated at Dunsinane in 1054 when, according to legend, Malcolm slew one of MacBeth's chieftains, crossed his own sword over that of the vanquished, and danced in exultation over them. The pipe tune for this dance, the "Gillie Chalium," was composed to mock the tax gatherers of Malcolm (Calum aChinn Mor—"Malcolm of the Big Head," literally translated from the Gaelic).

According to the ancient *Legends of the Braes of Mar,* Malcolm also figures strongly in the athletic events of Scottish Games. He is purported to have inaugurated a hill race to the summit of Craig Choinnich, the purpose being to select a gille-ruith (running footman or messenger). Competitive selection of this kind was another reason, or excuse, for track events as well as the strength-testing heavy events so beloved by Scots.

We find mentions of Highland gatherings in various forms throughout the centuries. For example, when Lord William Harwood came to Scotland as the envoy of Henry VIII (1491–1547), a Games program was arranged in honor of the visit. There are good descriptions of Highland dances in the sixteenth century and evidence of the unrelenting fight of the Kirk (the Church of Scotland) to put an end to such activities. Two centuries later Bonnie Prince Charlie enjoyed watching his men compete in athletics between battles, and it was his Rebellion of 1745 that led to the Act of Proscription and the banning of all things Scottish in character. Along with the understandable

LISTEN MEN

THIS is bringing before all the *Sons of the Gael*, that the King and Parliament of Britain have for ever abolished the Act against the Highland Dress; which came down to the Clans from the beginning of the world to the year 1746. This must bring great joy to every Highland Heart. You are no longer bound down to the unmanly dress of the *Lowlander.* This is declaring to every Man, young and old, simple and gentle, that they may after this put on and wear the Truis, the Little Kilt, the Coat, and the Striped Hose, as also the Belted Plaid, without fear of the Law of the Realm or the spite of enemies.

Act of Proscription, 1746

THAT from and after the first day of August 1747, no man or boy within that part of Great Britain called Scotland, other than such as shall be employed as officers and soldiers in his Majesty's forces, shall, on any pretence whatsoever, wear or put on the clothes commonly called Highland clothes—that is to say, the plaid, philabeg, or little kilt, trowse, shoulder belt, or any part whatsoever of what peculiarly belongs to the Highland garb; and that no tartan or party-coloured plaid or stuff shall be used for great coats or for upper coats; and if any such persons shall presume, after the said first day of August, to wear or put on the aforesaid garments, or any part of them, every such person so offending, being convicted thereof by the oath of one or more credible witnesses, before any Court of Justiciary, or any one or more Justices of the Peace for the Shire or Stewartry, or Judge Ordinary of the place where such offence shall be committed, shall suffer imprisonment, without bail, during the space of six months, and no longer; and, being convicted for a second offence before a Court of Justiciary or at the Circuits, shall be liable to be transported to any of his Majesty's plantations beyond the seas—there to remain for the space of seven years.

Repeal Proclamation of 1782

ban on weapons, this edict prohibited the wearing of the kilt, the playing of the pipes, and the gathering of persons. This drastically affected many Scottish activities, and it is a wonder that any traditions survived.

It was not until the last two decades of the eighteenth century that Highland societies managed to reverse the trends (see text of the Repeal Proclamation of 1782), but by that time some facets of Scottish culture were lost forever. Society gatherings such as the earliest one at Falkirk in 1781 first encouraged "social intercourse," but Scottish music, dance, and Highland dress were gradually introduced in a low-key fashion, perhaps to combat any accusations of or reprisals for nationalism. Almost unnoticed, groups of people in the Highlands again began organizing gatherings. The Braemar Wrights' Society held a procession in 1800, then added a dance, and gradually developed the full-scale gatherings that are held today. A Society at St. Fillans was well to the fore in 1819 with ambitious Highland Games in present-day form. Almost surreptitiously, a Highland Games structure or circuit came into being, although at that time the proceedings were essentially local in character. At about the same time this was happening, Scots were going to America, Canada, New Zealand, and Australia and doing the same things there to retain and develop their culture.

In 1847 the *Philip Laing* sailed from Greenock, Scotland, to Otago, New Zealand, with 247 colonists aboard. The passengers passed the time dancing jigs and reels and listening to the music of their beloved bagpipes; the men exercised themselves by wrestling. When the Otago settlement was a year old, these proud Scots celebrated the anniversary by organizing a Highland Games. In 1863 they formed the Dunedin Caledonian Society, which produced an outstanding crop of champions in wrestling, running, and field events within ten years. Caber tossing, track events, and Highland dancing also featured prominently in the programs. Many of these activities were taught in Otago by J. E. Lowe, son of the Balmoral dancing master who taught Queen Victoria's family when they made their annual visits to Scotland.

Scottish Highland Games came to the United States in 1836 when the Highland Society of New York held its first "Sportive

Meeting" in the Elysian Fields in Hoboken, N.J., the stated aim being "to renew the Sports of our Native Land." Canada's first Highland Games were held in Antigonish, Nova Scotia, in 1861, and many more Games sprang up in that area later. The abundance of gatherings in these places reflected what was happening on a greater scale in Scotland.

There were two major factors which greatly assisted in giving Highland Games their rightful place in the life of their home country. The first was the visit of King George IV to Edinburgh in 1822, ably stage-managed by Sir Walter Scott, who even prevailed upon the king to wear full Highland dress, thus setting the seal on an open revival of Scottish culture. The second and even more influential factor was Queen Victoria's affection for the Dee Valley. When Victoria came to Scotland, she showed great interest in all that went on in the district where she built Balmoral Castle. The Braemar Gathering did not escape her notice, and soon she was regularly attending the Games, taking huge parties of her friends to enjoy the sport and encouraging her retainers to participate. My mother's great-uncle was a ghillie (gamekeeper) on the estate, and I used to revel in the stories that the old man told of Queen Victoria. Charles Duncan, a keeper at Balmoral, was one of the great prizewinners of this time and was written into the queen's journals. Her Majesty also donated prizes for various events. On one occasion, a proud forester named Charles MacHardy received a sword and dirk from the queen's own hands. This was the sort of incentive she gave at a personal level, which reinforced her official influence. The "Royal" prefix was bestowed on the Braemar Highland Society by invitation of the queen. This was no frivolous compliment but the beginning of a personal link with the British monarchy that has lasted throughout every reign since.

The scene was now set for widespread development of the gatherings. Soon every little village had its own Games. With improved communication methods, competitors became aware of the contests and began traveling around the country to compete. As is inevitable among highly competitive and often aggressive contestants, major competitions and championships developed.

In the period from the beginning of Queen Victoria's active

interest in Highland gatherings in 1848 until the decline caused by World War I, the Games circuit grew at incredible speed. There were literally hundreds of gatherings in Scotland each year. Every weekend presented a choice of several events, and all seemed to flourish. After the war there was very little change in the Games scene; indeed, the crowds became larger and larger. Many gatherings, even those that laid no claim to being major events, attracted 20,000 to 30,000 spectators.

In the early post-World War II years, it is estimated that there were still around 200 Games. But things had changed forever. In Aberdeenshire, for example, where there were once eight Games within almost a ten-mile radius, only the largest gatherings survived. Fortunately, the decline was halted, and a full and excellent calendar of events combined with fine support from the general public (an estimated half-million spectators each season) now make the Games one of Scotland's leading spectator attractions.

Today most enthusiasts travel to the Games by bus or car—very different from what happened in years past. In those first upsurging years, families who could not walk to the Games would go by pony and trap; farmers would hitch up their largest carts and their strongest Clydesdales and load up their families, workers, and friends. When bicycles became a popular mode of transport, there were often thousands of bicycles at a major gathering. Some of the athletes bicycled from Games to Games; many would travel nearly 100 miles a day to subject themselves to the grueling competition.

The expansion and popularity of railways played an important part in developing Highland gatherings by giving Scottish city dwellers an opportunity to have a cheap day out enjoying pleasant entertainment in congenial surroundings. This increased mobility also allowed the better competitors to participate in more distant Games. Local champions would travel long distances to match their skills with those of their counterparts in other places. The cash prizes given for the major events were high compared to the poor wages paid in farming communities in those days, so some of the best contestants made their Games activities their main source of income. The age of professionals had arrived.

ENTER THE SUPERSTARS

In 1875 a Canadian newspaper published a rather petulant letter decrying the fact that professional athletes were traveling from one Games to another, winning everything and keeping local amateurs off the prize lists. The Games committees themselves encouraged professionals, recognizing that spectators wanted to see the best-known performers and that record-breaking efforts were much enjoyed by the crowds. Taking this philosophy to the ultimate conclusion, committees made tempting offers to the leading Scottish athletes. Accepting with alacrity was the greatest of them all, Donald Dinnie, the world's first sports superstar.

Born in Balnacraig, Aberdeenshire, in 1837, Dinnie turned professional at the age of 16 and in his remarkable 57-year career won more than 11,000 sporting contests. This incredible total included (in round figures) 2,000 contests in wrestling, 1,800 in jumping, 2,000 in hammer throwing, 1,800 in putting the stone, 1,500 in tossing the caber, 300 in weight throwing, 500 in running and hurdling, and 200 in weightlifting. These victories were supplemented by a great many in pole vaulting, Highland dancing, shooting, and even elocution. If a competition offered a cash prize, Dinnie would train for it and probably win. His earnings were phenomenal by the standards of that era. To quote figures on his winnings would be pretty meaningless in these days of rampant inflation, but suffice it to say that in one day he could earn the equivalent of three years' wages for an average worker of the time. It would have taken an ordinary farm worker 400 years to earn as much as Dinnie did during his lifetime. When Dinnie was not competing at gatherings, he gave exhibitions and issued or accepted challenges of the sporting elite of the area he happened to be in at the time. And the legend still lives. Recently a small collection of Dinnie's medals was sold to the Aberdeen Museum for over $12,000.

Donald Dinnie's admirers fondly believed that his achievements as a heavy events athlete could never be beaten, but even before the great old man died, some of his records were surpassed by A. A. Cameron of Dochanassie, Invernesshire. Cameron stood 6′ 1″ and weighed 238 pounds of solid muscle—incredible in an age when many people were familiar with malnutrition and poverty. Cameron eclipsed many of Dinnie's greatest feats and might have achieved even greater heights had not World War I erupted.

Great champions arose in the piping and dancing events as well. Just as in the heavy events, there emerged in each discipline colorful characters who endowed the Games with a charisma unsurpassed in any other sphere. Where in the world could you find a tradition of hereditary pipers like the famous MacCrimmons of Skye? For hundreds of years the MacCrimmons were the hereditary pipers to the Chief of Clan MacLeod (and, indeed, they still are; see the chapter on piping) and ran a piping college at Boreraig on that island off the west coast of Scotland. The college was said to have been established by Iain Ohar (Sallow John), who was well known prior to the 1600s. That seat of learning flourished until the 1800s, except during the time of the Act of Proscription, when playing the pipes was a punishable offense.

The piping tales that have been passed down through the centuries are a legacy almost as rich as the legacy of piping music itself. For example, the MacCrimmons' skills and techniques were closely guarded secrets, and legend has it that when one of the MacCrimmon women taught her sweetheart, who was not of the MacCrimmon clan, the fingering of a tune, the family cut off her fingers on discovering her actions so that she could not do such a thing again and others would not follow suit. According to another story, an officer and 60 of MacLeod's men, including Donald Ban MacCrimmon, were captured at Inverurie in December 1745. The Jacobite pipers of the opposition, greatly respecting the past master of piping, refused to play until MacCrimmon was released.

The MacCrimmons gave the world Ceol Mor or piobaireachd, the great music of the pipes, as well as salutes, laments, and the like. Their own compositions show not only significant events in the history of the clan but also minor incidents of importance to the pipers. For example, "A' Bhiodag Bhoidheach" ("The Bonny Dirk") is attributed to Patrick Og, perhaps the most famous of the MacCrimmons, who was offered a much-admired dirk (long dagger) if he would compose a tune extolling the qualities of the weapon.

The dancers, too, had their folk heroes: the MacLennans, the Cuthbertsons, Johnny Pirie, and much more recently, James L. MacKenzie and Bobby Watson. In the first Games, competitive dancing was a male domain. Women tended to heed the words of ministers throughout Scotland who said dancing was sinful. Also, the old laws that had forbidden the wearing of the kilt everywhere except in Highland regiments gave Scottish soldiers, who practiced the spirited Highland dances as a form of exercise, a little more latitude than civilians to practice this nationalistic tradition. Therefore, the men had a significant advantage when Highland dancing was again recognized as a worthwhile activity deserving of encouragement and promotion. Women gradually gained a footing (pun intended) on the Games platform and soon eclipsed the males in open competition, which in turn led to a decrease in the number of male competitors. Some gatherings took positive action and followed the lead of the Aboyne Highland Games, which reinstated the graceful feminine dances for women and kept the more vigorous, warlike dances for men. Others such as the Braemar Gathering, probably the last bastion of dancing chauvinism, held out strongly until the mid-1970s.

Clearly there was parallel development in piping, Highland dancing, and heavy athletics, and the competitive structure that evolved led to higher standards than could ever have been envisaged a hundred years earlier. Because of the intense rivalry, the frequency of competitions, and the wide geographic spread of the circuit, Scottish music, dance, and sport were developed to a greater, more sophisticated degree than their ethnic counterparts in other countries. This is particularly interesting in view of the almost rural background of the events. Yet when we witness the zeal of the Scots in becoming administrators, inventors, and international leaders in railways, politics, and banking, it is not surprising that they would demonstrate the same enthusiasm in recreational and artistic endeavors.

It is almost impossible to compare the respective merits of modern-day Highland dancers and pipers with those of the past.

The massed band salute their sovereign as they pass the royal pavilion at the Braemar Gathering. Prince Charles returned with Princess Diana to this same spot in their first public appearance as husband and wife a few years after this photo was taken. (Courtesy of British Tourist Authority)

Donald Dinnie, Scotland's first sports superstar. (Courtesy of David Webster)

The piper's hollow at Braemar, a quiet nook placed away from the main arena where most of the 30,000 spectators gather to watch the other events—and the royal family. (Courtesy of David Webster)

Young aspirants at a Gaelic Mod with two of Scotland's most renowned musicians: James L. MacKenzie, left, and Seumas MacNeill. (Courtesy of David Webster)

Some modern heavy events athletes at the 1981 World Heavy Events Championships in Lagos, Nigeria: from left, Fred Vaughan, U.S.; Geoff Capes, England; and Grant Anderson, Bill Anderson, and Hamish Davidson, Scotland. (Courtesy of David Webster)

We must, therefore, look to the heavy events, where measurements are available, to get some idea of the rise in standards. In order to assess the great champion "heavies" (heavy events competitors), we can look at the accomplishments of four Herculean athletes who were dominant in their own eras during the last hundred years: Donald Dinnie (1837–1916), champion from 1856–69 and 1871–76, a span of 20 years; A. A. Cameron (1877–1951), champion from 1903–14, a span of 11 years; George Clark (born about 1908), co-champion with Ed Anderson from 1929–40, also 11 years; and Bill Anderson (born 1937), champion from 1959–62 and in 1964, 1967, 1970, 1972, and 1973, a fine career of nearly 25 years.

In the 1840s Alistair MacHardy held the 16-pound hammer record of 88′ 10″. Dinnie threw the light hammer 107′ 10″ at Aboyne in 1867. By 1904 Cameron had pushed the record up over 117′, and in 1969 Bill Anderson set the still-unbroken world record when he threw the light hammer 151′ 2″. Dinnie's 1867 record in the 16-pound stone was 45′ 7″, compared with a 1980s-era winning put, which is over 60′. In tossing the 56-pound weight for height, there are at least four men who could beat any throwers of ten or more years ago. The biggest and heaviest cabers have been turned by Anderson, Clark, Cameron, and Dinnie, in that order. This is based on the measurements of known cabers at long-established Games. The cabers now regularly used at most Games are much more impressive than those of long ago. At the end of 1984 it was announced that a new caber was being sought to replace the mammoth one (19′ 9″ long and 132 pounds) that had been in use at the Braemar Gathering for 30 years. Although only a few of the "heavies" have turned this caber, the Games' organizers wanted to present a more difficult challenge in this event.

THE GAMES TODAY:
BRITAIN'S FINEST

It cannot be disputed that the modern "heavies" are better than any of the past, including those who were invincible in their heyday. Grant Anderson, Geoff Capes, Hamish Davidson, and Doug Edmunds, to name a few Britons active in international

Games at this writing, could totally outclass the giants of the past. It would, therefore, be unfair not to mention briefly some of these contemporary stalwarts.

Grant Anderson of Dundee is 6'1" and weighs about 290 pounds. A town planner, Anderson (no relation to nine-time champion Bill) is one of the growing number of brawny and brainy athletes with good educational backgrounds and respectable professions. While competing as an amateur, he won a bronze medal for weightlifting at the 1970 Commonwealth Games. Anderson has proved to be a strong contender—in more ways than one—since he began competing at the professional level. He won the first World Heavy Events Championships in Pomona, California, in 1980 and has also been named overall champion for 1981–84 at the Games held in Santa Rosa, California, which is the main American event attracting international competitors. He has been the world record holder in tossing the 56-pound weight for height (his personal best being 16' 7" at Oban in 1981) and is the current world record holder in the heavy hammer (123' 8½", set at the 1983 Santa Rosa Games).

At the end of 1980, thousands of miles from Scotland, an imposing figure in international sports quietly made his debut in professional Highland Games. There, on the coast of Africa, Geoff Capes (dubbed Geoff Dubh Laidir—"Black Strong Geoff") left the amateur ranks after a career that included the British, European, and Commonwealth shot-put championships. Capes is a stellar attraction on the Games circuit because of his achievements as an amateur athlete. His Highland Games accomplishments match his others: he set the world record in the 56-pound weight toss (16' 9½") in 1981 and two years later won the World Heavy Events Championships in Carmunnock, Scotland. The former policeman from Spalding, Lincolnshire, has twice won the "Britain's Strongest Man" competition and has placed second in the "World's Strongest Man" competition behind American powerlifter Bill Kazmaier, who has also competed in Scottish Highland Games. At almost 6' 6" in height and weighing sometimes as much as 330 pounds, Capes is by far the largest competitor at the Games.

The first man to beat Geoff Capes on the pro circuit was

Hamish Davidson, a 29-year-old mink farmer from Cawdor, near Nairn. Davidson, also a disillusioned amateur shot-put champion, was the first Scot to break Bill Anderson's stranglehold on the heavy events title. Turning professional in 1978 after being left off the Commonwealth Games team, he quickly made his mark, breaking 38 ground records in putting the stone and winning the Tamnavulin Trophy (awarded to the best all-around heavy events athlete on the basis of points accumulated at stipulated Games) in 1979. As an amateur, he had won 17 Scottish titles in athletics and powerlifting, and after turning pro, he won the Scottish and British Highland Games heavyweight titles. He holds the world records in the 56-pound weight throw (43' 7") and the 28-pound weight throw (88' 10½"). Nicknamed "Mr. Five-by-Five," he stands 5' 9" and weighs nearly 300 pounds.

Douglas Edmunds was first brought to my attention by Scotland's national athletics coach, Tony Chapman, who told me of a young schoolboy from Glasgow at St. Joseph's College who handled enormous weights in training. I introduced Edmunds to the Scottish Amateur Weight-lifters Association and watched with delight as he won the Scottish Junior Championships in his very first weightlifting competition. He eventually became an outstanding caber tosser, winning the World Caber Tossing Championships from 1976 to 1978 and being the only competitor to toss the Braemar challenge caber in 1979. Edmunds has hundreds of prizes and awards to his credit in a number of sports, but his travels and employment in Africa have curtailed his athletic career. However, he has continued to compete and even organize major events; the Games in Lagos, Nigeria, were a result of his endeavors, and the splendid organization of this Games testifies to his abilities.

To complete this brief review of the current "heavies," mention must be made of Bill Anderson of Bucksburn, Aberdeenshire, the king of them all. Anderson is already in the legendary class along with Donald Dinnie, as he has been a top athlete for a quarter of a century. Like Dinnie, Anderson has gone to the farthest corners of the earth, competing with great success on every continent and crowning an illustrious career by winning the heavy events world championship in Melbourne, Australia, in 1981. Anderson came on the scene when Jay Scott of Inchmurrin, Loch Lomond, was champion. In one eventful season, Anderson laid claim to the crown and never looked back. Long-standing records from the days of Dinnie and Cameron have fallen before him like skittles. This stalwart athlete's abilities seem almost limitless: in 1983, at the age of 47, he competed in 41 Scottish Highland Games. His record of achievements may never be surpassed.

These, then, are some of the interesting participants in Scottish Highland Games who make the results more open than ever before. Whereas in the past the results were fairly predictable, it is now anybody's guess who will come out on top each season— which is always good.

THE GAMES IN THE 1980s

The Games today are in a healthy state, despite the fact that there are not as many in Scotland as there were 80 to 100 years ago. There is comparative stability and a good blend of the old, established gatherings like those at Aboyne, Braemar, and Ceres. Some Games have waxed and waned depending on their current leadership, weather, and many other factors that affect the narrow division between success and failure. There are other lesser-known but captivating and charming gatherings with their own special appeal. The splendid Lonach Games and the lovely west coast and island Games are good examples of those providing variety and contrast to the summer scene.

Sponsorship has become a major factor, especially for important competitions. I could not arrange the World Heavy Events Championships without the support of commercial companies. The status of these championships is now higher than any previous Games competitions. During the world championships held in Melbourne, Australia, in 1981, athletes and officials received VIP treatment from a number of notables, among them Australia's prime minister and minister of sport. Such treatment on the other side of the world shows the prestige that Scottish Highland Games have now achieved internationally. Back at home in Britain, Princess Diana's first public appearance after her wedding to Prince Charles in 1981 was at the Braemar

Gathering, further evidence of the strong link between the royal family and the Games that has existed since the young Queen Victoria first visited Deeside.

The Highland Games arena of the 1980s is a vibrant and ever-changing scene. Although old champions retire and new ones come along, although the emphasis and topical interests may change, the philosophies and traditions remain as they always were. I think that if Malcolm Canmore saw the Games today, he would not want to fall on his sword. I also believe that Donald Dinnie would prefer to judge the "heavies" rather than match his muscles against theirs.

2

The Games
in the United States

Scottish Highland Games are flourishing in the United States. Over 80 such gatherings are held each year. But this is the second time around, so to speak. For 20 to 30 years after the Civil War, the Games in this country were at their summit, their number being as many as 125. Many of the Games were also larger in scope than today's Games. Several cities that once boasted large Scottish gatherings now have none; on the other hand, Games today suddenly appear and take hold in seemingly unlikely places.

In Scotland the Games originated as, and for the most part remain, local affairs. Both native and international competitors and spectators still abound there, which is to be expected in the Games' motherland. In North America, Scots at first gathered to seek out and share their Games heritage, but these activities, with their opportunities for display of and reward for brawn, soon attracted non-Scots as well. In Scotland and Canada, the Games have experienced a fairly unbroken reign. In the United States, however, their history would take the shape of an hourglass with a slim bottom.

A few of today's Games in the U.S. may be considered old-timers, though by Scottish and Canadian comparisons they are youngsters. Our one claim to fame as far as authenticity and longevity are concerned is the Games of the Caledonian Club of San Francisco, celebrating their 121st consecutive year in

1986.* The Games in Round Hill, Connecticut, and Costa Mesa, California, have been around for over 50 years. Central New York holds its 47th Games in 1986. Others in existence for more than 20 years include those at Everett and Spokane, Washington; Portland, Oregon; Grandfather Mountain, North Carolina; and Ligonier, Pennsylvania. But what happened to those that were prospering at the end of the nineteenth century? And just how secure is the footing of the Games today?

THE BEGINNING:
SCOTTISH SOCIETIES

With the few exceptions pointed out by David Webster in the first chapter, Scottish Highland Games in Scotland began a period of rapid development in the 1820s; the momentum began in Canada and the U.S. about 40 years later. There were—and are—Games in other countries to which Scots have migrated, but the story of the United States' Games cannot be told without referring to those in Scotland, which were their source, and Canada, with whom they still share the Games tradition.

The first Scottish organizations formed in the United States were economic—beneficent groups aimed at helping indigent fellow Scots. The oldest charitable society of any sort in this country was the Scots' Charitable Society, founded in Boston in 1657. The first of those societies named for St. Andrew, the patron saint of Scotland, appeared in Charleston, South Carolina, in 1729. This group, open to any male at least 18 years old and of good moral character, called itself the St. Andrew's Club, since most of the original members were native Scots.

According to the *Register of Scottish Societies in the United States and the Dominion of Canada,* issued by the Philadelphia St. Andrew's Society in 1903, the St. Andrew's societies, except the one in

---

*Detroit, Michigan, advertised its 137th annual Games in 1986. According to Professor Rowland Berthoff of Washington University in St. Louis, Missouri, the *Scottish-American Journal* carried notices of the first Games in Detroit on July 25, 1867, and the second Games in San Francisco on November 28, 1867. Eventually the Games were dated from the founding of the sponsoring society. The Detroit St. Andrew's Society was founded in 1849 and is still active.

Charleston, were restricted to men of Scottish birth or descent. They had a threefold purpose: "To relieve indigent and unfortunate Scotchmen or their families; to foster and encourage a love of Scotland, its history, literature and customs, and, for a number, is added *encouragement of the national athletic games* [italics mine]; and to promote friendly and social relation of members."

One may study the dates and locales of these early St. Andrew's societies in the *Register* and see reflected there the periods of immigration and expansion of Scots on this continent. On the East Coast, societies were organized in 1729 in Charleston; in 1749 in Philadelphia; in 1750 in Savannah, Georgia; in 1756 in New York City; in 1803 in Albany and Schenectady, New York; and in 1806 in Baltimore. Then came a gap of nearly 35 years. In 1840 Buffalo, New York, reported a St. Andrew's Society. From then until the end of the century these societies appeared across the country as the West developed—Chicago; Cleveland; Detroit; Milwaukee; San Francisco; Saginaw, Michigan; St. Paul, Minnesota; Portland, Oregon; Oakland, California; and Tacoma, Washington, in that order. In 1894 Newark, New Jersey, brought the trend back to the East Coast.

In a similar fashion, St. Andrew's societies in Canada first appeared in 1798 in St. John, New Brunswick. In 1825 they began a steady spread westward from Fredericton, New Brunswick, to Ontario, Quebec, British Columbia, and, by 1897, Indian Head, Northwest Territory.

Organizations with social or cultural emphases for the most part followed the lead of societies formed primarily for the mutual benefit of fellow countrymen. Notable early in this movement were the North British Society or Scots Club of Halifax, Nova Scotia (formed in 1768); the Scots' Thistle Society of Philadelphia (1796); the Caledonian Society in Lexington, Kentucky (1798); and the Burns Club of New York City (1847).

In Scotland, even before the official repeal of the 1746 Act of Proscription (see chapter 1), steps were being taken to assure that the elements of Scottish culture that had been repressed by the act would be revived. In 1781 the first Highland Society Gathering at Falkirk took place and gave birth to Games similar to those we know today. In 1819, the same year that the St.

Fillans Society of Scotland held its first Games (including the sword dance as a competition for the first time), a Highland society was organized in Glengarry, Ontario, Canada, to promote the Scottish sports by means of a Highland gathering. Though short-lived, this society was probably the first in North America to sponsor a rudimentary Games.

After the middle of the nineteenth century, Scottish societies in North America with a social or cultural purpose began to flourish, perhaps given impetus by the royal patronage and favor bestowed upon the Braemar Gathering in 1848. There were Scottish clubs, Burns clubs, Thistle clubs, Gaelic clubs, clubs for members from specific areas of Scotland—all organized to cater to the mutual specialized interests of Scots and their descendants.

Caledonian societies and clubs also emerged. According to the previously cited *Register*, the general purpose of these groups was "to unite more closely Scottish people and their descendants in this country. To advance their interests by friendly methods and in frequent social meeting. The cultivation of a taste for Scottish music, history, and poetry, and the *encouragement of Scottish games, costumes and customs*" [italics mine].

Though emigration from Scotland to the United States continued into the twentieth century (and indeed continues today), Scottish-Americans had become well established here by the mid-1800s and had been woven into the fabric of America. But they were still Scots, and many felt the need to band together to share and revel in their common heritage. For Scots everywhere, the Games eventually became an embodiment of their endemic spirit.

"TO RENEW THE SPORTS OF OUR NATIVE LAND"

Perhaps the initial attempt at a Scottish gathering in the United States was the "first Sportive Meeting" held by the Highland Society of New York in 1836. Its expressed purpose was to "renew the Sports of our Native Land." Though its sports program was unlike that ordinarily associated with Highland Games, it did include dancing to the accompaniment of bagpipes and a parade of the costumed chief and clansmen to the site—trimmings of ceremony so prevalent in later Games. This event represents an early culling of nostalgic pride among Scots far from home. This Society seems to have lasted only until 1841.

By this time Highland Games were well established throughout most of Scotland. In Canada, the oldest continuous Games are those sponsored by the Antigonish Highland Society, founded in 1861. Its first Games were held on nearby Apple Tree Island two years later. Before confederation in 1867, Scottish Highland Games had spread across the whole of Canada.

Before the Civil War there were four Caledonian Games instituted in the United States—in Boston, New York City, Philadelphia, and Newark, New Jersey. (Curiously, areas in the Southeast such as North Carolina that attracted large Scottish communities did not champion the Games until more than 100 years later.) These first Games were similar in that athletics—which included dancing, as it was considered an athletic event and performed only by men for many years—played the major role in the program. The athletic events were the ones that we still see today, as well as those now considered track and field events and various novelty events. The number of events was considerably larger, ranging from twelve to twenty-five, as opposed to our more common five to eight.

From the beginning, prize money or extravagant prizes or both were the mode. At many Games there was a prize for the best-dressed Highlander. (Ladies, of course, never wore the kilt, which is a male garment; when one did appear in this garment at the Boston Games in 1913, the men were shocked.) Also from the beginning, the clubs realized that an admission fee could serve as an important, and often the sole, source of income for these popular events.

BOSTON

The Boston Caledonia Club was founded in 1853 and held its first Games that same year. Before the club's official founding, groups had been getting together annually for several years to participate in the sporting activities of Scotland. The Boston Scottish Club advertised its tenth annual Games in the August 11, 1866, issue of the *Scottish-American Journal*. After the Boston Caledonia Club merged with the Boston Scottish Club in 1868 to form the Boston Caledonian Club, the September 5, 1868, issue of the *Journal* included a report of the twelfth annual Games of the new organization—signifying that the club was using the date of the first Boston Scottish Club Games, 1857, as the beginning of its series.

The Boston Caledonian Club was incorporated in 1869. Article I of the club's constitution set forth the objectives of the club (among which was the "encouragement and practice of the athletic games of Scotland") and called for at least two annual celebrations: one on the Friday nearest January 25 to commemorate poet Robert Burns's birthday and another "on such day as the Club may determine, to be devoted to the athletic sports of Scotland." Also specified in the constitution was a Games committee, seven men elected annually to work with the club chief and chieftains in arranging the Games. These arrangements were to conform to the spirit expressed in the preamble of the constitution:

> Whereas, physical culture is considered by all in our day to be an essential element in the education of young men, in order to qualify them for the more important duties of active life; and believing that no physical exercise conduces more to a perfect physical development than the Scottish national games; and knowing, also, that the practice of those games fosters and keeps alive the associations, social customs, and the memory of the land of our or our fathers' birth; therefore, we, the members of the Caledonian Club of Boston, for our better physical and mental improvement, do hereby agree to the following Constitution, By-Laws, and Rules of Order.

The Boston Caledonian Club sponsored Games for more than a century; the last one was held in September of 1956 at Brookline Town Field. The 1870s and 1880s were the heyday of the Boston Games, attracting crowds of almost 20,000. According to the present chief of the club, Herbert A. MacLeod, the club experienced its "days of glory" from 1905 to 1922 with about 500 members. The Games still drew reputable crowds of 10,000–20,000 during this period.

Today the Boston Caledonian Club is still in existence, though its membership is down to nine stalwart sons of Scotland. Its Games legacy is only a proud memory, but the other celebration delineated in the club constitution continues to thrive. The

Robert Burns Celebration (the 132nd annual event was held in 1986) has restricted its attendance of late to 400.

NEW YORK

The New York Caledonian Club was formed in 1856 and began its 77-year Games streak in 1857. This club became one of the largest and most successful in the country. In the thirtieth program of the Games (1886), a brief history was recorded:

> Like most of the national organizations in New York, the Caledonian Club had a very small beginning, although the want of some such social, charitable and public-spirited society had long been felt among the Scottish residents of this city. A meeting of a few Scots was held on November 28th, 1856, for the purpose of considering the advisability of forming an organization, and it was determined to go on, creeping ahead "cannily and warily," as the old national maxim expresses it. The first regular business meeting was held on December 29th in the same year, when officers were elected. The progress made was, for a time, decidedly slow, although three and sometimes four members were admitted at each meeting. From the first it was agreed that a field-day should be held, at which the old-fashioned games, practised from time immemorial on every haugh in the Lowlands and every hillside in the North, should be the feature. The project was taken up with much enthusiasm. Stones, hammers, etc., were secured, as were also two dozen "shinties." The first games were held in October, 1857, at the St. George's Cricket Grounds, Hoboken. The Athletes were genuine amateurs—their records were hardly worth being kept—but the pleasure experienced by both spectators and competitors was boundless. Many of the old members still reflect on the day's episodes with evident delight, tempered, however, by the reflection that such a large proportion of those who were then active, willing participators in the fun have since passed away to the silent land. On every side the games were voted a success; they brought the Club prominently before the Scottish residents of this city, and in a measure established the organization in the community. No charge was made for admission, and the entire expenses of the day's proceedings amounted to $38.35—not enough at the present time to pay the prizes in a single competition. By the end of the same year its membership roll included fifty names in good standing, and the success of the Club was fully assured, although we question if those pioneer members had any idea, even then, of the importance the Club was afterwards to assume in the list of the national societies of this city.

A 25-cent entry fee was charged at the second Games. These and all following events were advertised, an action which helped assure their success. The events at this second Games were throwing the light and heavy hammers, putting the light and heavy stones, caber toss, blindfolded wheelbarrow race, sack race, standing high jump, running long jump, running high leap, short race, and sword dance. Within five or six years this list expanded to 20 and eventually more than 25 events.

The New York Caledonian Club established a format that was more or less adhered to for many years and eventually adopted by other Games. Club pipers would lead costumed members and their guests, usually officers of other Caledonian clubs in the United States and Canada, from club premises to their cars (or horse cars). Upon arrival with much pomp at the Games site, all would join in a "Scotch" reel, after which the Games would commence. During a midday intermission, the members and guests would adjourn for luncheon and speech-making, and the Games would resume in the afternoon. The festivities ended with dancing for all at the close of the day.

Since this club was highly esteemed and its position was considered preeminent, a closer look at its activities will clarify both its nature and that of its era. The following fragmented sketch is drawn from reports in various issues of *The New York Times* from 1864 to 1933.

In 1864 there were 25,000 attendees and 20 events on the New York club's program. In 1866 the club leased permanent quarters, since its membership roll had so substantially increased; the Games that year drew a crowd of 20,000. Donald Dinnie and James Fleming, the champions from Scotland, competed in the 1872 Games, which helped draw 25,000 spectators. Four years later, at the 20th Games, it was advertised that some of the best-known athletes in the United States would appear.

Attendance was down to 5,000 in 1878, due in part to a railway strike in New York City. By the next year, the club had outgrown its leased building and purchased land to build its own clubhouse at 8 and 10 Horatio Street. In 1880 12,000 people watched a program of 24 events. The September 2 *New York Times* carried a nostalgic notation on the Games' participants:

The young men who had big lumps of muscle on their arms when the New York Caledonian Club began its yearly display of brawny Scotch lads are glad nowadays to get a soft-cushioned seat in a shady spot, and let their grandchildren play about their feet, for that was 24 years ago—near enough to a quarter of a century to make old Father Time's head swim. And in this quarter of a century, although new lads have come to take the places of the old, not a bit of the old Scotch brawn and muscle has been wasted. The young club members of today, some of them fresh from the banks of the Tay and the Dee, others having their knowledge of the land of great tradition only by inheritance, are in no way behind their ancestors in throwing the hammer, running, jumping, or any of the other athletic sports that amused young and old Scotsmen a century ago, and still amuse to this day.

On the 25th anniversary of the New York Games in 1881, the gathering attracted more than 20,000 spectators. Four years later attendance was down to about half that number, with the number of competitors down, too. The prizes awarded were fairly evenly shared among Caledonian Club members from New York, Boston, and Canada. Attendance was up a bit to 15,000 at the 30th Games in 1886; a tug-of-war was added to the program. In 1887 the crew of the Scottish ship *Thistle* was among the 7,000 spectators. In 1888 the club announced that it was completely out of debt and owned property valued at $50,000.

The 37th Games in 1893 attracted 10,000 people. Some of the events were open to sister societies (Boston, Brooklyn, and Ontario members were listed as prize winners), some only to members of the New York club, and some to all. In 1894, 3,000 attended the Games, and nearly double that number gathered for the dance at the end of the day.

By 1923 the program consisted solely of track and field events, with no traditional Scottish events included. In 1925 open Amateur Athletic Union (AAU) events were held in conjunction with the Scottish Games; again, no Scottish events were included. At the 75th Games in 1931, a member of the New York Athletic Club won the one-mile race. All events were track and field, with much acclaim given to the winner of the senior 15-mile Metropolitan Association AAU championship run. At the last Games in 1933, there were 1,000 attendees; 3,000 people attended the dance in the evening. One of the major events of the day was the pipe band contest, which was won by the Lovat Pipe Band of Manhattan. The band was awarded a prize of $75.

From these gleanings one can clearly see the gradual decline of the New York Caledonian Club's Games. The club's decision to emphasize general track and field events at the expense of traditional Scottish events did extend the life of the Games for a while, though in the end it was not enough. Before its demise, this tenacious club sponsored 77 Games, an admirable record. (The New York Caledonian Club was revived in 1981. Its headquarters is not far from the old headquarters: 30 Horatio Street. It has a new logo and a new enthusiasm. Perhaps one day we shall again see notices of Games of the New York Caledonian Club.)

The two other pre-Civil War Games were those of the Philadelphia Caledonian Society, founded in 1858, and the Newark Caledonian Club, founded in 1861.

POST-CIVIL WAR GROWTH: SAN FRANCISCO

On November 24, 1866, seventeen men met to organize a Scottish club in San Francisco, thereby kicking off the post-Civil War expansion of Scottish Highland Games. Their primary intent was to establish a club for the propagation and practice of the athletics of their native land, as elucidated in the preamble to their bylaws:

> Being well assured that man is so constituted as to require occasional seasons of relaxation and amusement; believing also, that athletic exercises, duly regulated, are conducive to the healthful invigoration of both mind and body; and being, moreover, desirous of assisting toward the establishment and maintenance of friendly relations among those who are of Scottish blood or extraction; and keeping alive in them an interest in Scottish manners and usages, we do form ourselves into a Club, bearing the designation of The Caledonian Club of San Francisco, whose chief objects shall be, the encouragement and practice of the Games, and preservation of the customs and manners of Scotland, the promotion for a taste for her language and literature, and the binding more closely in social links the sons and daughters, and descendants of our mother country.

Five days later, on Thanksgiving Day, the first Games of the Caledonian Club of San Francisco was held—the only event in the club's history that was not advertised beforehand. That a full-fledged Games complete with prizes, two judges, and nine events could be organized and successfully accomplished in five days speaks well for the determination and enthusiasm of the founding members.

The inaugural Games was a small invitational affair. As with the Games in Scotland, the San Francisco Games started with an athletic program. Musical competitions were added to the program later. The events and their winning measurements (where applicable) were: quoits, throwing the 22-pound hammer (78′ 6″), throwing the 16-pound hammer (92′), putting the 26-pound stone (22′ 1″), hop-step and jump (35′ 6″), running leap (15′ 7″), running high leap (4′), blindfolded wheelbarrow race, and three-legged race. Only seven contestants competed.

The following year the club had a membership of 95, many of whom—as is still the case—were also members of the San Francisco St. Andrew's Society. The second Games, held November 28, 1867, and attended by 4,000 people, had fourteen events, thirteen athletic and one musical: quoits, throwing the hammer, running leap, three-legged race, hitch and kick, running high leap, wheelbarrow race, 22-pound stone throw, caber toss, 100-yard dash, running hop-step and jump, race for men over 45, 300-yard race, and piping. The prize for winning the caber toss was a set of quartz sleeve buttons. Two medals were given, a gold for the stone and a silver for the hop-step and jump. The winner of the 45-and-over men's race received a silver mounted cane. The best piper (who happened to be the club's piper) received a silver goblet.

This Games instituted the tradition of the chief's message. All activities ceased at noon and the president of the club, Donald McLennan, addressed the assembly in these words:

> We are assembled here this morning to participate in the sports so dear in the memories of our native land. Though transplanted, as it were, to the shores of the Pacific many thousands of miles from bonnie Scotland, still the hearts of her children warm at the recollections of their youth, and beat more strongly at the mention of her name. It has been one of the peculiarities and the pride of our people, in whatever portion of the globe we may dwell, to honor and cherish all that reminds us of our earlier years; and in those fond recollections we harbor our national Games, to celebrate which we are met here today.

The 1868 Games took place across the bay in Sausalito and were marked· by the addition of the Highland fling to the program. Because of the early emphasis on advance publicity, the Games received wide recognition. The July 25, 1868, issue of the *Illustrated London News* reported on the Games, complete with a woodcut illustration (most likely from the artist's imagination, but a remarkable depiction). This is the earliest-known published illustration of a Caledonian club affair. That same year, in keeping with its policy of advertising, the club began listing itself in the city directory. The club also broadened its social function in 1868 by holding its first ball. (By 1874 the Games had become so popular that special gatherings were held to distribute the prizes formally; this annual event soon became one of San Francisco's social highlights, continuing until 1895. In 1888 an estimated 10,000 people attended the event.)

At the fourth Games in 1869, members of the press began live coverage of the 23-event gathering. In 1870 the sword dance was added to the competitions. An unusual prize—a cow and a calf—was given to the winner of the handicap race for men over 45.

More than 4,000 spectators attended the 1871 Games. For the first time a foot race open to all comers, not just club or sister club members, was held, with a gold medal awarded to the winner. A second Games was held that year to raise funds for the victims of the Chicago fire; the event netted $1,200. The competitions were open to all, with eligibility based on novice, amateur, or professional standing as well as on age and other characteristics. (This has remained the club policy.) The second chieftain of the club, Andrew Foreman, won most of the events at this gathering. His prize was a specially designed gold and silver medal. Now owned by the California Historical Society, it is the oldest club medal still in existence.

By 1873 the Games had assumed a traditional format which encompassed four segments: Games in the morning, intermission at noon, resumption of the Games in the afternoon, and dancing for all at the end of the day. During the intermission there was often entertainment and events for nonmembers, including an old ladies' race, girls' handicap race, and married ladies' race.

In 1875 the San Francisco club's articles of incorporation were filed with the State of California. Another officer—club physician—was added the following year. His duty was to attend the Games and any other club-sponsored athletic event in case his expertise were required.

By 1877 the all-comers policy was broadened to include boys' and girls' events, and age groups were instituted to equalize the competitions. The 1877 program of closing dances was as follows: Scotch reel, quadrille, lancers, waltz, schottische, Scotch reel, mazurka, Virginia reel, and repeat. In 1878 the highly popular tug-of-war contest was added, pitting married men against single men. The 1887 Games included contests in Highland fling for lads and lassies, Highland fling for girls in costume, and reel of Tulloch for boys and girls in costume. Membership in the San Francisco club numbered 650 in 1894; two years later, the number had nearly doubled to 1,225.

Some of the prizes awarded before the turn of the century were purely practical and certainly unconventional by modern standards: a ton of coal, a half-dozen shirts, a box of handkerchiefs, a pistol, and a "lightning calculator," to name a few. In 1891 the winner of the young ladies' race won a quart of milk daily for a year. Other such perishable prizes included 100 pounds of oatmeal, 20 pounds of finnan haddies (smoked haddocks), and a case of champagne. By the 1890s nearly all prizes were monetary.

More than 8,000 people attended the 36th annual Games in 1902. Honored guests included the mayor of San Francisco and his wife, five Superior Court judges, and Jimmie Britt, a popular boxer. Sixty boys and girls in Highland costume danced simultaneously on the platform at Shell Mound Park, the site to which the Games had been moved in 1884. Members of the host club were victorious in two of the forty events held.

The Games continued even in 1906, the year of the tragic April 18 earthquake in which Scottish Hall, the mutual home of the Caledonian Club and the St. Andrew's Society, was destroyed, along with much of the city of San Francisco. The May 1 date was obviously cancelled, but the Games were held on August 25. There were twenty-three events, fewer than in previous years, but the Games tradition was upheld.

Special mention should be made of club member Jim McEachern, who joined the club in 1910 and began competing the next year. He was an outstanding athlete of his day who went on to represent the United States at the 1920 and 1924 Olympics. In 1918 he broke the world 21-pound hammer throw record.

The date of the San Francisco Games was changed to Labor Day weekend, the prevailing date, in 1950. The Games were moved twice before settling in their present location, the Sonoma County Fairgrounds in Santa Rosa, in 1962. The present two-day schedule was established in Santa Rosa as well.

Statistics on a recent Games paint an encouraging picture of the present state of Scottish Games. One hundred forty-five events filled two and one-half days at this 1980s-era gathering; the early starting time accommodated the large number of contestants for the Friday piobaireachd competitions. The Games were the largest in the country with two-day crowds in excess of 30,000. There were nearly 1,000 competitors and participants from the western United States, Canada, and Scotland, including over 175 pipers, 265 dancers, 33 pipe bands (creating a massed band of nearly 300 pipers), 6 invited international professional athletes, and a host of amateur athletes.

Today's Santa Rosa Games are the site of several important championships: the Western United States Open Highland Dancing Championships, the United States Heavy Events Championships, and the United States Caber Tossing Championships, with a challenge caber weighing over 120 pounds. All cabers are imported from Scotland for this Games. There is competition at every level of dancing, piping and drumming, and athletics. And the competitions continue to expand. At the 1983 Games the Niel Gow Scottish Fiddling Competition was begun, as well as the Invitational Piping Contest, featuring five of North America's outstanding pipers.

The Games of the Caledonian Club of San Francisco are tightly organized and tightly run. The 50th Games in 1916 was run by a committee of 45; today the committee numbers about 35, working under seven division heads. The committee works throughout the year to make the Games flow as smoothly as possible. Every consideration is taken to anticipate and accommodate the needs and desires of each competitor and spectator. For so large an undertaking, it fits together amazingly well. These Games, the only ones to have continued so strongly in the face of varying adversities, serve as an inspiration to other clubs. The story of their success recalls words from the club's preamble: "Being...desirous of assisting toward the establishment and maintenance of friendly relations among those who are of Scottish blood or extraction; and keeping alive in them an interest in Scottish manners and usages." Seventeen men banded together to perpetuate a common love. One hundred nineteen years later, 160 men happily uphold a tradition in which all who are of Scottish descent may delight.

ORGANIZING THE GAMES

The seed had been planted and its germination assured. By 1880 Games were being held across the country; in another 40 years they had appeared at more than 125 locations. Add to that number those in Canada, and it becomes apparent that many opportunities existed for people to show their skill in the ancient sports of Scotland or to marvel at the skill of others. Considering this number, it is not surprising that an organization to represent and regulate the Games came into existence.

In 1866 representatives of Scottish clubs in the United States and Canada met at the New York Caledonian Club to "discuss matters of mutual concern and cooperation." All agreed to hold an international gathering of the clans the following year. On July 1, 1867, the first International Highland Games was held at Jones Wood in New York City. In 1870 delegates from nearly all the United States and Canadian Caledonian clubs met to discuss standardization of implements, measurements, and rules—a meeting that had become necessary because of the increased number of Games and the wide variations in rules and equipment.

Out of the 1870 convention evolved the North American United Caledonian Association (NAUCA), which became the governing body for member Games in the United States and Canada. Its membership qualifications were simply and specifically stated: "No club or Society shall be eligible for affiliation with the North American United Caledonian Association except

such as are composed entirely of Scotchmen and their descendants and organized for the encouragement and practice of
Scottish Games, and the promotion of a taste for Scottish Literature, Poetry and Song." The exact date on which this organization ended is uncertain, but it is known that as of 1902 it was still
in its position of authority over member Games.

In his book *The Sporting Scots of Nineteenth Century Canada,* Dr.
Gerald Redmond has captured the spirit and significance of
NAUCA's nomenclature:

> The formation of the North American United Caledonian Associa-
> tion...was also a significant indication of Scottish cultural pride in
> North America, which in this case transcended national consider-
> ations. The Scots concerned did not form two separate national
> associations, one in Canada and one in the United States, as one
> might have expected. Instead of an "American" or "Canadian"
> Society, it was a "North American" Society, but the crucial adjectives
> in its title seem to have been "United" and "Caledonian." Many
> Scots might well have agreed with [Alexander] Muir's sentiment
> expressed in "The Maple Leaf Forever"...but as far as the Caledonian
> Games were concerned, an international and Scottish outlook prevailed
> whether they lived under the Maple Leaf or the Eagle. The ethnic
> pride in their cultural identity superseded any national pride which
> might have existed in 1870....Caledonian Games should be regarded
> as a North American phenomenon in the nineteenth century, and a
> sporting product of Scottish self-esteem throughout the continent.
> One cannot look at the development of these Games in Canada
> alone, or only in the United States, during the nineteenth century,
> without an imbalance in historical perspective.

Not only did athletes from the United States and Canada
compete in each other's Games, but outstanding athletes from
Scotland, too, found it exhilarating as well as profitable to
compete on this continent. American spectators in the 1870s
were thrilled at the opportunity to see such stellar greats as
Donald Dinnie and James Fleming; the Games committees knew
that the attraction of such names would assure larger crowds
and, hence, revenues.

American interest in participation sports was on the rise, and
the popularity of Scottish Games was certainly one indication of
that fact. The Americans' fervor was heightened by the knowledge that Britons were adopting athletics as a form of recreation.

In the midst of this trend, an event occurred that was to shape the future of American track and field athletics: the organization of an amateur club for the promotion of this interest in sports.

In September of 1868 William B. Curtis, John C. Babcock, and Henry E. Buermeyer formed a club called the New York Athletic Club. It was similar in intent and function to the recently formed London Athletic Club, the purpose of which was to foster competition among postcollege athletes. The events of the Highland Games (most often known as Caledonian Games in this era) played a major role in this new track and field program. The newly formed club held its first Games on November 11, 1868, and a special invitation was extended to members of the New York Caledonian Club. The Caledonians won the events most familiar to them—hammer, shot put, pole vault, standing high jump, and running long jump—and the "Americans" won the running and walking contests. (A noteworthy aside: William Curtis, one of the founders of the new club, caused a sensation by wearing spiked shoes. This innovation was already the vogue in England, but this was their first appearance in the United States.)

The Caledonian influence was to weigh heavily on the New York Athletic Club in many respects, not the least of which was the choice of its first director of athletics, George Goldie, who took the post in 1885. A native of Edinburgh, Goldie came to the United States as a boy and began his athletic career as a gymnastics teacher and circus performer. He achieved great success in Highland Games as a member of the New York Caledonian Club and was as well known in the U.S. as Donald Dinnie and James Fleming, the Scottish Games champions. As director of Princeton University's gymnasium, he was the inspiration for the school's Caledonian Games, which were held from 1873 to 1947. Goldie was the first proponent of the Scottish sport of pole vaulting in America and a world record holder in the standing high jump and standing broad jump.

Within 20 years of the founding of the New York Athletic Club, amateur clubs for track and field athletics had sprung up across the country and the popularity of the Caledonian Games as such was dwindling. The Games, once strongholds for the

Scottish athletic events, were being supplanted by the very clubs that they had helped to start.

Track and field athletics had their start on United States college campuses at Columbia in 1869, mainly the result of the enthusiasm of one of its graduates for the Oxford-Cambridge meets (begun in 1864). While it is true that the events of these English meets did have a bearing on their American counterparts, the greater influence came from the events prevalent at the Caledonian Games. But it was not only in the college arena that track and field activities were taking hold. More amateur athletic clubs were being formed and expanded to include this burgeoning sport. To standardize and regulate these clubs, the National Association of Amateur Athletes of America was formed in 1879. Nine years later the Amateur Athletic Union of the United States was created to have jurisdiction over all amateur athletics, not only track and field.

END OF THE BOOM

By this time, Scottish Games were clearly losing their appeal. The attraction of the new amateur athletic clubs was stronger than that of the predominantly professional Scottish Games. The clubs offered more frequent opportunities for competition than the annual Games did, and amateur meets were devoid of such peculiarly Scottish contests as caber tossing, best-dressed Highlander, best piper, and Highland dancing.

Other new pursuits were also distracting competitors and spectators from the Games. Baseball had been an amateur sport for nearly 30 years and had been played on an intercollegiate basis for nearly 10 years when the first professional team, the Cincinnati Red Stockings, was formed in 1869. By the 1880s football was appearing on college campuses; the next decade brought professional teams in this sport. Professional boxing was faring well in the 1890s; 1892 saw the first official heavyweight United States boxing championship fight, between Jim Corbett and John L. Sullivan.

The Caledonian clubs, which had depended on the popularity of the Games for financial support, began to feel the effects of America's sporting boom. A Games was expensive to stage, and decreasing gate receipts were causing many clubs to run in the red. Soon only the larger clubs remained successful. The International Highland Games was still attracting crowds and competitors, however, and in 1875 the New York Caledonian Club reported not only a large cash balance but its largest membership to date. During "Scottish Week" in Chicago in 1893, held in conjunction with the World's Fair, a highly successful three-day Games was held under the auspices of the NAUCA and officially hosted by the Chicago Caledonian Club. It was advertised nationwide and drew participants from all over the world.

Those in Scottish circles were suggesting that it was time for a return to the original purpose of the Games: Scottish events for the enjoyment of Scots and their descendants. As early as 1875 the NAUCA decreed that the open policy of the Games was to continue. However, 10 years later the prestigious *Scottish-American Journal,* voice of North American Scots from 1858 to 1919, carried a long article predicting the end of the Games's heyday and calling for a reevaluation of their direction.

Sure enough, the Games fell, one by one. It was inevitable. The lavish productions were playing to nonexistent audiences. Clubs often knowingly went into debt to stage a Games, hoping to recoup their expenses. Even the large and affluent New York Caledonian Club, which had stood its ground for so long, could not sustain its Games in the face of the Great Depression. The 1933 Games showed a deficit of over $400, which quietly bespoke its demise. All but two were gone from the greatest era of the Games in the United States.

North of the border, the Games in Canada were faring better. When the track and field craze hit there, it turned heads, but eventually the athletic events joined forces with Scottish Games. Perhaps this was to be expected in Canada, a country with a stronger Scottish tradition.

REBIRTH

As the older Games in America continued to die in the 1920s, the current rebirth of the Games began, slowly and at random. Connecticut was the site of the first of these, the Round Hill Games, which began in 1924. The Games of the United Scottish

Artist's rendering of the International Caledonian Games held at
Jones Woods, New York City, on July 1, 1867. (Courtesy of
Museum of the City of New York)

This woodcut illustration of the Games of the Caledonian Club
of San Francisco appeared in the July 25, 1868, issue of the
Illustrated London News. (Courtesy of *Illustrated London News*)

George Goldie, early U.S. Games champion and sports pioneer. (Courtesy of Princeton University Archives)

Highland dancing participants at the Athena (Oregon) Caledonian Games, circa 1900. (Courtesy of Donald R. Duncan)

Spectators and participants at the Athena Caledonian Games, early 1900s. (Courtesy of Donald R. Duncan)

Societies, Inc., of Southern California followed in 1927, originating as the Los Angeles Highland Games and taking its current title upon incorporation of the society in 1952.

The year following the last of the Games of the New York Caledonian Club, 1934, saw the birth of the Central New York Scottish Games; New York added another Games in 1946 near Albany, the Capital District Games. The latter continued until 1969, then was reinstituted in 1978. The Pacific Northwest Games in Everett, Washington, began in 1945. Portland, Oregon, held its first Games in 1952.

The year of 1956 heralded the appearance of the United States gathering that has probably received more national and international attention than any other: the Grandfather Mountain Highland Games and Gathering of the Scottish Clans. Its site is MacRae Meadow, a slope of the beautiful mountain (elevation 5,964') in Linville, North Carolina, from which it takes its name. Part of the lure of this gathering is undoubtedly the setting, which with its rhododendrons, rowan trees, thistles, and frequent mist is reminiscent of Scotland. Equally addictive to clansmen and curious spectators alike is the rallying of clans. At no other Games—or any Scottish event, for that matter—are so many tartans seen. Clan and Scottish organization tents reach more than halfway around the extensive field, forming a double row where the terrain allows.

The Games of Grandfather Mountain have been the subject of numerous tourist attraction guides, newspaper features, magazine articles, and television news and documentary programs. In 1981 a film entitled "America's Scottish Highland Games at Grandfather" produced by Hugh Morton, son of one of the Games' co-founders, won the CINE Golden Eagle award, the top award of the Council on International Non-Theatrical Events, in the culture film category. In 1982 the American Bus Association named this Games one of the top 100 annual events in North America.

ORIGINS OF GRANDFATHER MOUNTAIN

When one mentions Grandfather Mountain in Scottish circles

around the country, the name is repeated with such ethereal reverence as to sound almost mystical. Prospective visitors conjure up visions of pipers piping, dancers dancing, and athletes contending against a backdrop of instant nostalgia in the best Scottish tradition. Past visitors block out memories of the clogged single road of ascent and the ubiquitous tartan throng to conjure up the same vision. For there *is* a mystique about this event. Much of this aura was engendered by the enthusiasm with which it was imbued by its founders.

Donald Francis MacDonald and the late Agnes MacRae Morton shared a deep love of their Scottish heritage. More than that, they had a desire to make others aware of and rejoice in their common bond.

A journalism graduate of the University of North Carolina and a reporter for the *Charlotte News,* MacDonald was co-organizer of Clan Donald, U.S.A., and its first North Carolina commissioner. Lord Macdonald, father of the present high chief of Clan Donald, appointed him vice convener to fellow North Carolinian Reginald MacDonald. The American organization was the first Clan Donald society formed outside Scotland. A true rouser of Scots, Donald MacDonald organized the first Clan Donald gathering in this country in 1955 and co-founded the Robert Burns Society of Charlotte.

Agnes MacRae Morton attended Vassar and Massachusetts Agricultural Colleges (the latter became the University of Massachusetts in 1947), after which she returned to her home in Linville, North Carolina. Her father, Hugh MacRae, establihsed the resort village of Linville and with his father built the Yonalassee Road connecting Linville and Blowing Rock. Wishing to organize a clan gathering in 1956 and foreseeing MacRae Meadow as its ideal location, Agnes, who had married, contacted MacDonald for advice and assistance because of his well-publicized Scottish activities.

Their Games experience was, to say the least, limited. MacDonald had spent the summer of 1954 in Scotland and had attended the celebrated Braemar Gathering; Morton had read of the Games in Connecticut. But they decided to stage a full-fledged Scottish

Highland Games in North Carolina, using the Braemar souvenir program as a guide. MacDonald recalls the beginning of their venture thus: "Neither of us had a clue as to what we were letting ourselves in for—the hard work, the slogging, the personal expense, the bewilderment, the uncertainty of success." But they were determined and dedicated.

The date of the Braemar Gathering commemorates the raising of the standard during the Rebellion of 1715, the first attempt to regain the throne for the Stuarts; in the same spirit, August 19 was chosen as the date for the Grandfather Mountain gathering, as that is the anniversary of Prince Charles Edward Stuart's raising the standard at Glenfinnan during the Rebellion of 1745. (MacDonald is a descendant of Flora MacDonald, a young woman of Skye who helped the prince escape to France after the Stuart cause was lost.) Since the Games were an unknown event in the South, heavy use was made of the press and direct mail to alert as many as possible who would be interested. "Mrs. Morton wrote her fingers to the bone," remembers MacDonald, "sending out fliers and answering queries, arranging overnight accommodations for guests, etc. She was really a miracle worker."

MacDonald and some of his friends journeyed to Linville on weekends to assemble building materials, for there were no accommodations or facilities at the site. MacDonald and company spent the day before the Games putting up borrowed bleachers and fence posts, setting up the athletic field, roping off areas for the pipe band to march, and erecting the one big tent that the organizers could only afford to rent because of a last-minute donation of $100 from a native Scot. The gratifying result of all this hard work was the massing of approximately 7,000 Scotiaphiles. After their initial success, the Games' organizers decided to make it an annual event.

The first Grandfather Mountain Games, held on Sunday, commenced with a worship service. A choir of native Scots sang metric psalms. Since a native-born minister could not be obtained in time, Donald MacDonald preached a "sermonette." He also served as master of ceremonies, tossed the caber, entered the wrestling contest, competed in Highland dancing, and sang at the ceilidh the previous evening. The first guest of honor was the aforementioned co-organizer of Clan Donald, U.S.A., Reginald MacDonald, then living in Pittsburgh.

Nearly all the events listed in the Braemar souvenir program were included in Grandfather Mountain's program. Among the first athletic events were the shot put (the stone throw appeared later), caber toss, sprints, 440-yard dash, high jump, broad jump, pole vault, tug-of-war, and wrestling. Lawrence Brown, Jr., was the director and judge of track and field events.

Sally Southerland, a physical education instructor from Charlotte, was in charge of Highland dancing. She was also one of the first judges, along with Mrs. E. M. Bosworth and Mrs. Ralph Santoro. A Braemar rule was (and still is) followed concerning dancing: there must be more competitors than prizes. Clan Donald had donated three dancing medals; there were three contestants entered. Donald MacDonald, who had learned the Highland fling several years earlier, entered as the fourth contestant, assuring propriety—and placement for his competitors.

Since The Citadel, a military college located in Charleston, South Carolina, had probably the only pipe band in the South at that time and its student members were unavailable, the first guest pipe band (Grandfather Mountain has never had a pipe band competition) was the St. Andrew's Society Pipe Band of Washington, D.C. There was one other kilted band, a brass band representing the "Fighting Scots" of Laurinburg (North Carolina) High School. The solo piping competition attracted several amateur pipers as well as members of the pipe band. Pipe Major Millard F. Crary of The Citadel, Pipe Major Jack Smith, an Ayrshire native then living in Winston-Salem, and Tom Moore of the pipe band served as judges. (The first director of piping, Pipe Major Lewis Davidson of Pittsburgh, was not appointed until 1958.)

In 1961 MacDonald and his wife, who was from the Hebridean Isle of Lewis, moved to Edinburgh, where he began writing for *The Scotsman* and the *Edinburgh Evening News*. In the 1960s he also wrote a column in *The Weekly Scotsman* called "The Story of the Clans." The column, which ran for three years, related the

One of the first Highland dancing competitions at the Grandfather Mountain Games. (Photo by Hugh Morton)

Nestor J. MacDonald, left, head of the Grandfather Mountain Games for 25 years, and Agnes MacRae Morton, co-founder of the event. (Photo by Hugh Morton)

Kilted heavy events athletes join in a tug-of-war at an early Grandfather Mountain Games: from left, Bill Bangert, Ron Short, Arnold Pope, and Gordon Varnedoe. (Photo by Hugh Morton)

The 1977 Grandfather Mountain Games as seen by Keith Nichols, then-U.S. hang-gliding champion. (Photo by Hugh Morton)

history of a different clan each week. Since 1973 he has been teaching journalism at Napier College, keeping up his freelance writing, and writing a book on the history of the Games that he co-founded.

When Donald MacDonald emigrated, Nestor J. MacDonald took over as president of the Grandfather Mountain Games, and under his direction the event has grown immensely. In 1978 Nestor MacDonald became chief of the Games and chief executive officer of the Grandfather Mountain Highland Games, Inc., and that same year, Robert Groves, Jr., assumed the presidency of the Games. He and his wife, Cornelia, have attended every one of these gatherings.

Though Donald MacDonald has returned to the motherland, his legacy remains, and not in fact alone. His sister, Flora MacDonald Gammon, is director of music for the Games; her daughter, of the same name, is her assistant; and her husband, the Rev. Richard R. Gammon, is in charge of AAU-sanctioned events. MacDonald's nephew, James R. "Jamie" MacDonald, is the current North Carolina commissioner for Clan Donald, U.S.A., and follows in his uncle's versatile footsteps, being an accomplished athlete, singer, country dancer, and fiddler.

Agnes MacRae Morton died on April 22, 1982. Though her health had been failing in the preceding years, she continued to attend the Games. She enjoyed witnessing the realization of her dream and, like MacDonald, her family's involvement. Her son Julian is a director and officer of the Games. Son Hugh, mentioned earlier, is president of Grandfather Mountain and an excellent photographer; samples of his work appear in the Games programs. And Morton's "family" considerably increased during the 27 years that she nurtured the Games; she was known and loved by thousands who continue to flock to her mountain and share her heritage.

Reginald MacDonald, in his capacity as convener of Clan Donald, U.S.A., established the Clan Donald Educational and Charitable Trust early in the organization's history to further strengthen the ties between Scotland and America. Because of the success of the Grandfather Mountain Games, he founded a similar event in the Pittsburgh area in 1959: the Ligonier Highland Games. These Games eventually came under the sponsorship of the Clan Donald Trust. Donald MacDonald served as guest of honor at this Games in 1960.

The Grandfather Mountain Games today provide nearly every Scottish activity one could imagine. At each Games there is a pre-Games picnic, two ceilidhs, a tartan ball, and a kirking of tartans at the conclusion of the worship service. Recent Games have included over 150 competitions in the areas of heavy events, AAU events (Grandfather Mountain is the only Games in the United States where these appear), Highland dancing, piping, and drumming. In addition, there are also fiddling and sheepdog demonstrations. The notorious 26-mile mountain marathon encompasses a part of the road built by Agnes MacRae Morton's father and grandfather. Over 100 clans and Scottish organizations are usually represented.

One moving ritual recently introduced is the raising of the clans on the Thursday night before the Games weekend. Designees of each clan gather in four groups, one group at each corner of the main field. As "Scots Wha Hae" is sung, the representatives, each bearing a lighted torch, march toward the center of the field, forming a fiery cross of St. Andrew. Each representative is asked, "Who comes to raise the clans for this celebration?" and responds appropriately.

THE SPIRIT SPREADS

With the establishment of the Grandfather Mountain Games, Scottish Highland Games in the United States were taking root again. Revivals of this form of Scottish culture and tradition began to happen across the country as more and more Scots felt the desire to exalt their heritage with a colorful and unique display. In 1958, a small Games was held in Coeur d'Alene, Idaho; this event evolved into the Spokane, Washington, Games. In the 1960s Games appeared (chronologically) in Sacramento, California; Bellingham, Washington; Fair Hill, Maryland (the Delaware Games); Long Island, New York; Salado, Texas; Denver; Dunedin, Florida; Phoenix; Houston; Devon, Pennsylvania; Kansas City, Missouri; Alma, Michigan; and Tacoma, Washington.

During the next decade, which Donald MacDonald calls the "seventies explosion," new Scottish gatherings took place on California's Monterey Peninsula; in St. Paul, Minnesota; Quechee, Vermont; Charleston, South Carolina; Dallas; Stone Mountain, Georgia; Marin County, California; Salt Lake City; Alexandria, Virginia; Bucks County, Pennsylvania; San Diego, California; Athena, Oregon (originally estalished in 1899); Loon Mountain, New Hampshire; Jacksonville, Florida; Glens Falls, New York; Red Springs, North Carolina; Orlando, Florida; Savannah, Georgia; Oberlin, Ohio; Ft. Ticonderoga and Altamont, New York; Fresno, California; Estes Park, Colorado; Williamsburg, Virginia; Huntingtown, Maryland; Virginia Beach, Virginia; Waterville, Maine; and Campbell and Chino, California.

Since 1980, the Games have spread to Tulsa, Oklahoma; Trenton, Maine; Batesville, Arkansas; Waxhaw, North Carolina; San Fernando, California; Honolulu, Hawaii; Gatlinburg, Tennessee; Modesto, California; Ft. Collins, Colorado; Lubbock, Texas; Chicago; Eagle River, Alaska; Ft. Myers, Florida; Aurora, Colorado; Colorado Springs, Colorado; Selma, Alabama; Miami; Pittsfield, Massachusetts; Essex Junction, Vermont; St. Louis; Vashon, Washington; Payson, Utah; Litchfield, Connecticut; Plano, Texas; Mt. Vernon, Georgia; and Biloxi, Mississippi.

THE ASGF: TOWARD THE FUTURE

With the expansion of the Games came the creation of an interdependent organization. However, unlike the NAUCA of the 1800s, this organization was not intended to be a universal governing body. The Association of Scottish Games and Festivals (ASGF) grew from a small seed planted in the mid-1970s by the late Bob Dickey of the Delco Games in Devon, Pennsylvania, and Dave Peete of the Ligonier Games near Pittsburgh as they pooled efforts and ideas for the mutual facilitation of their respective Games. Eventually the Colonial Highland Gathering of Fair Hill, Maryland, and the Virginia Scottish Games of Alexandria partook of this informal cooperative. The first official meeting of the association took place in February of 1979, when representatives of these Games and the Capital District Games of Altamont,

New York, met during the Delco Scottish Games workshop. The group agreed that the association was beneficial and should be perpetuated. They met twice in 1980 and decided to organize formally. In March 1981 a statement of organization was approved and charter membership rolls were opened until August of that year. The rolls closed with 15 charter members. (As of July 1985, the ASGF had 37 members.)

At the first annual meeting of this group in Alexandria, Virginia, in December 1981, the following officers were elected: president, L. C. "Chuck" Bearman, Virginia Scottish Games; vice president, James McCaig, Tidewater Scottish Games; secretary and treasurer, Mary Beth and Charles "Chuck" Dent, respectively, Southern Maryland Celtic Festival.

The purpose of the ASGF is expressed in these words: "To encourage, support and assist member organizations in the production and presentation of Scottish Games and Festivals. Such endeavors provide a means of celebrating, encouraging and perpetuating the rich heritage accruing to persons of Scottish heritage and descent, and present, for the enjoyment and benefit of all people, those aspects of Scottish culture and tradition for which the Scottish people are known the world over." Among the ways ASGF members are mutually assisted is through the sharing of ideas, equipment, and personnel. Another important benefit of membership is participation in group liability insurance. This, more than any of the other advantages, has broadened the geographical realm of the association. (ASGF members are noted in the Games listings in chapter 8.)

The worth and effectiveness of the ASGF has created a natural expansion of what were originally considered geographical limitations. The organization has proved beneficial to member Games and it was quite by accident that I stumbled upon a similar, though smaller, group on the West Coast. The Pacific International Highland Games Association, headed by David Rickard of Tacoma, Washington, was incorporated in 1952. This organization has members in Washington, Oregon, and British Columbia. There are two U.S. Games as members: Seattle and Portland. This group is a sounding board for Games associations, with its primary purpose being to create harmony among Games along the Pacific Coast. At its formation it allowed Games to set dates that would not conflict with other Games and to establish standard rules for competition. Other members include piping and dancing organizations, which have cooperated in setting the contest standards.

Canada is still very much in our Games picture. At Games there and in the U.S., it is not uncommon to see listed among the competitors—or to see among the spectators—visitors from the adjoining country. There are currently more than 40 Games in Canada, including the North American Heavy Events Championships held at Fergus, Ontario (organized 1946), and the North American Pipe Band Championships held at Glengarry, Ontario (organized 1948).

As a matter of fact, one may attend any Scottish Highland Games anywhere and, though the accent and milieu may differ, the spirit of Scotland and its people is pervasive. For in the boldness of the kilt, the bravado of the music, and the fierceness of the sports, this small country—considered so bleak and barbaric as to have been walled off by Hadrian—unapologetically proclaims to itself and the world that here is a spirit irrepressible and immortal.

Part 2
THE EVENTS

Introduction to Part 2

Competition has always been the heart of the Scottish Highland Games. Even in what may be considered the rudimentary forms of the Games—gatherings in which clansmen vied for positions as bodyguards and couriers for their chiefs and friendly interclan athletic contests in which claims of strength were contended—the top honors were bestowed on the best competitors of the day. The primary purpose of reviving the ancient Games in the eighteenth and nineteenth centuries was to reinstitute and perpetuate the aspects of Scotland's culture that had been banned by the 1746 Act of Proscription. These evidences of nationalism—the music, the dances, the dress—were revitalized and even enhanced by competition. Two hundred years later, whether the gathering is in a wee glen or thousands of miles away in a bustling city, competition is still the cornerstone.

When one considers the relatively short history of the current Games in the United States, it is amazing to think that we are living in the era of the American champions. This is not to say that the first phase of the Games in this country in the late nineteenth century produced no champions; quite the contrary. There were many notable athletes, pipers, and dancers who traveled the early Games circuit competing with each other for top honors. For the most part, though, these were native Scots or first-generation Americans who had an inherent appreciation of their rich heritage. Thanks to those early Scots, the Games became a haven for tradition, until a combination of such diverse events as the birth of track and field athletics, the absorption of second-generation Scots into the American way of life, a world war, and the Great Depression caused the Games to fade into oblivion for the most part.

The Games today are the result of a new desire among Scots to learn about, appreciate, and preserve our heritage. Today's competitors glorify our traditions. For the first time ever, Americans are going to Scotland to compete with the best athletes, pipers, dancers, and fiddlers in the world, and they are leaving their mark. Although they may not often capture the top prizes, they still prove that the Games here are capable of producing some of the very best representatives of each of these pursuits.

The three main competitive events—athletics, piping, and dancing—are found in some form at all Games in the United States. Fiddling is also included in this book, since it is a growing area of competition at American Games. The chapter on other events and Games activities covers features of Games that are just as important to the Scottish tradition as any of the main competitive events, including the increasingly popular clarsach competitions. All of these areas are illustrative of the spirit of the Scottish people—their tenacity, ingenuity, and zeal. These pursuits are unique, and most are quite demanding. The bagpipe has been called the most difficult of the wind instruments to play. Highland dancing is said to require more stamina than any of the other "athletic arts" (i.e., football). The heavy events, which often last six or more hours, require great endurance along with strength and skill. The Scottish style of fiddling differs from all other styles and has made two distinct contributions to the music world.

What, then, is the attraction of these events for a competitor? Is it the fact that the competition is unique and demanding? Is it the material rewards that come with expertise—the tangible evidence of mastery of an art? Or is it something that encompasses and, at the same time, transcends competition? There is no single answer to these questions, but multiple manifestations of the lure of the Games can be found on Games stages and fields across the United States.

The athletes, musicians, and dancers I've talked with at various U.S. Games all say that competition is captivating. It becomes a way of life. Their devotion to competition in general is heightened by the pride they feel at accomplishing these unique Scottish feats.

As a prelude to the segments on the events themselves, I wanted to present some personal stories to serve as examples of the depth of commitment and devotion found in Scottish Highland Games. I tried to find competitors for whom the Games have represented a real challenge. I think the stories I've recorded truly exemplify the spirit of competition at the Games.

THE ATHLETE

On September 10, 1977, Dave Bryson of Albemarle, North Carolina, had one of his best days in the Scottish Highland Games heavy events competition, winning third place at Ligonier, Pennsylvania. That year he had shown marked improvement in the Games; the 6' 6" Scot even started winning some prize money. He had competed at places other than his "home" Games at Grandfather Mountain, including the Virginia Scottish Games in Alexandria and the now-defunct Games at Ellerbe, North Carolina, where he tied veteran Ed McComas for first place in the sheaf toss.

Bryson's love of things Scottish came naturally; he is a second-generation Scottish-American. He was born in upstate New York and attended Games there. His family moved to North Carolina when he was nine years old, and the Brysons began to attend the Grandfather Mountain Games regularly. At that time the athletic events were open to anyone, and competitors were not required to compete in all of them. Bryson started wrestling at the Games when he was 14 years old, tried the caber a year later, then tackled the sheaf. When he first started entering the competitions, he found that the professional athletes were helpful and encouraging, freely giving suggestions. "I've always enjoyed competing," he says, "and this is good competition because it's real free. In other competitions you can't joke around with the guys, whereas here it's real relaxing and the guys give you pointers."

The heavy events differ a bit from their nearest relatives, the field events. Difficult techniques must be mastered. Technique was especially important for Bryson, since he was lighter (a disadvantage in most events) but taller (which could be worked to a real advantage in such events as the caber and sheaf) than most of the competitors. To excel in these events, it is essential to have your own implements and lots of time to practice with them. Bryson had acquired 28- and 56-pound weights, and in the late summer of 1977, his hours of practice were starting to pay off.

His professional life was starting to come together, too. He was a recent graduate of Appalachian State College in Boone, North Carolina. He worked at various jobs all summer while searching for a job related to his major, parks and recreation, and had just been hired by the Department of Recreation in Albemarle. He was to report for work in late September.

The night before he was to begin his new job, he fell asleep at the wheel of his van and crashed into the back of a lumber truck. He received serious injuries above his neck and below his knees. His right leg was so badly damaged that doctors initially thought it would have to be amputated at the knee; there was extensive damage to his muscles, nerves, and circulatory system. His lower jaw was broken in four places; his upper jaw was pushed up behind his nose, which was also broken. Skin grafts had to be performed on his right leg, and the multiple cuts on his face required numerous stitches. For two weeks after the accident, he had no recall at all.

Bryson remained in the hospital for a month, during which time he lost 50 pounds. When he was released, he wore a full-leg cast on his right leg; he was told that he would never walk on that leg. Later, when physical therapy caused some improvement, he was told that he would walk with a limp. His knee would not move at all at first, and he was told that he would never have more than a 30-degree range of motion in it. He was also told that he would never run. Bryson took all these pronouncements as challenges. "I never did like sitting still, even before the accident," he says. "I always liked staying active and staying in shape. And I liked competing on whatever level I could. I wasn't about to just sit there and let this change my life so drastically. So I did my best to become active again."

Six months later his cast was removed, though his bones did not completely mend for another three months. He began a swimming regime to strengthen his atrophied leg. After walking with the aid of crutches for a month, he used a cane for another couple of months, then was able to walk unassisted. He still had an appreciable limp, but the most important thing to him was the fact that he was walking on his own again.

In 1979 Bryson was hired for the summer staff of the Albemarle Department of Recreation. Before staff training began, he ran almost a quarter-mile a day for a month. On the first day of staff training he ran a mile; on the second day, two miles—slowly, but he did it. At an outdoor workshop that August, he camped with two marathon runners. He regularly ran about six miles of their customary ten-mile run with them. After that experience, he decided to enter a ten-kilometer race. He kept running to beat his own records.

Bryson found that running helped his leg tremendously. He set a goal to run a marathon but found that this was physically too much. Ten miles, which seemed like a marathon to him, is the most his body will take. Along with all of his victories in rehabilitating his body, he had learned how far to push himself.

In 1978, the year after his accident, Bryson went to the Grandfather Mountain Games supported by his cane. "I can come [to the Games] in any condition and enjoy just watching because it's a fun two days," he said at the time. But that year he was also equipped with two still cameras and a movie camera. He photographed the form of the competitors—that was the year the great Bill Anderson was entered—and then studied the photographs and movies he had taken.

Bryson continued to work toward the goal of competing again in the Games he loves so much. To do so, he cut back on running, put on some weight, and concentrated on lifting weights. In 1983 he went to the Tidewater and Grandfather Mountain Games to compete. Even though his efforts were equal to those he posted in 1977, everyone else had improved in the meantime, so his scores were at the bottom of the list. His upper body strength was good, but he did not have the strength in his legs necessary to compete in the heavy events. Plus, he had lost the flexibility in his right ankle, and the extra weight he had put on to compete in the Games was causing circulatory problems.

When Bryson realized just what he was up against, he did a lot of serious thinking. He had to face the fact that he was restricted in his movements and strength. It was a difficult decision— whether or not to relinquish what he had worked for so long and diligently and seemingly against all odds—but he had to give up the heavy events. But he hasn't given up the Games. He still has attended every Grandfather Mountain Games since he was nine years old, and he plans to continue doing so and to help out in any way he can.

The accident brought about another change in Bryson's life. He is presently a full-time student at the University of North Carolina in Charlotte beginning work toward a master's degree in physical therapy.

THE PIPER

When you talk for any length of time with piper Chip Reardon, you forget that he is blind and has been since birth. He is so accomplished and so excited about life that his physical limitations seem to disappear.

It was obvious early on that music would play a major role in Reardon's life. The Philadelphia native began playing the piano by ear when he was three years old, started lessons when he was eight, and started playing the organ as well at thirteen. His lifelong infatuation with the bagpipe began when he heard them being played on a television program when he was two. But it was not until he was in college that his desire to play the pipes was fulfilled. His first direct encounter with the pipes came when he was a sophomore studying organ at Oberlin College in Ohio. He was practicing for a boomerang tournament that was to be held as part of the college's British Commonwealth of Nations Fair, and a beginning piper was practicing his music on the same field. On one of Reardon's throws, the wind suddenly changed direction and threw the boomerang off course. The piper yelled a warning. Reardon ducked out of the wayward boomerang's path, then ran to check on the condition of the piper. Reardon picked up the pipes in a completely unorthodox manner and attempted a tune. The piper asked him where he had learned to play the pipes, and Reardon replied that he had just held them for the first time. The piper told him about his teacher, a fellow student, and ceased lessons himself. (Incidentally, Reardon won the boomerang contest.)

Reardon eventually got in touch with Bob Gilchrist of Newark, Delaware, though they did not work together directly except in workshop situations until 1979. In the meantime Reardon bought a set of Granger-Campbell pipes, graduated from Oberlin, and went to West Germany for a year on a Fulbright scholarship. He took his pipes with him and found that they were a tremendous aid in making friends and crossing cultural barriers because of the curiosity they created—especially since he was the only piper in the area.

While in West Germany, Reardon continued to study the pipes on his own through records and the music of the Frankfurt Scottish country dance club, for which he became the piper. By listening to the instructor as he taught the club members how to do the various dances, Reardon counted along and picked up the rhythm. He also played the pipes at the officers' club on an American military base and at some dance clubs to which the country dance group was invited.

One of Reardon's greatest joys and honors in piping came while he was in West Germany. Bob Nichol, the Queen's Piper, was invited to open a British trade fair in Frankfurt. The Scottish country dance group was also invited to participate. Nichol played, then Reardon played a solo before playing for the group. Nichol came up to Reardon afterwards and asked him with whom he was studying. When told that Reardon was studying on his own, Nichol suggested that he get a teacher to correct his bad habits. Nichol then gave Reardon an impromptu lesson for about an hour and a half. At Nichol's request, Reardon returned to play that night. Nichol told him approvingly that he could tell he had gone home and practiced.

Upon returning to the United States, Reardon began graduate studies at Eastman School of Music in Rochester, New York. He received his master's degree and became director of music at what is now Valley Forge Christian College in Greenlane, Pennsylvania. In 1981 Reardon became music minister at Faith Assembly Church in Poughkeepsie, New York. He left that position in December 1983 to work on his doctorate in organ/church music at Eastman. He completed his dissertation in the spring of 1985 and is seeking a teaching position at the university level. He is married and has a ten-year-old son who is also studying the pipes.

Reardon's love of the pipes is intense and obvious, and he is always eager to learn more about them. He has attended all of the Delco Scottish Games Workshops and several other piping schools and workshops. He has been able to study with such renowned pipers as Donald Lindsay, Jim McIntosh, and Murray Henderson through lessons recorded on cassette tapes.

The quality of piping in the United States is high and continually on the upswing. Reardon and other pipers as well say that this is largely due to the fact that workshops and piping schools have given American pipers the opportunity to work with some of the greatest names in piping today. Of the workshops Reardon says: "One of the things that intrigues me about this art is that every time I attend a workshop, everyone there is as zealous and enthusiastic about this as I am. And that just thrills me to death. When I'm at these schools I even sweat piping. I have the time of my life with this. I sit there and listen to the instructors and I'm almost hanging on their every word. If you don't, then you really don't belong in a thing like this."

Reardon has come a long way since his first competition at Fair Hill, Maryland, several years ago. At that competition he did everything wrong: he arrived late and was almost disqualified; he played pipes that he tuned quickly after they'd spent five hours closed up in the hot trunk of the car; and he played tunes that were too much for him at the time. He placed fifth out of 34 contestants and was told by the judge, John Wilson, that he needed more practice. Two weeks later he competed at the Delco Games in front of noted piper Duncan McCaskill, Sr. He played simpler tunes and did everything right in preparing to play. The result was a score thirteen points higher and fourth place in that competition; he was one point short of a medal.

Reardon is currently a member of the Fraser Highlanders Pipe

Band of Rome, New York, and competes about six times a year. He is ranked by the Eastern United States Pipe Band Association as Amateur Grade I, soon to be changed to open. (See chapter 4 for an explanation of the EUSPBA grading system.) Before his ascendancy to Grade I, he said that no matter how anxious he was to keep progressing in his piping—"I do play to win"—he did not want to advance in grade until his teachers told him he was ready. "Grade I in piping is like the Triple A of minor-league baseball, so I don't want to go up with bad habits." Obviously, he has not. In one recent competition in the amateur class, he was one of eight top-ranked amateur players in the region participating in the first Robert Nichol-Robert Brown Amateur Invitational Piobaireachd competition at the Berkshire Indoor Games.

He enjoys playing piobaireachd, the masterful classical music of the pipes: "You realize just how complicated an art form it is and, to a degree, [that it is] innate on the part of the performer— if it's not in your blood, it's hard to teach it.... The more I see of the *art* of piping and the more I see of piobaireachd, the more I can understand what a deep, dark mystery it has been for so long."

Reardon's drive as a piper is representative of his whole outlook on life. "If you want something bad enough, it's not going to come to you by itself; you've got to go get it. So, I went and got it. I'm *still* going to get it. I consider it of vital importance to me to play the pipes. As I said to my pastor, 'When the time comes for me to meet my Maker, the need for playing the pipes better be satisfied in heaven!'"

THE DANCER

Elaine Burgin is now an assistant chef in a French restaurant in Charlotte, North Carolina. Her mother, Anne Burgin, teaches Highland dancing and has been director of dancing at the Grandfather Mountain Games for several years. So it was only natural that Elaine would become a dancer.

Elaine's dancing career started at age six. She competed in the open class for nine years and became one of the most outstanding Highland dancers in the South. She won 200 medals and 75 trophies in U.S. competitions as well as one title at the Great

Dave Bryson

Chip Reardon

Elaine Burgin

Lakes Open (Detroit), two at the Atlantic International (Grandfather Mountain), and three at the Southwestern Open (Houston) championships. In July 1981 she was one of two representatives from the southern region in the 17-and-under age group to compete at the first United States Inter-Regional Highland Dancing Championship, held at the Virginia Scottish Games in Alexandria. She has also given demonstrations of Highland dancing at various Games and functions and on educational television.

Perhaps one of the biggest thrills for any Scottish Games competitor outside of Scotland is to compete in the motherland. Burgin has known this thrill and the accompanying joy of placing in competition in the land where it all began. Her Scottish honors are the Inverkeithing Challenge Shield, first runner-up at the Montrose Games, second and fourth places at the Edinburgh Festival, and fourth place at the prestigious Cowal Gathering.

Competing in Scottish Games has been more than a mere hobby for Burgin. She realizes that there are areas of her life that are richer and fuller because of Highland dancing. She has been able to travel widely and has made special friends whom she never would have known if not for her involvement with dancing. It has also taught her self-discipline and the ability to accept defeat as well as victory.

In the fall of 1978 Burgin began experiencing pain in her feet while dancing. The diagnosis: tendinitis. She continued dancing—by then it was a very important part of her life—but the painful condition worsened. To alleviate the situation she took periodic breaks from dancing, eventually as long as four months at a time. In 1979 she went to Scotland to compete, and while performing at the Edinburgh Festival that August, her feet hemorrhaged. She did not dance at all during the remainder of her trip or for the next couple of months. She competed at the end of the season back in the United States and then decided to forego her dancing until the next season.

The pain continued to intensify in the summer of 1980. She attempted to compete several times but usually ended up dropping out after the first dance. Her feet again hemorrhaged at the 1981 Inter-Regional Championship; the pain, especially toward the end of the competition, was excruciating. She did herself great harm—more than she realized at the time and more, she says, than any championship could ever be worth. "I have learned that all the fun and reward goes out of it [competing] when you're unable to dance at a level you used to and when you can't relax because of the pain. If all the enjoyment is gone, then you know it's just not worth it. I kept on competing probably because I love competition. It becomes a part of your life. You depend on it to show you've worked at something you love."

After the 1981 championship Burgin gave up dancing and began therapy for the tendinitis problem. She tried to dance again in 1983; she did well at the regional championships, and in representing the South at the national championships that year was third runner-up in her age group.

Her desire to dance remains strong, but between the long hours of work and therapy for the tendinitis problem, she competed only twice in 1984.

There is a happy ending to Burgin's story. In spite of her injury and a lack of competition time, Burgin capped her career and captured part of her dream by finishing second runner-up in the 18-and-over category at the 1985 U.S. Inter-Regional Highland Dancing Championship. Adding to the importance of this accomplishment was the fact that the competition was held at the Grandfather Mountain Games under the direction of her mother.

As a tribute to Burgin's leadership in the South, two awards have been named for her. One is an achievement award presented at the Charleston Games to any open dancer under 15 years of age. The other is a trophy given at the Stone Mountain Games to the Southeast dancer with the highest number of points at the end of a year's competition. The Charleston award has been won every year by a student from Anne Burgin's school of dancing; the Stone Mountain prize has gone to the same school two out of three years. These dancers consider it an honor to win the Elaine Burgin awards—and a joy and an inspiration to have her visit their classes.

3

Heavy Events

This is where it all began—athletics. This is also the competitive area most often associated with the Games. Mention "Scottish Highland Games" to the average person and the most ready response, particularly from those who have had only slight exposure to the Games, will refer to the tossing of the caber. Longtime caber champion Ron Short calls this event "the essence of the Highland Games."

But the tossing of the caber is only one of seven different contests most often included in the heavy events competition at the Highland Games. The others are the stone throw, the 28-pound weight throw, the 56-pound weight throw and toss, the Scottish hammer, and the sheaf toss. (Strictly speaking, an implement is *thrown* for distance and *tossed* for height.) When all seven different events are included in a competition, it is often referred to as a Scottish heptathlon, an apt term originated by Maclean Macleod, president of the Colonial Highland Gathering in Fair Hill, Maryland. However, these seven events are not included at every Games having a heavy events competition. The sheaf toss is frequently eliminated or replaced by an extra hammer or stone event. For a competition to be considered major, five to seven events must be included, and there must be at least five competitors who are experienced in the sport.

In Scotland the heavy events program is generally comprised of five to seven events, but it differs from most of ours in that it has two stones, two hammers, the 28-pound weight throw, the 56-pound weight toss, and the caber toss. A few Games in Scotland have the 56-pound weight throw. Canada's heavy events program is similar to ours, with the sheaf toss generally excluded.

The sheaf toss is only included in two Games in Scotland: those at Halkirk and Lochearnhead. It is not considered one of the heavy events in Scotland but instead is listed by the Scottish Games Association as a farming sport. When it is contested, a sheaf of sticks is tossed (unlike in the U.S., where burlap bags of hay or straw are used). An American witnessed this event at Lochearnhead about 25 years ago and took the idea back to the Games at Grandfather Mountain, where it was instituted. As other Games appeared in that region and existing Games sought to keep up with Grandfather Mountain's innovations, the sheaf toss spread. Today the sheaf toss is found in most Games in the eastern part of the United States; it is gradually spreading westward. (At the Alma Highland Festival and Games in Michigan, the event is made indigenous by the use of a 25-pound bag of Michigan beans!)

Some of the athletes would like to see the sheaf toss removed from the heavy events competition, but others insist that it remain because it is popular with Games spectators; like the caber and the 56-pound weight toss, they can easily see what is happening. Besides, there is something innately gratifying about watching such an anachronistic event.

At some Games the heavy events competition follows the same invitational format as a heavy events championship; that is, certain professional athletes are invited to participate. Most Games, however, have all-comers meets that are open to everyone. Some of these open meets are professional, with the prize monies often determining which athletes will appear; some are amateur; and some have both categories.

The United States offers three heavy events championships: the North American Heptathlon Championship at the Ohio Games in Oberlin in June, the U.S. Highland Heptathlon Championship at the Virginia Scottish Games in Alexandria in July, and the U.S. Heavy Events and Caber Tossing Championships at the Games of the Caledonian Club of San Francisco (CCSF) in

September. Several of America's top athletes compete in foreign championships as well. The Canadian Heavy Events Championships are held at the Fergus (Ontario) Games in August. In Scotland the Games in Dundee and Lochearnhead in July and Crieff in August include the European, British, and Scottish Heavy Events Championships, respectively. There are three caber championships in Scotland in June: the World Championship in Aberdeen, the Scottish Championship in Forfar, and the British Championship in Old Meldrum. The World Heavy Events Championships, initiated in 1980, have been held in Pomona, California; Melbourne, Australia; Prestonpans, Scotland; and Carmunnock, Scotland. In 1984 three sites in Scotland were chosen for the world championship series: Blair Atholl, Carmunnock, and Kilbirnie. Rankings are compiled from the results of all three events. The United States was represented by Fred Vaughan of Bishopville, South Carolina, Keith Tice of Clovis, California, and Tom Johnson of Charleston, South Carolina, at the 1980 contest and by Vaughan and Tice again in 1981. Vaughan, Tom Carmichael of Knoxville, Tennessee, and Bill Kazmaier of Auburn, Alabama, represented the United States at the 1983 event. Tice and Vaughan were the representatives at the 1982 world championships and Tice returned in 1984. Newcomers (to the professional ranks) Jim McGoldrick and Kevin Brady competed at the 1985 competition.

The overall championship in the heavy events in Scotland each year is based on the total accumulated points earned at the 10 Games that are a part of the Tamnavulin Trophy Circuit. Each of the athletes desirous of that title and its concomitant reward and recognition is certain to appear at the member Games. This guarantees a hearty contest for the competitors at the member Games and an opportunity for spectators to see Scotland's world-renowned athletes. Several American athletes would like to see something like the Tamnavulin Trophy series organized in this country as well. Such a series, however, would need a sponsor to promote it. As it now stands, only those who can afford the time and cost are able to compete in a number of Games. A limited attempt at a series was made here in 1979 when five eastern Games—those at Fair Hill, Maryland; Devon and Ligonier, Pennsylvania; Alexandria, Virginia; and Altamont, New York—participated in the American Scottish Games Tour Championship, which was won by Fred Vaughan.

THE HEAVY EVENTS IN AMERICA

In 1967, Bill Bangert of Missouri became the first American to compete at the Games in Scotland. There were less than 20 Games in the United States at that time, and very few had any types of heavy events in their athletic programs. Those that did had a caber toss and an array of track and field events. This was quite different from the Games in Scotland, where athletics have always been paramount. Bangert brought the proper Scottish weights back to the Games here and gave exhibitions throughout the country to help spread awareness and adoption of the events. This was the turning point for the heavy events portion of the U.S. Games.

Thanks largely to the enterprising efforts of Fred Vaughan (and the undergirding of Pete Hoyt of Pittsburgh), the heavy events competitions are well-structured and significant components of many Games today. A 1968 history graduate of Virginia Polytechnic Institute, Vaughan was the Southern Conference discus champion in 1964 and 1965. After college he shifted his athletic prowess to the AAU fields. In 1970 he was the Virginia-North Carolina AAU discus champion, and in 1971 and 1972 he was the Tri-Cities Super Heavyweight Powerlifting Champion. In 1975 and 1976 he won the weight pentathlon in his age group at the Southeastern AAU Masters Championship. He first learned of the Highland Games in a *National Geographic* article about Grandfather Mountain. The description of the athletic events, so closely related to track and field, made him take notice. (Grandfather Mountain started the shot put and caber toss in 1960, added the sheaf toss in 1963, and switched to a full heavy events program in 1972.) Vaughan was living in Kingsport, Tennessee, in 1972 and decided to go to the Grandfather Mountain Games. Intrigued, he entered two athletic events. A couple of years later he moved to North Myrtle Beach, South Carolina, and read about the Games in Charleston. It was at the 1974 Charleston Games that the Games bug bit.

As Vaughan became more involved in the Games here, he saw the need for an organization like the Scottish Games Association (SGA) in Scotland to guide and regulate the heavy events, keep official records, and report on the competitions. In 1976 he founded the North American Scottish Games Association (NASGA), which, according to its preamble, "is dedicated to the promotion and understanding of Scottish Heavy Events competition in the United States and Canada and the appreciation of our Scottish heritage." Vaughan's organization followed the basic SGA rules governing the various events but differed from the SGA in that it was concerned solely with the heavy events. (The SGA regulates *all* athletic events at the Games.)

Although the NASGA was originally founded to govern the Games in all of North America, Canada formed its own heavy events organization in 1981. The Canadian/Scottish Heavy Events Association, or HEC for Heavy Events Canada, was organized to promote and encourage participation in the heavy events at Games there. (Unfortunately, it has not yet become fully functional.) Its founder and president, Dave Harrington of Old Chelsea, Quebec, was Canada's top Scottish Games athlete for several years before his retirement at the end of the 1984 competition season. And in Scotland, David Webster has branched out and formed a heavy events organization. These activities of the past few years show the high regard in which the heavy events are held by earnest athletes and the high standards by which the sport is governed.

Fred Vaughan has put much time and effort into the development of heavy events competitions in the United States, and the results reflect his success. When the NASGA was founded, there were fewer than 10 Games offering a full heavy events program; today there are nearly 50, with approximately 35 at the professional level. Vaughan served as president of the NASGA from its inception until the end of 1981, when former vice president Pete Hoyt, a 14-year veteran of the Games, took over the top post. Hoyt is an able successor: he has worked tirelessly since his first involvement with the Games to establish heavy events contests and keep up with the myriad statistics that today deluge the organization's office.

Vaughan's position of leadership in the heavy events competitions also extends to the events themselves. As of mid-1985 he had competed in more Games than any other American—over 140—and had won more than 50 of those contests. He held the U.S. records in the 28-pound and 56-pound weight throws from 1981–84 and 1980–84, respectively. Vaughan was the 1979 Canadian caber champion, the 1980 and 1982 U.S. Highland Heptathlon champion, and the 1981 Canadian Heavy Events champion. He has competed in more than 25 Games on nine trips to Scotland, seven to Canada, two to Nigeria, and one to Australia. He competed in the world championships from 1980–83. In 1980 he placed third at the World Heavy Events Championships and in 1981 he placed sixth at that event. Vaughan has traveled nearly half a million miles in his Games career. Why does he do it? "I enjoy it. Seeing the world is a big turn-on. I enjoy the travel and going to the Games and also knowing that it's not just one Games that makes you good. You have to be able to travel, go the whole year, and do well over the entire span. Sometimes I get tired *of* traveling, but I don't get tired *when* I travel. You forget how tired you get. The trip to Australia was awesome—something like 54 hours with no sleep. At 6' 5½", it's virtually impossible for me to sleep on a plane; there's no place for me to put my head."

Another athlete, Gordon Varnedoe, has built on Vaughan's work promoting the heavy events by helping to get them recognized as a legitimate professional sport. Varnedoe's father, grandfather, and great-grandfather all served as president of the Savannah (Georgia) St. Andrew's Society. Varnedoe moved to Oakland, California, after graduating from the University of Georgia in 1961. During one of his visits home, his father took him to the Games at Grandfather Mountain and suggested that he try the caber toss. Varnedoe had always participated in sports—he wrestled and played football in college—and so was attracted to this unique event. "I was challenged by it—the way I was in...getting a pilot's license, learning how to surf or ski, or whatever. The challenge of the event really stirs my adrenalin. So I went out there to try to do the caber toss and I experienced the same frustration most people do the first time—the balance and the timing and the other things you need to do it just aren't there the first time you try it. I wouldn't give up.... I started practicing and I'd really wear the skin off my shoulder a half an hour a day trying to do this thing."

A photograph of George Clark (one of Scotland's great heavy events athletes) in a book helped Varnedoe in his endeavor to succeed. "[This book] had a picture of George Clark taken just at the moment he was letting the caber go. All the veins in his neck were standing out. I got my wife to come outside and hold the book so I could see it... and I leaned the caber against my house and backed away until I had that right moment where he was putting all the effort into the toss. Then I went back and tried it a few more times and waited until the caber got to that point and heaved it. And it was amazing to me that once the timing came I could stand flat-footed and let the caber start to fall and just pop it over. The same one I had been working with for weeks got to be simple. It was easy to do after that." That was the summer of 1971. Varnedoe then started tossing the caber at Games in California.

Over the years he has become increasingly involved in organizing the heavy events. He served on the committee of the CCSF Games at Santa Rosa and since moving back to Savannah in 1982 has been closely aligned with the Games at Grandfather Mountain, Stone Mountain, and Savannah. He has managed to obtain private sponsors for several heavy events competitions, which has enabled the world's top Scottish Games athletes to compete in America. A true believer in the importance of finishing touches, he has imported cabers from Scotland, hand-selected by some of the greatest athletes there, for use in various Games here.

The caber toss is the only heavy event Varnedoe competed in, and he won over 25 championships in his Games career. Several years ago he was able to bring the event to the attention of millions of West Coast residents by tossing the caber in an Olympia Beer commercial. In 1975, after having twice won the caber toss at the CCSF Games, Ballantine's Scotch, which sponsored the caber toss, sent him to Scotland to represent the company at the Aboyne and Braemar Games.

At the 1981 Grandfather Mountain Games, the site of his Games debut a decade before, Varnedoe officially retired from caber tossing. His decision to leave competition was partially due to the fact that athletes and cabers have gotten bigger and better over the years. But more importantly, he has come to believe, as do others, that the outstanding Games athlete is not the person who stars in one or two events, but the one who is the best and most consistent in *all* events. The athletes he met in Scotland chided him for only competing in the caber toss; they enter all of the events. This is generally the case here in the United States as well.

The Games will continue to hear from Gordon Varnedoe, though—in more ways than one. He is the athletics announcer at Savannah and Stone Mountain, and he continues to work toward making the heavy events an even more appreciated and widespread sport. One of the ways he has done this is through the institution of Scottish athletic schools in 1984. The purpose of these schools is to allow athletes to learn from the experts just as pipers, drummers, Highland dancers, and fiddlers do in their workshops. The students' training sessions are videotaped and later critiqued by the coaches. Fred Vaughan was the coach for the first school, held in conjunction with the Savannah Games; Ed McComas, Keith Tice, and Michael Reid coached the school held during the Alexandria Games weekend.

The Scottish Games scene in Colorado has taken on new life with the developments introduced by the Scottish Athletic Group of Colorado. This group was formed by Greg Bradshaw of Denver in the early 1980s. Bradshaw has also been instrumental in the formation of three Games in that state since 1982. Games in Colorado include athletic events for men and women, a junior caber toss, and special events such as the manhood stone (more on that later). The heptathlon is contested among the men. The women compete in the caber toss (with a downsized caber), 28-pound weight toss, 11-pound Braemar-style stone throw, and the 12-pound rolling pin throw. A scoring method similar to that used in the decathlon is used to determine the winner of all-around trophies.

On the West Coast there is another recently formed athletic group, the Scottish-American Athletic Association. It was formed by athletes there (though they consider the group national in scope) to assist the Games upon request by providing judges, implements, and standards. The president, Dave Taddeo of San Diego, has served as athletic chairman of Games. Keith Tice is vice president.

WHAT MAKES A CHAMPION?

I learn a lot by spectating—not just about the events, but about the spectators as well. I have often heard big, strong-looking men at heavy events amateur all-comers competitions boast about how effortless such feats would be to them. When they are goaded by their companions into trying, they are usually quite surprised at how difficult the events are. Knowing that more than strength is required for the heavy events is the first step to learning them, for a great deal of finesse and skill is needed to learn these events. Many weightlifters, for example, cannot do these events well, because they lack the necessary agility, quickness, and sense of timing.

It goes without saying that frequent practice is what makes the desire and the ability work together well. As Fred Vaughan says: "Anybody who's got the quickness and the timing and some kind of strength can learn to throw the events. One of these has to stand out or you have to have them in balance. It's training—it's mostly practice.... You can't go into a competition when you're questioning what you're doing. All of these things have to be decided before you throw because you have to be aggressive when you throw. You can't hang back or you won't do anything. If you think about what you're doing when you're throwing, you're probably going to be too slow to do any good. You have to know what you're doing before you get in the ring. That's why you practice."

The Games career of Michael Reid of Maryland is a prime example of the value of practice. At 5′ 10″ and 175 pounds, Reid is the smallest of the professional athletes. He trains daily, concentrating on technique and strength. In 1985, after seven years of competing in the Games, he had steadily improved to the point that he often finished ahead of competitors who were well over 6 feet tall and 200 pounds.

THE HEAVY EVENTS
EXPLAINED

Although there are established standards for all of the implements used in the heavy events except the caber, all implements are not identical. They vary in shape and weight—often by more than two pounds—which, of course, makes a considerable difference in the measurements recorded. In Scotland every Games has its own weights that are used from year to year; some have been in use for over a century. This practice is becoming the vogue in the U.S. as well. Using the same implements at a Games from year to year allows an accurate appraisal of the performances at that Games to be made. A comparison of measurements using the same weights over the course of a few years at the Games would also show an athlete's progress. (Note: Records and other statistics in this chapter are current as of July 1985.)

The throwing weights are all done behind a trig, a wooden toeboard measuring 4' 6" long, 6" high, and 6" wide. If an athlete touches any part of the trig except the side nearest him or steps over the trig, a foul is called. The throw is measured from the point on the inside edge of the trig closest to where the throw was made to the nearest break in the ground made by the implement (not its handle).

The Stone Throw

All of the heavy events reflect their rural origins and the natural accessibility of their implements. The stone throw is believed to be related to the "stone of strength" or clachneart (the Gaelic name often used in Games today) that was often found at the gates of Highland chieftains' homes; visitors were encouraged to test their strength by throwing the stone.

A more difficult ancient test was the manhood stone, which usually weighed between 100 and 200 pounds. Men would challenge each other to lift such stones onto low walls or to carry them from one spot to another. Some Games in Scotland and Canada include versions of the manhood stone challenge; a few in the U.S. do, too. The Fergus Games include a Fergus walk in which an athlete walks as far as possible with a four-foot section of railroad track in each hand (total weight: 370 pounds). The Games in Chicago and Aurora, Colorado, have similar events: Chicago's weights total 400 pounds and Aurora's total 320 pounds.

The stone throw is usually the first of the heavy events contested. It is like the shot put except that the implement is a stone that is as round as possible and weighs between 16 and 32 pounds. A river stone is preferred for its smoothness. Most athletes glide or twirl and then propel the stone, taking advantage of the 7' 6" approach to the trig allowed them. The best stone-throwers use their legs as well as their upper bodies. The throw seems to start in their feet, rush through their bodies, and end with the last flick of their fingertips. The Braemar style of throwing—standing still—is being seen more often in the U.S. It is included in the Virginia and California championship Games.

Brian Oldfield, the 1972 Olympic shot-put champion, turned professional in 1973 and competed in the Highland Games for six years. After a lengthy but successful struggle to regain his amateur status in track and field athletics, he left the Games. (But he is still setting records. He put the shot 72' 9¾" in 1984 for a new American record in that event.) Two of his Games records still stand—an American and world record of 63' 1" in the 17-pound stone throw at Campbell, California, in 1979 and an American record of 46' 5" in the 25-pound stone throw at Fergus, Ontario, the same year—but the world and American records set in many events by this phenomenal athlete are slowly being surpassed. In Scotland the stone records he left behind in 1973 stood for nearly ten years before they were wiped out by the mighty Geoff Capes. Oldfield's spectacular distances are attributed to his style of throwing, which incorporates a spin similar to that used in throwing the discus. Fred Vaughan, another champion, also uses the Oldfield style.

Paul Ferency of Easton, Pennsylvania, one of the newest heavy events athletes, made a good showing for himself in his first Highland Games by establishing a new American record of 51' 9½" in the 20-pound stone. The 6' 5", 305-pound athlete added 5' 5" to the existing record at the 1984 Devon, Pennsylvania, Games.

Vaughan was involved in a classic prefer-to-forget incident at the Games. The stone throw was proceeding at the Charleston,

South Carolina, Scottish Games, which is held on the beautiful grounds of Middleton Plantation. Arnold Pope's throw landed directly atop one of the "traces" of the horses kept on those grounds. The athletes' laughter intensified when Fred Vaughan soberly realized that as the next contestant, he had to retrieve the stone.

The Weight Throws

Both the 28- and 56-pound weights are thrown for distance at U.S. Games. These weights are measured according to the British Imperial System, a hundredweight being 112 pounds. The implement may be squared off or spherical in shape. It is attached to a handle or ring by a chain, the overall length not exceeding 18 inches.

The 28- and 56-pound weights are difficult to distinguish by appearance alone, but the difference is obvious when the weights are thrown. (For a greater appreciation of the implement and the athlete, consider that the 56-pound weight is a bit over the weight of eleven five-pound bags of sugar.) The weights are thrown with one hand only. A 9-foot approach to the trig is allowed; the athletes usually use the whole distance, since the secret to a good throw in this event is speed and momentum. The athlete stands facing the trig, slowly swinging the weight from side to side and behind him. He then goes into a spin, gaining momentum as he approaches the trig. He must be standing when the weight is released. With the combination of a heavy weight in one hand and a swing breaking into a spin, it is understandable that half the battle in the weight throw is to hang on to the weight until the proper moment.

Keith Tice holds the American record in both weight throws. He set the 28-pound record, 83' 5", in Costa Mesa, California, in 1985 and the 56-pound record, 40' 10¾", in Modesto the same year. Hamish Davidson of Scotland holds the world record of 88' 10½" in the 28-pound weight throw, set in 1978, and the 56-pound weight throw record of 43' 7", set in 1981.

The Hammer Throw

American athletes have made tremendous strides in the heavy

events and are highly respected by the Scots, but there seems to be something about the hammer throw that lets the Scots shine forth. Many of our athletes have fine form and are stunning to watch in this event, especially Keith Tice of California, who holds the American records in the light and heavy hammers. The Scots, however, are simply awesome. I was fortunate enough to witness the stunning athletic display put on by Bill Anderson and Grant Anderson at the 1981 Santa Rosa Games; they upheld the Scots' reputation of being phenomenal hammer throwers.

The Scottish hammer is not like the Olympic one but is derived from the village blacksmith's hammer. The implement thrown at the Games today is a metal ball weighing 16 or 22 pounds that is attached to a wooden or cane handle. (Cane is more flexible than wood and tends to withstand the force of impact better.) The hammer throw requires a precise combination of speed and timing. To make matters more difficult, the competitor is not allowed to move his feet while throwing; he may lift his heels while turning, but his feet must not move until the hammer leaves his hands. Many athletes wear shoes with metal spikes under the toes, which they drive into the ground before the throw. The athlete stands with his back to the trig and a firm grip on the handle of the hammer. (Sticky resin is applied to the hands to improve the athlete's grip.)

When the competitor is ready, he places the hammer on the ground far out to one side. He then swings it in front of him and up and over his head in a circular motion three to five times. When he feels he has gained enough speed, he releases it directly behind him, using his last turn to push the hammer on its way. Watching the great Scots Bill and Grant Anderson is a special treat; they swing the hammer around with amazing speed, especially considering their sizes. (Bill is 6' 1" and 280 pounds; Grant is 6' 3" and 290 pounds.) It is spectacular to watch—an unforgettable experience.

The American records are earning great respect. Keith Tice's American records are 137' 5½" (set in Estes Park, Colorado, in 1984) for the 16-pound hammer and 114' 11" (set in Costa Mesa, California, in 1985) for the 22-pound hammer. Bill Anderson has held the world record in the 16-pound hammer, 151' 2", since 1969. Grant Anderson broke Bill's 22-pound hammer record, also set in 1969, with a throw of 123′ 8½″ in 1983.

The Caber Toss

One of my pet peeves is to hear the caber toss called "throwing the telephone pole." Perhaps I even called it that before I became so infatuated with the Games; I do not recall. It is true that the caber does look like a you-know-what, and one does more commonly view trees right side up and with branches and leaves. But to settle any doubts, let it be known that a caber (from the Gaelic *cabar*) is a trimmed tree trunk.

The type of tree used largely depends on the native woods available. Cypress is said not to dry out so quickly (and thus become lighter in weight) as some of the others. Cabers are often immersed in water during the year to keep them from drying out. Regardless of its species, a straight, tapered caber is preferred. At Red Springs in 1980 there were two cabers, each with characteristics which made selection almost a moot point: one was quite crooked and the other was bowed into a huge arc. It should have taken more than the three tries allowed in this event just to decide how to handle either of them, but expert Ron Short undauntedly made three good tosses.

Since cabers vary from Games to Games and year to year, no records are kept in this event. Bill Bangert, Arnold Pope, Gordon Varnedoe, and John Ross were all early U.S. caber champions. The American at the Games today who is most adept at tossing the caber is Ron Short of North Carolina. He performs with such finesse and apparent ease in this event that he makes it look almost effortless.

Short started going to the Grandfather Mountain Games and tossing the caber in 1963 when he was in high school. He has won the caber toss at least once at every U.S. Games in which he has competed. In 1976 he won the caber toss at Lonach, Scotland, and in 1979 he placed fourth in the World Caber Toss Championship in Aberdeen.

It takes a great deal of skill, strength, and timing to master this event. Cabers are generally 16 to 20 feet long and weigh 90 to 120 pounds. The longer the caber, the more difficult it is to turn. Championship or challenge cabers are occasionally offered at Games; these are usually monstrous cabers weighing 130 to 160 or more pounds. A challenge caber is kept from year to year, and prize monies are added on if no one is able to turn it. The 19-foot, 140-pound Grandfather Mountain challenge caber has never been turned.

In the caber toss, the stewards upright the caber on its tapered end, and the athlete is on his own. With the caber resting on his shoulder, he interlocks his fingers and works them down to the bottom of the caber, all the while holding his position so the caber does not topple over. He quickly grasps the bottom and lifts it off the ground. Balance at this point is crucial; if the athlete loses control here, it is virtually impossible to regain. Once the caber is up and balanced, he is ready to run. He may run as far as he likes in any direction. When he feels he has built up enough speed, he stops short and dips down, letting the caber start to fall forward. At the right moment, the athlete must heave the caber with all of his might; discerning that moment is the trick of the trade. Ideally, the caber hits the ground on its large end and flips over, the narrow end flipping up and away from the athlete.

The judge follows the competitor as he runs. When the caber is tossed, the judge stands immediately behind the athlete, who must remain in place so the caber may be "read." The toss is judged according to an imaginary clock face. The athlete is considered to be at 6 o'clock; a perfect toss points to 12 o'clock. Tosses landing between 9 o'clock and 3 o'clock are considered valid. If no one is able to turn the caber, a portion of the large end may be cut off or the scores judged according to the degrees of a circle, with the most vertical of the tosses meriting first place.

I have heard stories about Brian Oldfield and Bill Anderson psyching themselves up for a Games. Gordon Varnedoe tells the following story about how he surprised everyone, including himself, by winning the caber toss at Grandfather Mountain. He attributes his victory to an unexpected surge of adrenalin. The caber toss and the heavyweight wrestling were being contested at the same time, and Varnedoe was entered in both events. "I

Keith Tice throws the hammer. (Photos by Ed McComas)

Rick Porter pulls himself out of a bend and stretches his whole body to heave the 56-pound weight up and over the bar.

Balance and a firm grip are essential in preparing for a caber toss, as Michael Reid demonstrates.

tossed *at* the caber the first time—I threw a perfect 6 o'clock. The other guys got the caber over with 10 o'clocks and 11 o'clocks or whatever. They called my name for the finals in wrestling, so I went and wrestled. I won that tournament. I'd just finished the match—I'd just gotten up off the ground and they'd raised my arm in victory—when my name was called for the second round of the caber toss. I went over there and my hands were still trembling from the wrestling match—the excitement of it. Wrestling is done barefooted, and I figured I wasn't going to waste these guys' time by stopping to put my hose and flashes [garters with colored ribbons worn around the calves to hold up the hose] back on, I'd just toss barefooted. I picked the caber up and ran out there and flipped it and the thing went right over to 12 o'clock! I stood there in disbelief; Ross Morrison [the judge] stood there in disbelief. Then everybody else finished their third turns and the next highest toss to mine was 11 o'clock. When it came my third turn they said, 'Let's see you do it again.' So I went out there and threw another 6 o'clock."

The 56-pound Weight Toss

The weight used in this event is the same one that is thrown for distance, yet the casual manner in which this event is performed often causes spectators to wonder if they have heard the weight correctly. Charlie Allan, a former Scottish champion and author of a book on the Games in Scotland, made a very good analogy that puts the event in perspective. At the time Allan was writing, Bill Anderson held the world record in this event: 15′ 7″. Allan likened this feat to tossing a seven-year-old boy over a double-decker bus with one hand.

In the weight toss, the athlete stands with his back to (but almost directly under) the crossbar and takes brief notice of its height. He then grasps the weight with one hand, lifts it out in front of him, swings it far back between his legs, and brings it all the way back out in front of him and up in one smooth motion, releasing it to go over the bar in a backward arc. The experts do it with ease, and unless the weight hits the bar, it usually lands right at their heels. It takes a great deal of practice to toss the weight so that it arcs perfectly. Too wide an arc decreases the maximum height of the toss. Too narrow an arc would require the athlete to step out of the way quickly lest the weight land on top of him.

Each athlete is allowed three attempts at each height. If he fails to clear the bar in his three turns, he is eliminated from the competition. If the crossbar is dislodged, the throw is considered a miss; if it is hit but not dislodged, the throw is usually considered good.

For an athlete, above-average height and weight are obvious advantages in the weight toss. Brian Oldfield (6′ 5″, 270) set a five-year American record of 16′ 7″ in this event in 1979 at the Ohio Games. The world record of 16′ 9½″ is held by Geoff Capes (6′ 5½″, 340) of England, who beat Oldfield's record in Scotland in 1981. Kevin Brady (6′ 5″, 295) of Campbell, California, moved the American record closer to the world mark when he tossed the weight 16′ 8″ at the 1984 Monterey Peninsula Games.

The Sheaf Toss

It takes a lot of practice to develop effective form for the sheaf toss. Tossing hay onto a stack with a pitchfork is one thing, but hurling a bag of it straight up in the air over a crossbar is quite another. The rules governing this event take this factor into account; the 16-pound sheaf may be tossed "by any method possible." Even if the competitor tosses the sheaf high enough into the air, the size of the bag means a greater possibility of the bar being dislodged.

Ron Short has been successful in the sheaf toss for many years. He has won and set the Games record in this event at almost every Games in which he has competed. He had the second highest sheaf toss—25′—in the 1984 season.

Over the past few years, more athletes have gotten the hang of tossing the sheaf. At the U.S. Highland Heptathlon in Alexandria in 1981, Ron Short, Keith Tice, and Tom Carmichael finished in a three-way tie for second place in this event with 24′ tosses; Ed McComas came in first by six inches. McComas went on to break the American record of 25′ 4″, which had been set by Brian Oldfield in Alexandria in 1979, with a toss of 25′ 7″ at the 1981 Ligonier Games. Carmichael tied McComas at a height of 25′ 10″ at Ligonier in 1982 to share top honors in the event, but

McComas boosted that record to 26' at the Tidewater Games in 1983. McComas stayed at the top of the rankings in 1984 by tossing the sheaf 25' 2½", higher than any of the other major athletes. This record fell in 1985; Keith Tice broke it with a toss of 26' 1" at the Delco Games, and Jim McGoldrick boosted it to 27' at Alexandria.

THE COMPETITORS

Considering that the proper heavy events implements and standards were introduced to the Scottish Games in this country only a little over 20 years ago and that the Games have been run according to authentic rules for only about 10 years, it is obvious that the heavy events portion of the Games and the athletes who compete in them have made astounding progress. Although there might be as many as 100 athletes who compete at the professional, or open, level at the Games, there are about 25 who can be called the core group. These are the ones who are dedicated to the sport and who strive for excellence in the events. Many were drawn to the Games from track and field, where they were stellar performers. Any athlete who has had the opportunity to compete with members of this group in all-comers competitions quickly sees how seriously they take the sport.

Though the heavy events are individual sports, these athletes can be likened to a team in that most of them usually show up at Games where heavy events are taken seriously, the events are run efficiently, and the prize money makes the traveling and sacrifice of family time worthwhile. (Most of the professional athletes live in the eastern U.S., which is where most of the major heavy events competitions are held. However, they all log a great number of travel miles in the course of a year's competing, especially those who journey to the West Coast, Canada, and abroad.) A sense of closeness has developed in this group after many years of competing with each other several times a year for five, seven, or more hours a day. Camaraderie is at a high level. They are quick to encourage each other and to help each other with friendly advice. But although their attitudes may be relaxed and friendly, the competition itself is keen and tough; each man wants to do his best and win, or at least better his personal record. By the end of the day, each athlete has swung, hoisted, dragged, and hurled over 1,000 pounds of unwieldy weights— not including the warm-ups. They do not stop; they ignore the whims of weather and seldom take lunch breaks. Only in cricket or a 14-inning baseball game, perhaps, are the participants together for so long.

Bill Bangert of Missouri was introduced to the Scottish Highland Games in 1967 when a business associate who was a native Scot entered him in the Braemar Games as a lark. As mentioned before, Bangert was the first American to compete in these Games, and he made a lasting impression in more ways than one. Since Braemar is the Royal Highland Society Gathering, the royal family is always in attendance. The queen and her family were seated in the royal stand. When Bangert's turn came to toss the caber—which he was doing for the first time ever—he slipped with it on the wet grass. Prince Philip laughingly took his photograph and the announcer piped across the field, "Big Bill, you're supposed to bow before the queen, not sit down!"

Despite this embarrassing incident, Bangert liked the Games and began competing in them in the United States. "When I first appeared on the scene in the Highland Games in North America, they were practically a track meet in kilts. The iron shot was tossed, there was the sheaf toss...and the caber. Contestants were not even made to wear the kilt." Things began to change when he brought news of how things were done in Scotland.

Bangert was well equipped to follow through on that lark of an entry at Braemar; at 45 years of age, he was 6' 5" and weighed 280 pounds. He had been an AAU shot and discus champion (he won an AAU shot put championship in Madison Square Garden and auditioned for the Metropolitan Opera on the same day one year), an NCAA discus champion, and a Midwest boxing champion. In a national AAU boxing championship, he came within one fight of meeting Rocky Marciano. In his U.S. Games career Bangert won the heavy events competitions at the United Scottish Society of Southern California Games four times as well as the competitions at Grandfather Mountain, Alma, Dunedin (Florida), Salado (Texas), and Honolulu, the last of which he helped promote. He also won at Maxville, Ontario, and competed in the Diamond Jubilee Games in Melbourne, Australia. An engineer with a degree from Purdue University, Bangert now lives in Anaheim, California.

Arnold Pope of Fayetteville, North Carolina, emerged as the next heavy events notable. An ordained Methodist minister, he holds a bachelor's degree and a master's in divinity from Duke University and a master's in education from North Carolina State University. Pope was an AAU weightlifting champion. In 30 years of participation, he won 27 North Carolina championships and six Southern championships.

His involvement with the Games began in 1966. He was overall champion at Grandfather Mountain and the now-defunct Norfolk Games twice. Over the course of his career, Pope has won first place in every event except the stone throw. His best event has always been the caber; he has won that event at Grandfather Mountain, Charleston, Charlotte, Norfolk, St. Louis, and the Flora MacDonald Games in Red Springs, North Carolina. He won the North American Caber Championship in 1976 and was the first American ever to win an open caber championship in Scotland. On his 1970 trip to compete in Scotland, he placed fifth at the World Caber Toss Championship in Aberdeen, fourth at the Ceres Games, and first at the Newburgh Games.

He still competes in the Games, though not as regularly as in the past. He particularly enjoys Grandfather Mountain, Tidewater, and Red Springs (which is close to his home). He was on the faculty of Methodist College in Fayetteville until 1981 and now works for that city's school system. (Pope is the only athlete who also plays the bagpipe.)

Before the heavy events competition was reorganized into an all-Scottish program, Paul Bidwell, a former member of the Pan American and Olympic weightlifting teams, was doing astounding things in the 56-pound weight toss and the caber. At the Fair Hill Games his weight tosses cleared the bar at 16′ in 1971 and at 16′ 1″ in 1972, using the two-handed toss that was later banned. When the Americans started crossing the ocean to compete in Scotland on a regular basis, Bidwell's reputation had already landed there. Ed McComas has said that he never met anyone who had beat Paul Bidwell in the caber toss. (Bidwell retired from the Games in the early 1970s.)

John Ross started competing at the Games in his hometown of Santa Rosa, California, in 1964 and has not missed a year at those Games since. His longevity as a competitor is second only to that of Ron Short. A 1962 graduate of San Jose State with a degree in physical education, Ross is another track and field convert. In college he threw the shot and discus and participated in the decathlon. He continued to compete in track and field until 1968, when the Games became his main sporting interest.

Ross was one of the Games' early caber champions. In 1975 he won the U.S. Caber Toss Championship at Santa Rosa. He has been overall champion many times at Santa Rosa; Monterey, San Diego, and Campbell, California; and Portland, Oregon. He competed at four Games in Scotland in 1976. He currently works for Santa Rosa Water Systems.

Ron Short of Winston-Salem, North Carolina, began competing in Scottish Games in 1963. A 1968 graduate of the University of North Carolina with a degree in Latin, Short was a shot and discus star in college. He also fenced sabre on the UNC fencing team for two years. Short has won more than 20 Games championships. He has been a multiple winner at heavy events competitions at Grandfather Mountain, Charleston, Stone Mountain, and Alexandria. Short and Bill Anderson are the only athletes ever to have won six events in the same year at Grandfather Mountain, the former in 1975 and the latter in 1978. He has also won the Houston, Virginia Beach, and Altamont Games. In 1977 he won the Canadian Heavy Events Championships in Fergus. While competing in Scotland in 1976, he tied Bill Anderson for first place in the caber at Aboyne and also tied Australian champion Colin Mathieson at Glenisla. He graduated from Wake Forest University Law School in May 1985 and is in private practice in Winston-Salem, North Carolina.

About the same time that Gordon Varnedoe was introduced to the Games, Pete Hoyt of Pittsburgh discovered them. Hoyt is a graduate of Lehigh University, where he was a track and field competitor. He has competed in AAU track for over 25 years and has won more than a dozen district championships in the hammer throw, weight throws, and weightlifting. His first exposure to Scottish Games came in 1972 at Fair Hill. He enjoyed the Games so much that he journeyed down to Grandfather Mountain the next month. He entered that Games' first full heavy events program and won the 22-pound hammer throw.

Hoyt was instrumental in getting the heavy events established at several Games, including Ligonier, St. Louis, and Ft. Ticonderoga, New York (the Memorial Scottish Games). He moved to Florida in 1974 and helped establish heavy events at Orlando (where he served as athletic chairman for several years), Dunedin, Jacksonville, and Ft. Myers (the Scottish Highland Games of Southwest Florida). An executive with Westinghouse in Pittsburgh, he has been president of the NASGA since 1981. He has competed in nearly 125 Games and has been overall champion at Jacksonville, the Rocky Mountain Games in Golden, Colorado, and Ft. Ticonderoga. He has been a frequent winner in the sheaf toss.

In the mid-1970s, the major heavy events athlete was Ed McComas, a Johns Hopkins graduate from Lutherville, Maryland. He was a high school swimming standout, but his forte was track, especially the shot put and discus. He competed for the Baltimore Olympic Club for over 25 years. He won over 60 gold medals in South Atlantic AAU competition. In 1975 he defeated competitors from 23 countries to win the shot put and discus at the World's Masters Championship in Toronto.

McComas first went to the Games at Fair Hill in 1972 to compete in the stone throw. He was impressed with the Games, especially the heavy events and the way so many people seemed to really enjoy watching them. Since then, McComas has competed in over 120 Games and has won 59 of them, more than almost any other athlete. His consistency in all of the events is unmatched by any other American. After more than a dozen years of competing, he continues to hold his own. In 1980 Fred Vaughan won nine overall competitions and McComas won eight; the next highest number won was three. In 1981 Vaughan again won nine and McComas won four; the next highest number won was two. In 1982 and 1983 McComas won seven Games each year. In 1984, the year he turned 50 years old, he won six Games. He remained unbeaten in the sheaf toss from May 1983 until June 1985.

He competed in Scotland in 1976 and won the Braemar stone throw by throwing the 28-pound stone 34' 1". He missed winning the overall championship by one point. At Aboyne he won the 16-pound stone throw, which earned him the Donald Dinnie Trophy, one of the most prestigious heavy events awards in Scotland.

After a recent competition, McComas discussed what he likes best about the Games: "The competition. Just like this weekend; it was super! Even though I only tied for third place, the point spread was incredibly close. One event I lost by three-quarters of an inch. That's the kind of thing that makes you keep going. If I had been trounced on or had won by a wide margin, the feeling wouldn't be the same. I probably would have lost interest in the Games by now if I had kept winning. It's just not very satisfying. A lot of people say, 'Oh, it must be nice to win!' But I've won so many things for so many years, I guess it becomes hollow after a while. Losing a close competition becomes maybe as thrilling as winning. You'd like to win the close competition, but you still want the competition to be close." In professional life, McComas is president of his family's home heating oil business, which dates back to 1871.

McComas has been recognized in a special way for his dedication to the heavy events. A trophy named for him is the top prize awarded in the masters classic heavy events competition first held at the 1985 U.S. Highland Heptathlon Championship at the Alexandria Games. Fred Vaughan was the first recipient of the Edward R. McComas Award.

Brian Oldfield splashed onto the Games scene in 1973, traveled all over the world to compete in them, and splashed out again in 1979. The only time I saw him compete was in the 1979 U.S. Highland Heptathlon in Alexandria. When I saw him that day, I was not aware that it would be one of his last Games performances; of course, neither did he. At the end of that year, he was allowed to return to track and field athletics as an amateur.

In 1976, two years after Fred Vaughan got into the Games, he

Ed McComas, another enduring competitor, shows the effort required in the sheaf toss.

Pete Hoyt, current president of the NASGA, follows through on a stone throw.

Fred Vaughan, NASGA founder and a consistent performer in the heavy events, displays his mastery of the weight throw.

Arnold Pope demonstrates the form that made him the first American to win a caber championship in Scotland.

A gathering of heavy events athletes at the 1982 Gatlinburg Games: from left, Dave Harrington, Tom Carmichael, Pete Hoyt, Jim Pauli, Larry Satchwell, judge Ed Holcombe, George MacAulay, Ed McComas, Wayne Thompson, Ron Short, Rick Porter, Keith Tice, Fred Vaughan, and Bob Kidder.

started his long Games winning streak. Also that year, at Lonach, he became the first American to win an overall Games championship in Scotland. Although he does not compete in as many Games today as he once did, he is still a strong contender. He still spends much time traveling as well in his job as a sales representative.

Keith Tice holds bachelor's and master's degrees in education from California State University at Fresno. Tice competed in the hammer throw at the NCAA University National Championships during his junior and senior years of college. Since his debut in Scottish Games in 1973, he has won more than 30 overall championships. He won the U.S. Heavy Events Championships at Santa Rosa in 1974 and 1975 and placed third there in 1976, 1977, 1978, 1982, 1983, and 1984. He was third in the U.S. Highland Heptathlon at Alexandria in 1978, second in 1985, and won the event in 1981 and 1984. At the Canadian Heavy Events Championships in Fergus, he won second place in 1978 and 1981 and first place in 1982, 1983, 1984, and 1985. He took second place at the 1981 World Heavy Events Championships in Melbourne, Australia, with a score 1½ points behind champion Bill Anderson and won the first Gatlinburg heavy events competition in 1982, defeating a field of 13 seasoned competitors. He finished fourth in the 1984 worlds and second at Santa Rosa in 1985. He holds the American records in the light and heavy hammers. Tice teaches advanced studies to junior high school students. A true Californian, he makes special-order hot tubs and is a eucalyptus tree farmer.

Canadian Dave Harrington received a psychology degree from Stanford University in 1968. He participated in the shot put and discus in college and was Canada's discus champion in 1970 and 1971. Harrington began competing in the caber toss in 1965 at the Maxville, Ontario, Games; in 1978 at the Fergus Games, he began competing in all of the events. He was one of the leading heavy events contenders of the past few years. Because of recurring injuries and an increasingly heavy business schedule, he retired from the Games at the end of the 1984 season.

Harrington left an impressive record of accomplishments in the Games. He was the Canadian champion for seven years and won

35 U.S. and Canadian championships. He represented Canada at all of the world championships; his best showing was fourth place in 1981. In 1983 he won the U.S. Highland Heptathlon Championship in Alexandria. Harrington's most outstanding event was the hammer throw: he was the first North American to throw more than 100′ in the 22-pound hammer. At his retirement from Games competition, he was ranked third out of nearly thirty competitors in the 16-pound (120′ ½″) and 22-pound (102′ ½″) hammers. Harrington is a management consultant and motivational speaker.

George McAulay of Stratford, New Jersey, is a first-generation American whose father was born and raised in Glasgow. His father played the bagpipe and enjoyed going to Games here, and it was he who got George to go to the Grandfather Mountain Games in 1975. The younger McAulay has been competing ever since. When his job took him to the Bahamas for two and a half years, he would often fly to southern Games to compete. His best event is the hammer, but he has also scored victories in the caber toss. (He was the only athlete to turn the caber at the nationally televised Glenfiddich Games in New York's Central Park.) In 1984 he was ranked ninth out of nearly 30 athletes in both hammer events. He won his first Games championship (Southern Maryland) early in 1985. He is participating in a work-study program in which he studies engineering at Drexel University and works on the U.S. Navy Aegis weapons system.

When Michael Reid, the relatively diminutive (5′ 10″, 175) athlete from Monkton, Maryland, was a student at Towson State University in Towson, Maryland, Ed McComas used to practice the heavy events at the school's athletic facilities. Reid had heard about the Games from a friend who had been to Scotland but had never gone to one himself, so when he watched McComas practice, he didn't know what the champ was doing. He went to the Virginia Games in 1977 and saw McComas win the championship. Reid was impressed with the events and with the friendliness that pervaded the competition. The next week he approached McComas and told him that he would like to learn the events. They still spend practice time together, although the roles of teacher and student have long since dissolved.

Reid started competing in the Games in 1978. He competed at the Glenisla Games while visiting Scotland in 1979. Fred Vaughan once described him as the best competitor pound for pound. His top events are the hammer throw and the sheaf toss. Reid is a skilled cabinetmaker specializing in eighteenth-century reproduction furniture.

Jim Pauli, who lives in Saxonburg, Pennsylvania, also started competing in the Games in 1978. In 1972 and 1976 he was the Pennsylvania State Olympic Weightlifting Champion. From 1975 to 1979 he competed in the shot put, discus, 16-pound hammer, and 35-pound weight throw in Sub-Masters track and field. (Since his fortieth birthday in 1983, he has competed at the Masters level.) He read about the Games in Ligonier and, as they included several track-type events, he went there to see what the Games were all about. He discovered not only familiar events, but familiar faces, including Pete Hoyt, whom he knew from weightlifting competition.

Pauli is becoming increasingly proficient in the heavy events. The culmination of his Games career came in 1984 when he was named overall champion of the Chicago Games. He also won both extra events at those Games, the farmer's walk and the beer keg toss. He is a strong contender in the hammer throw and has won that event at several Games. He placed third in 1982 in the hammer among 13 top athletes in Gatlinburg. At the end of the 1984 season, he was ranked tenth out of 31 competitors in the 56-pound weight throw. Professionally, Pauli is president and general manager of a sprinkler company in Pittsburgh.

Tom Johnson graduated from the University of Kentucky in 1972 with a degree in physical therapy. In college he participated in track and field and was the National Collegiate Powerlifting Champion (super-heavyweight class) in his senior year. In 1976 he moved to Charleston to begin graduate studies in physiology at the Medical University of South Carolina. He worked with The Citadel's track and field program as assistant track coach in charge of weight events.

Johnson competed at the Charleston Games from 1976 to 1978 and began competing on a full schedule of 10 or more Games a year in 1979. He set an American record of 45′ 4″ in the

20-pound stone at the 1979 Charleston Games and returned in 1980 to better that mark by 5″, a record that stood for three years. In 1980 he won the stone throw at Grandfather Mountain (setting a new Games record), at Alexandria, and at the first World Heavy Events Championships. In 1981 he was ranked number one in the 17-pound stone throw. He has been overall champion in Jacksonville, Orlando, and Charleston. Internationally, he has competed at Fergus and at two Games in Scotland. He now resides in Phenix City, Alabama, where he works as a physical therapist. Unfortunately he has not competed since the 1981 season and he is sorely missed. Heavy events fans and athletes hope he will return to the Games and continue his outstanding accomplishments.

Also in 1979, another Charleston athlete, Rick Porter, began competing in the Games. He graduated from The Citadel, where he was an education major, in 1972 and earned his master's degree in school administration three years later. In college Porter competed in the shot put and discus. Most of his post-college sporting involvement before the Games was in helping other athletes: he has been coach of the varsity football team at a Charleston high school since 1974, leading the team to first and second place in its conference. He also coaches varsity softball and junior varsity basketball.

Porter's best heavy event is the 56-pound weight toss. He was ranked thirteenth out of 32 competitors at the end of the 1984 season. He placed fourth at the 1981 Antigonish Games in Nova Scotia (the oldest Games in North America); this Games is more accessible to his summer (native) home of Orr's Island, Maine, than to his adopted Charleston. He has also given heavy events demonstrations at the Games now held in Waterville, Maine, and won the first competition at this Games in 1984. He placed second in the 1984 Chicago Games, winning the 20-pound stone, 35-pound weight throw, and the sheaf toss. He tied for first at the Essex Junction, Vermont, Games in 1985.

Tom Carmichael of Knoxville, Tennessee, is a 1971 graduate of the University of Tennessee, where he majored in English and history. He was Southeastern Conference champion in shot put and discus twice and was captain of the track team.

Carmichael attended the heavy events competition at Grandfather Mountain for four years before competing in 1980. In this, his first sports competition since college, he placed third in the stone throw and fifth overall. In 1981 he won the caber toss at Orlando and Jacksonville and the overall title at Houston. He was ranked fifth in the season's standings for the 22-pound hammer throw and was part of a four-way tie for second in the sheaf toss. In 1982 he shared the sheaf toss record with Ed McComas; he finished the season fourth in the 20-pound stone and tied for fifth in the 56-pound weight throw. In 1983 he was a U.S. representative at the World Heavy Events Championships in Carmunnock, Scotland, and placed third in the stone event. He won his first Games in 1983 when he was declared overall winner at the special Glenfiddich Games in New York. Millions of TV viewers saw him show honorary Games chieftain Charlton Heston how to toss the caber. In 1984 he won second place at the U.S. Highland Heptathlon Championship in Alexandria, Virginia.

Carmichael was a member of the board of directors of the first Great Smoky Mountains-Gatlinburg Highland Games and was responsible for bringing thirteen of the best North American Scottish Games athletes together for this special competition. Because of his efforts, a huge crowd of 1982 World's Fair visitors was treated to a demonstration of the heavy events by nine of these top contenders. Carmichael is an account executive with Blue Cross-Blue Shield.

Larry Satchwell of Lawrenceville, Georgia, came into the Games as an amateur at the 1980 Stone Mountain Games and joined the professional group the next year. He holds bachelor's and master's degrees in physical education from Northern Illinois University and has done work toward his doctorate. In college he was named all-American in the 35-pound weight throw and also excelled in the 16-pound hammer. He participated in AAU hammer events from 1975 to 1979 and in the first Summer Olympic Sports Festival in Colorado Springs in 1978. He has served as an AAU hammer coach.

In 1981 he set a new 16-pound hammer record at the Jacksonville Games and won the sheaf toss. He finished that year tied for second in the rankings for the sheaf toss, sixth in the 16-pound hammer, and ninth in the 22-pound hammer. In 1983 he was invited to give a heavy events demonstration at the first competition held in Alabama. At the end of the 1984 season he was ranked sixth in both the light and heavy hammers out of a field of nearly 30 contenders and eighth out of 25 in the sheaf. He is director of the Children's Movement Center in Lilburn, Georgia.

Jim McGoldrick, a bank loan officer from Cupertino, California, is a 1976 graduate of the University of Texas, where he majored in business management. He has accumulated an impressive string of discus titles: national high school champion, 1971; national collegiate champion, 1975; ranked tenth in the world, 1977. McGoldrick competed in the Games as an amateur for ten years before turning professional in 1984. During his amateur tenure, he was consistently ranked among the top ten in the nation. In his first year as a professional he won the San Diego, Fresno, and Stone Mountain Games. At the 1984 U.S. Heavy Events Championship in Santa Rosa he placed second overall, losing to international standout Grant Anderson by a mere one-half of a point. He won the 17-pound stone throw, the 28-pound weight throw, and set a new Games record in the 56-pound weight toss, bettering Grant Anderson's 1982 record of 16' by 6½". He won the 1985 U.S. Highland Heptathlon Championship and the U.S. Heavy Events Championship and was second in the 1985 world championships.

At 28 years of age, Kevin Brady of Campbell, California, is the youngest of the professional athletes in this group. Like Ferency, he wowed the heavy events world by setting a new American record in his first professional season: he boosted the 56-pound weight toss record to 16' 8". Brady, who is a theater arts major at San Jose State College, competed as an amateur from 1981–83. In that category he won 15 Games, including the U.S. Heavy Events Championships in 1983, and held the record in the 17-pound stone throw and the 28-pound weight throw. He was named athlete of the day at Campbell (twice), Monterey (twice), Modesto, and Honolulu.

When Brady began competing as a professional in May 1984, he kept his place at the top. He won three Games in his first professional season and was named athlete of the day at Campbell,

Monterey (where he set the new American record in the 56-pound weight toss), Sacramento, and Modesto. He tied for first place in Honolulu. At the 1984 U.S. Heavy Events Championships in Santa Rosa, he placed fourth overall out of a field of 12 international competitors, winning the caber toss and setting a new Games record in the 26-pound Braemar stone throw. He finished fourth in the 1985 world championships.

Brady also came to the heavy events by way of track and field. In college he competes in shot put and discus. He also does Olympic weightlifting and powerlifting.

Paul Ferency of Easton, Pennsylvania, stunned the athletes and onlookers alike at his first Scottish Highland Games (Devon, Pennsylvania, 1984). Not only did he exceed the American 20-pound stone record by nearly six feet, but in his elation he smartly whirled his 6' 5", 300-plus-pound body in a back flip. He finished his inaugural Games by winning the 28-pound weight throw and the 56-pound weight toss and placing second overall to veteran Ed McComas.

The 1979 graduate of East Stroudsburg (Pennsylvania) University was a college shot-put standout. He was an NCAA all-American in the event for three years, All-East ICAAAA in 1978 and 1979, and Pennsylvania Conference champion in 1976, 1978, and 1979. He was the Keystone State Games shot-put champion in 1982 and shot-put and discus champion in 1983. He was a member of the East team at the U.S. Sports Festival in 1979.

At the end of the 1984 season, Ferency had competed in four Games and had left his mark on all of them. At the championship Games in Alexandria in July, he won the 17-pound stone throw—again hurling the implement over 51 feet—and the 23-pound Braemar stone throw, setting a new Games record of 40' 11¼" in the latter. At the Capital District Games in Altamont, New York, he set new Games records in the 20-pound stone, the 28-pound weight throw, and the 56-pound weight toss. He ended up his whirlwind season by placing third overall at the Ligonier Games, setting new Games records in the 20-pound stone throw and the 28-pound weight throw. He continued to excel in 1985 with a first at Fair Hill and excellent showings in the 17-pound stone.

Not only is Ferency one of the strongest new contenders, he is excited about the Games and eager to compete in as many as he can. He is a supervisor in a children's detention center.

THE JUDGES

In Scotland the heavy events are usually judged by ex-Scottish Games athletes. America, however, does not have many ex-athletes because the resurgence of U.S. Games occurred so recently. Many Games have their own judges and officials to run the heavy events; Jimmy Flynn, for example, has faithfully served at Fair Hill since 1970. But Games competitors and fans are fortunate to have a dedicated group of men who are devotees of the sport and cover most of the major competitions.

Horace Crow was head judge at Santa Rosa for many years. He was also an AAU track official. The major West Coast heavy events judge now is Stan Russell of San Jose, California. He is an ex-Games competitor who starred in the caber toss at many California Games. He is also ex-president of the Northern California Highland Dancing Association and has two daughters who competed in Highland dancing.

In the East, John Severance of Paoli, Pennsylvania, officiates at the national heptathlon championships in Alexandria and the Games at Devon and Ligonier in his home state. Severance has been judging for more than ten years, usually accompanied by Betsy Roberts, his chief assistant and official recorder. Dave McKenzie, who took over as director of athletics at the 1985 Virginia Scottish Games, judges regional Games including Southern Maryland, Delco, Tidewater, Ligonier, and Williamsburg.

Before his recent retirement, Guy Soule of Charlotte, North Carolina, covered Games in the South. Ross Morrison of Harrisburg, North Carolina, continues to do so. Morrison has been connected with the Grandfather Mountain Games for most of its existence and is its current chairman of Scottish athletics. In 1981 Morrison judged the U.S. Heavy Events Championships in Santa Rosa.

Art Rigg's home Games is Stone Mountain, but he also travels to other major Southern Games to help officiate. Ed Holcombe of Charleston has been judging athletics at several Southern

Games for many years. He judged the first World Heavy Events Championships in Pomona, California, and the Santa Rosa Games in 1980.

A final note on Ed Holcombe: most of the athletes have him to thank for their practice implements. Before he cast the first weights and hammers, many athletes had to devise their own practice implements of approximate regulation weight. Arnold Pope used to practice the weight throws using a car battery; Dave Harrington swung an old sewing machine. The athletes' scores showed considerable improvement when they were able to get their own practice implements of regulation size and weight.

4

Piping and Drumming

There is a legend about a parade that was held in Chicago in the late 1800s to kick off a Scottish gathering. According to the legend, the sound of bagpipes startled a horse, which reared up and threw its rider through a shop window. The court case that resulted was decided on the basis of whether or not the bagpipe was a musical instrument. The verdict went against the pipes.

On July 24, 1982, Chicago held its first PipeFest USA. Abundant travel money was available to pipe bands that were invited to compete for prize money totaling $20,000. Regional and foreign bands were enticed to converge upon the city that had once legally declared that the bagpipe was not a musical instrument.

This turnabout illustrates the wide acceptance being enjoyed by Scotland's Great Highland Bagpipe in the United States today. People flock to parades and gatherings to hear the stirring sound of pipes and drums and to watch the colorful and impressive march of the tartan-clad band members. The lure prevails: there is something rousing about the combination of pipes and drums and tartan.

ABOUT THE PIPES

Historical evidence suggests that bagpipes were used in scattered parts of the ancient world. Several countries today have some form of the instrument, but none are as prevalent or revered as the Great Highland Bagpipe of Scotland. It is unlike any other instrument of this classification—or any other musical instrument, for that matter.

The bagpipe consists of a blow pipe, three upper pipes called drones, a chanter (the lower pipe with eight holes that produce the different notes), and a bag. The instrument takes a bit of coordination to play: the blow pipe hangs from the mouth, the drones go over the shoulder, the bag rests under the arm, and the chanter hangs down within easy reach of the hands. There are four reeds in a bagpipe: a double one in the chanter and a single one in each of the drones. These reeds are adjusted to the piper's blowing strength. The chanter reed is set to produce a bright A note, and the drones are tuned as follows: the tenor drones are one octave below and the bass drone two octaves below the low A, giving the bagpipe a three-octave range (although the notes of the bottom two octaves, the ones produced by the drones, never vary). The drones are tuned by moving them up to flatten or down to sharpen. Moisture and temperature changes cause the pitches to change. In order for the pipes to stay on pitch during performance—one of the first things a judge listens for in a competition—the instrument must be adequately tuned, which takes 15 to 30 minutes.

Air is not forced in by vigorous blowing, but blown into the bag and kept there by breathing naturally through the mouth. Pipers generally take anywhere from 12 to 55 breaths per minute, with an average of about 30. When the piper takes a breath, he applies slight pressure to the bag—just letting his arm gently press the bag toward his body—to maintain the essential steady flow of air. The bag must be absolutely airtight. If any air escapes, it will affect the sound. To check the bag for leaks, the piper plugs the stocks and fills the bag with air. At full extension, the bag should be as hard as a football. The bag itself is subject to a lot of moisture and must be seasoned regularly to keep it pliable and airtight. In Scotland, bags are usually made of sheep hide; in Australia, kangaroo; and in the United States, cow or Canadian elk. The climate of a particular area determines which hide is best for the bag.*

*Jim Ling, a recent president of the Eastern United States Pipe Band Association, tells a story about bringing his bagpipe cover to the dry cleaner's with some other items. The unknowing dry cleaner noted it on the itemized

The scale of the Highland bagpipe makes it unique. Simply put, it is the scale of A with the notes C and F slightly sharpened and an extra G below the low A. However, this is not the chromatic scale (the 13-note scale covered by the white and black piano keys in one octave) that most people are used to hearing. The Great Highland Bagpipe, unlike other instruments (including other bagpipes), has a fixed 9-note scale all its own. Accordingly, most music for this instrument is written with no key signature, since it can only be played in one key. This fixed scale has intervals that vary from the familiar intervals of the chromatic scale, which often causes the uninitiated to think that the instrument is out of tune. One must appreciate the uniqueness of the instrument and familiarize oneself with its sound to enjoy its music fully.

Because of its fixed scale, when the bagpipe (the term I use hereafter, along with *pipes,* to refer to Scotland's Great Highland Bagpipe) is played along with other instruments, the other instruments must be played in the key of B^b, and notes that would be discordant because of the bagpipe's differing intervals are deleted. Bear in mind, however, that the bagpipe originated as a solo instrument. As Francis Collinson states in his book *The Traditional and National Music of Scotland,* "The notes of the bagpipes are never intended to be *sounded together in harmony,* as are wind instruments in an orchestra. The bagpipe is a *solo,* or at least a *unison, melodic* instrument which is only required to harmonize to the sound of its own drones."

The bagpipe has been called the most difficult of the wind instruments to play. Sandy Jones, director of bagpipes at The Citadel in Charleston, says this may be true, because the pipes, unlike other wind instruments, cannot be "tongued" to produce special effects. Since the mouth is used only to keep a steady flow of air going to the bag, everything that is done with the lips, tongue, and fingers on other wind instruments must be done with the fingers alone on the bagpipe. This brings up another important part of playing the pipes: the grace notes. Since there is no way to stop the flow of music once it begins—the bagpipe

---

receipt as "1 dog coat." (This caused Jim some confusion at first, since the Lings did not own a dog—especially not a five-legged one.)

sounds even when all of the chanter holes are covered—musical embellishments called grace notes are struck between the melody notes. The grace notes give character and rhythm to the music. (One type of variation in piobaireachd or classical pipes music, the crunluath, requires *seven* grace notes after each melody note. Needless to say, extreme dexterity is required of the fingers when playing this type of music.) So a piper is not only playing the melody with his fingers but the rhythm and the special effects as well.

Roderick (Roddy) MacDonald of Newark, Delaware, emphasizes the importance of the mechanics of the pipes. It is a very temperamental instrument; to produce the best sound requires knowledge of and strict attention to its working order. In other words, proper teaching—knowing *how* to blow the pipes—is fundamental.

Learning to play the bagpipe proficiently is a gradual process. A piper spends a minimum of three to six months learning the scale, grace notes, and movements on a practice chanter. Special miniature chanters allow students as young as five or six to learn the instrument. Once the student masters the practice chanter, he begins coordinating all he has learned with the mechanics of the actual bagpipe. An old school of thought derived from the MacCrimmon legacy says that it takes seven years to make a piper. This may not be entirely true, but it does take a great deal of determination to become an adept piper. It takes a good deal of money, too; the least expensive set of pipes available today costs about $400. Heavily ornamented pipes can cost thousands of dollars.

The Gamesgoer who does not understand the significance of what is occurring in solo bagpipe competitions but is thrilled at the sight and sound of the massed bands—which is an altogether natural and desired reaction—is perhaps taking for granted the full merit of this instrument. Knowing the preparation that must go into playing of this special and demanding instrument should elicit greater appreciation for both the pipes and the piper.

BETTER THAN EVER

The overall quality of piping and drumming in the United States is reaching great heights today. This situation is the result of a number of influences, and much credit must go to the Scots themselves. Pipers in this country have enjoyed the benefit of the tutelage of some of Scotland's outstanding pipers, who have settled in the United States or come here every year to conduct piping schools and workshops for the new breed of pipers. Competitions today are keen and exacting; both judges and judged strive for the highest allegiance to the art.

The high standards of competition found at the Games keep the level of piping and drumming moving upwards. These criteria were established by three organizations that govern the competitions. Such organizations are quite common; Scotland has the Scottish Pipe Band Association and the Scottish Pipers' Association for solo pipers. The Piobaireachd Society promotes the classical music of the pipes. There is also the Institute of Piping, which is comprised of the Piobaireachd Society, the College of Piping in Glasgow, and the Army School of Piping in Edinburgh. In Canada there are five organizations: the British Columbia Pipers' Association, which governs solo piping in British Columbia; the Western Pipe Band Association, which governs bands in British Columbia as well as the states of Washington and Oregon; the Prairie Pipe Band Society, which governs Alberta, Manitoba, and Saskatchewan; the Pipers' and Pipe Band Society of Ontario; and the Nova Scotia Pipers' and Pipe Band Association.

Necessity caused the U.S. to adopt similar organizations. The few piping and drumming competitions that existed at Games in the United States in the early to mid-1900s were reportedly inefficiently organized and poorly judged. There were not many good solo pipers here, and the level of competition available did little to make the few that existed want to participate. The limited piping instruction available was usually obtained through a small number of bands. Now, however, thanks primarily to two separate organizations, the American piping scene has changed radically.

PACIFIC COAST PIPE BAND ASSOCIATION (PCPBA)

On August 31, 1963, mainly at the instigation of members of the now-defunct Caledonian Club of San Francisco Pipe Band, representatives of several pipe bands from Northern and Southern California met in Santa Rosa to discuss the feasibility of forming a pipe band association. Several factors led to this meeting, including inadequate judging and lack of rules for band competitions. The PCPBA was formally organized on January 18 and 19, 1964, in Santa Maria. A steering committee consisting of a chairman and ten members was elected to represent pipers and drummers from both areas of the state. They were: chairman, Sam Sweetman of San Francisco; Northern California members, Pipe Major Thomas Arthur, Pipe Major Thomas Kinnear, Drum Sergeant John Paterson, Drum Major G. Allen Smith, and Stan Patterson; Southern California members, Trevor Atkinson, John Hynd, Pipe Major James McColl, James Thomas, and Pipe Major John Rosenberger.

As delineated in its handbook, the PCPBA has the following objectives: "To promote and encourage the culture and advancement of Pipe Band music in the U.S.A.; to create and maintain a bond of Fellowship with all Pipers and Drummers; and to devise and operate a proper system of Pipe Band Contest Rules." The PCPBA does not govern solo events—only those events involving a multiplicity of pipes: trios, quartets, miniature bands, and bands. (A miniature band has four pipers, two side drummers, and one bass drummer. They are mostly seen on the West Coast.)

The PCPBA was founded to govern pipe bands in California and originally had two branches, the north and the south. The organization expanded in 1984 and went beyond the boundaries of California. The new intermountain branch includes bands in such states as Utah, Colorado, and New Mexico. The organization requires all contests in its domain to be run under its rules, although the organization works with the Scottish Games and other contests to incorporate agreeable local rules. All California bands that compete at a Games offering such a contest must be members of the association, but nonmember bands from elsewhere in the West and from Canada can and do compete at California contests under PCPBA rules.

The PCPBA places its more than 30 member bands into one of four grades. Until about 1982, the grading system of the PCPBA differed somewhat from the system used in other parts of the

United States, Canada, and Scotland, and there were several Grade I bands under its jurisdiction. Today, however, there are no Grade I bands in the PCPBA (although Grade I contests are held for visiting Canadian bands at Santa Rosa) and the grading system is more or less universal.

There are no championship Games for bands in the PCPBA region. At the end of the competition season, the organization lists the events held and the total points accumulated by each participating band.

The roster of approved PCPBA judges reads like an honor roll of piping and drumming greats from across the United States, Canada, and Scotland. The association prefers to employ judges from as far away as possible, but economy often overrules preference; it is less expensive to bring a judge from, let's say, another part of the state than from another part of the country. If local judges are used, those from Northern California are sought for the southern contests and vice versa to prevent subjective judging. As is done in Scotland, the PCPBA uses three judges to determine a band's score: piping, drumming, and ensemble (the total sound of the band).

Solo piping at Games in the western United States is judged by the PCPBA panel along local standards, although a basic format is followed. There are three categories: novice, amateur, and professional. A novice piper is one who has not won first prize in a major competition and has not competed in any amateur contests. The novice event is a march. An amateur is a piper who has never competed for or accepted cash prizes. A professional piper competes for cash prizes. The amateur and professional events are MSR (march, strathspey, and reel), hornpipe and jig, and piobaireachd. (A full explanation of these musical forms follows later in this chapter.) The professional category also has a four-minute medley event.

EASTERN UNITED STATES
PIPE BAND ASSOCIATION
(EUSPBA)

Duncan McCaskill, Sr., grew up in a small coal mining village in Scotland. When he started playing the pipes at age nine, he had to walk three or four miles to the home of his instructor, John Douglass, for lessons. McCaskill loved the pipes and was being primed as a solo player. (In Scotland, unlike the U.S., most solo pipers still do not play in bands.) But as McCaskill recalled in an interview, the lure of the band was too great. "You know how kids are—they see a band playing and want to get into that. I never let up on him [Douglass] 'til I finally got into a band. I played in 1921, 1923, 1924, and 1925 at Cowal with the band."

When McCaskill was 18 years old, his family moved to the United States. For five years before he left Scotland, he was receiving piping instruction seven nights a week. The last few months before coming to his new home in New Jersey he was taught by George Yardley, who had won the gold medal at Oban in 1911. "He was mad as a hornet when he found out I was leaving for America," said McCaskill. "He wanted me to stay with him for a couple of years and study." But McCaskill had a job waiting for him with Standard Oil Company, and his first allegiance was to his family. His father chose to come to America to establish a new life for his family and to give his sons a future other than the coal mines. McCaskill knew that his father would be needing his financial help. So Standard Oil's small pipe band became young McCaskill's only opportunity to practice piping. Piping instructors were scarce in the U.S. in the 1920s, so he never had another piping lesson.

He began competing in 1926 in a few Games in his area. The competitors in those days were few, and the judging was in name only: "I could figure on my ten fingers just who I had to watch out for in America in my day.... Some judges were has-beens; they never won anything in their lives. They could *talk* piping, but they really didn't know much about it." His first breakthrough came when he won a gold medal in Boston, and from then on he did very well. At one Games in New Jersey over a period of ten years, he received eighteen first prizes, two seconds, and a third. He also competed in Canada and won a number of prizes; McCaskill was prouder of his Canadian successes because the competition there was much stiffer than any he faced in America.

He became involved with other piping activities in this country as well. Soon after his arrival, he joined the Lovat Pipe Band in New York City, one of the top competitive bands of the day. When it merged with the Cameron Pipe Band in Kearney, New Jersey, to become the Lovat-Cameron Pipe Band, McCaskill became pipe major. He was piper to three clans and, when he started teaching later, gave private lessons and worked with several school pipe bands. He also piped for Highland dancing for nearly 40 years.

McCaskill never learned piobaireachd, nor were there any piobaireachd competitions in America when he first came. But he won the slow air competitions every year and, as for the MSR, hornpipes, jigs, and other small music, "I'd beat the best of them." He took his son (Duncan McCaskill, Jr., one of the top drum majors in the East today) to Johnny Miller in Kearney, New Jersey, to study piobaireachd, and in 1961, when Duncan Jr. was 16 years old, his father took him to Cowal to compete. The boy placed fourth in his division.

Through the years the Games slowly began to multiply. Several excellent pipers and drummers who were willing and eager to share their expertise with others emigrated to McCaskill's part of the United States. But the judging situation at the competitions still did not improve. When some of these top Scottish musicians took beatings here, McCaskill knew it was time for a change.

In 1964 representatives of several pipe bands met in Asbury Park, New Jersey, to form the United States Pipe Band Association, based on the Scottish Pipe Band Association, with McCaskill as the first president. The other organizers were Robert Gilchrist, James Kerr, George Bell, Maclean Macleod, and James Cairns. These piping enthusiasts had the welfare of the competing pipe bands at heart and wanted fair, competently judged contests. The members of this group traveled at their own expense trying to arouse interest in the new organization. It was a slow process, but Games organizers eventually began to see the worth of such a parent group.

McCaskill went to Scotland in 1968 to become certified as a judge by the Scottish Pipe Band Association. What he thought would be merely a matter of taking a test turned out to be nearly three months of intensive instruction.

In 1972 the organization's name was changed to the Eastern United States Pipe Band Association to reflect its main geographical realm. Also, awareness of the PCPBA precluded the use of the former name. McCaskill turned over the presidency of the EUSPBA to Roddy MacDonald, who came to this country from Dunoon. MacDonald was well qualified for the position. He started piping at age nine and won many major juvenile awards in Scotland. At age seventeen, he became the youngest piper ever to win the prestigious Territorial and Army Cup. He was a member of the Argyll & Sutherland Highlanders and of the renowned Invergordon Distillery Band, which was composed of the best, hand-picked Scottish pipers. The latter band won the Scottish, British, and European championships and placed third in world competition. In 1970 MacDonald won the Prince Charles Cup at an international competition sponsored by the College of Piping in Glasgow for composing a strathspey and reel. After emigrating to America, he won every major award for MSR and piobaireachd on the East Coast, including the Fair Hill Boreraig Trophy six times and the North American championship at Maxville, Ontario, twice. He was also instrumental in the founding of the Delco Scottish Games Workshop. MacDonald has been judging in this country since he was 27 years old—not because he wanted to start judging at such a young age, but because the lack of qualified judges here prompted it.

Under his guidance the EUSPBA was revamped to reflect its new attitude and future goals. This revamping shook the foundations of the piping tradition. In 1972 all competing bands in the EUSPBA were assigned a grade based on a full season's performance. The association expanded to include solo piping and drumming competitors, all of whom were also assigned a grade. It was in this area that the most dramatic changes occurred. The new grading system was based on the competitor's skill, not his age as in Scotland and Canada—which led to the motto "Stages, not ages." Four grades were created for the amateur class and two for the open (professional) class. The latter class was split to give those competitors advancing into the higher ranks breathing space before facing the more accomplished pipers. Piobaireachd became a required competition for both amateur and open classes. The concept of sanctioning assured competitors that they would be allowed to compete in their grades and according to accepted standards at all competitions run under this system. (This is no small feat: in 1984 there were approximately 90 bands and 900 individual members of this organization throughout five branches—Northeast, New York/ New Jersey metropolitan, Chesapeake, Southeast, and Southwest.) A program to expand the judges' panel was developed, and judging sheets were created to guarantee standardized judging. Such sheets proved to be such a sound innovation that they were soon adopted universally.

Ten years later, at the EUSPBA's annual general meeting in November 1982, the organization again stirred the piping world when it presented its adjudication program, which requires a strict examination regime for admission to the panel of judges. The United States is the only country having such an extensive program. Maclean Macleod, a founding member and past president of the EUSPBA, called this event "the greatest advance in piping in the last 100 years."

The area of judging has always been in dispute, and not just in this country. (There is even a Scottish pipe tune called "The Judging Was Bad.") The EUSPBA adjudication program marks the first concrete attempt to remedy this situation. Those now wishing to become judges for the EUSPBA must pass a stringent test to prove that they are authoritative in the field. The applicant must be fully knowledgeable in music and note-perfect in the music of the pipes. A minimum of 10 years' experience as a successful competitor is a prerequisite for taking the examination. Candidates who pass the examination become provisional judges. After judging three times in each of the categories in which they have applied, the EUSPBA Adjudication Advisory Board reviews their judging performance before they are admitted to the panel of judges. There are seven categories in which to apply: all areas of piping, amateur piobaireachd, open piobaireachd, Grades I and II pipe bands, Grades III and IV pipe bands, amateur piping—light music, and open piping— light music. Plans are for these seven levels to be eventually fused into three: piobaireachd, light music, and bands. The board also set standards for drumming judges, and there are two categories covered: snare, and tenor and bass.

Duncan McCaskill was named president emeritus for life of the EUSPBA at the revamping in 1972. Until his death in 1985 at age 78, he remained keenly interested in the piping scene. In an interview in 1982, I asked him what he thought of piping in the United States today. "The EUSPBA has made a big, big difference in piping. The piping today is way far superior to what it was in my day.... I would say that if I had to compete today, I would have a tough job."

MIDWEST PIPE BAND ASSOCIATION (MWPBA)

Like the other groups, the MWPBA was formed in 1964 and had ten member bands. According to a 1965 dance program (the organization used to sponsor Scottish dances), the officers were: president, William James; vice president, Donald Quig; treasurer, James Beecher; and Games secretary, Taylor MacDonald. The main event in the MWPBA calendar of events used to be a piping contest at Chicago's Grant Park.

The organization disintegrated in the early 1970s but was reformed in 1979, with Bruce Liberato as chairman of the organizing committee. It was officially started again in November 1980 with the following officers: president, Terry McHugh; vice president, Bruce Liberato; and secretary/treasurer, Nancy Taylor Campbell.

The MWPBA covers bands only; there are currently 35 members. There are three contests offering competitions under its sanctioning: St. Paul, Minnesota; Kansas City, Missouri; and Chicago (again at Grant Park and again the major event). Sanctioning at other Games is in the planning stages. Although the organization does not have solo memberships as yet, it sponsors several solo events in the Games' off season to keep the individual band members in competition shape.

PIPE BANDS

The phenomenon of pipe bands, always a big attraction at Scottish Games, is a relatively recent one. The drum, long considered a military instrument used to signal troops, has been in Scotland (and everywhere else, as it is also the oldest known musical instrument) since time immemorial. The special effectiveness of the pipes to incite soldiers, be they clansmen or army regiments, to battle has caused it to be called a weapon of war. However, not until the mid-nineteenth century did the pipes and drums come together as a military unit, the regimental band.

In his book *Scottish Highland Games,* David Webster states that the first massed piping event took place in 1745 when the clans and their pipes united under Bonnie Prince Charlie in his struggle to reclaim the Scottish throne for the Stuarts. In 1781, the year before the lifting of the Act of Proscription, the first solo piping competition was held at Falkirk. The first recorded competitive pipe band event, however, was not held until 1906 at the Cowal Highland Gathering in Dunoon. The first few competitions were open only to army pipe bands, but in 1909 the contest was broadened to include civilian bands as well. This was done at the urging of Scotland's famous entertainer Harry Lauder, who had worked as a miner and knew of several bands in the mining regions. The melding of pipes and drums that resulted outside the military proved that this move had been accepted.

Historian and author Rowland Berthoff, a professor at Washington University in St. Louis, has done extensive research into the history of U.S. Scottish Games. Though the facts are not as concrete in this area as a historian would like, his research has revealed that the first pipe band in the United States was formed in Chicago about 1895. The Pittsburgh Pipe Band Society was organized in 1900; in Boston, the site of the first regularly scheduled Games in this country (beginning in 1853), the Massachusetts Highland Dress Association appeared in 1902. About eight years later the Gordon Highlanders were formed in Buffalo, New York. By 1940 there were more than 30 pipe bands in the United States, more than half of which were found in the Northeast. Only two were on the West Coast: the Caledonian Club of San Francisco Pipe Band was formed in 1915, and a band was started in Seattle the following year. The remaining bands were spread throughout the upper Midwest. The Caledonian

Blue Ribbon Pipe Band of Winston-Salem, North Carolina, organized in 1946, was the first pipe band in the South.

Several of these early pipe bands are still in existence, including two of the top EUSPBA bands, the Manchester (Connecticut) Pipe Band (formed in 1914) and the Worcester (Massachusetts) Kiltie Pipe Band (formed in 1916). The oldest *continuous* pipe band in the United States today is the Holyoke Caledonian Pipe Band, which was formed in 1910. It competes in Grade IV at Games in the northeastern part of the country and participates in many private and charitable functions.

When one considers that the bagpipe is traditionally a solo instrument and appeared at the Games in Scotland as such for more than a century, pipe bands do seem relatively new. But when one considers the large number of bands, particularly competitive bands, in this country today—186 by one count— and the fact that the majority of them only date from the 1970s, pipe bands seem remarkably new. Their rapid rise is proof of the tradition they have become.

At the Games in Scotland it is unusual to see more than one pipe band. The exceptions, of course, are Games featuring pipe band competitions that attract large numbers of bands; at the 1979 Cowal championships held in Dunoon, the Games known for large numbers of pipe bands, 142 bands appeared. In the United States, on the other hand, it is uncommon to find a Games at which only one band appears. Most Games offer pipe band competitions, with those offering championships and the prestige that accompanies victories naturally attracting larger numbers of bands. The EUSPBA determines the top bands according to a scoring system based on the greatest number of points accumulated throughout the competition season, but it also offers championships at various Games. In a championship, a band can compete only in its own grade; in a regular Games competition, however, a band may compete one grade higher than its assigned grade, provided the prerequisites are met. The U.S. Open at Alma, Michigan, the Northeastern U.S. at Altamont, New York, and the Eastern U.S. at Fair Hill, Maryland, are the eminent championships.

The Games at Maxville, Ontario, host the North American

Pipe Band Championships. Top bands from Canada and the United States vie for the prestigious honors at that event. Canada has several fine Grade I bands that have competed on the West Coast and in the Midwest region, such as at the Chicago PipeFest. They are seldom seen in the area of EUSPBA jurisdiction except as guest bands because Grade II was the highest grade competition offered until 1986.

The Scottish Pipe Band Association World Championship in Scotland was first held in 1947. The site of this championship changes annually. As in the world-class solo competitions, Scotland has long been the possessor of these titles. Until recently, few North American bands competed in Scotland because of the cost involved in transporting a band across the ocean and the comparatively lower quality of the bands here. Both limitations, however, are being overcome.

In 1966, 60 years after the beginning of pipe band competitions, the City of Toronto Pipe Band placed fifth in the world championships at Inverness. This marked the first time that a band from outside Scotland had ever finished on the prize list there. In 1969 the Worcester Kiltie Pipe Band became the first U.S. pipe band to win a first prize in Scotland—in Lesmahagow, Lanarkshire. That same year the Seattle Boys' Pipe Band won the Robertson Cup, awarded to the best juvenile band in the world, in Edinburgh, making it the first band from outside Scotland to win the coveted prize. In 1973 the Prince Charles Juvenile Pipe Band of Marin County, California, was the first U.S. band to ever *appear* at the Cowal Games. The Manchester Pipe Band was named best overseas pipe band in Grade II at the world championships in 1977. The Prince Charles Juvenile Pipe Band returned to Cowal in 1978 and left its mark by becoming the first U.S. band to win in any division there. It also took first place at the Rothesay Games and at the Edinburgh Festival Invitational Games. At the world championships that year, the band placed first in piping, third in drumming, and eighth overall. In 1982 the Dunedin (Florida) Pipe Band placed seventh out of 38 bands in the Grade III competition at the world championships and was named best overseas pipe band. Dunedin also placed third, fourth, and fifth at Rothesay, Edinburgh, and

Cowal, respectively. The Midlothian Scottish Pipe Band (Mundelein, Illinois) placed eighth at the 1983 world championships and second at both Perth and Rothesay. The drum corps of the Denny & Dunipace (Washington, D.C.) and Charlotte (North Carolina) pipe bands have taken top prizes at the world championships as well.

PIPING SCHOOLS

Stiffer competition at the Games, particularly in the solo events, meant that competitors had to adhere to specific expectations in each grade in order to advance to a higher level. Many believe that the United States has the highest level of interest in the bagpipe of any country today. This is testimony to the fervor with which many students of the pipes approach the art. The success of piping schools, most of which provide short-term, intensive instruction by some of the greatest authorities in piping and drumming today, illustrates the fact that today's students are eager to learn as much as possible from the masters.

The first piping school in the United States was founded in Petersburg, New York, in 1961 by John F. Lindsay. He called it the Invermark College of Piping because the scenery of that area reminded him of his hometown, Invermark, on the east coast of Scotland. The idea behind the school, which began as a summer school, was that it would be similar in philosophy to the piping school that the famed MacCrimmons had established centuries before: it would be a place set apart for total concentration on piping. (More on the MacCrimmons later in this chapter.) American pipers were so eager for definitive instruction that they came from across the country to the live-in school, which housed about 40 students.

John F. Lindsay's main interest was piobaireachd (classical piping), the playing and knowledge of which was virtually non-existent in this country at that time. He had the idea of bringing top players from Scotland to teach students in this country. Until the 1970s, one of four experts would visit annually to share expertise. They were Thomas Pearston, co-founder of the College of Piping in Glasgow; John MacFadyen, who was later instrumental in forming the North American Academy of Piping; Bob Brown, the Queen's Piper at Balmoral; and Bob Nichol, successor to Brown as Queen's Piper.

In 1975 the school became year-round. There are no longer housing accommodations; the students, who now number about 200, come after work, after school, on weekends, or on vacations. The school is currently under the direction of John Lindsay's son Donald, who is a former president of the EUSPBA. Donald is the resident piper, and there are part-time instructors as well.

Donald F. MacDonald, co-founder of the Grandfather Mountain Highland Games, calls the last decade the "seventies explosion" in Scottish Highland Games. This assessment is also reflected in most of the individual parts of the Games. Most of the current pipe bands were formed in the 1970s, and at least nine more piping schools were established during that decade.

The Summer School for Piping held at Coeur d'Alene, Idaho, was established in 1967 by the late John McEwing. A native of Ontario, he retired from the U.S. Air Force to live in Spokane, Washington. He was an ardent proponent of piobaireachd and in 1969 formed the Spokane Piobaireachd Society, which took over the operation of the summer school in order to perpetuate the classical music of the pipes. Also in 1969 the school moved to its present site, North Idaho College, which became a co-sponsor of the summer event the following year. (North Idaho is the only two-year school in the country that offers a fully accredited course in advanced piping.) The staff of this school has included the late John Wilson, one of the leading authorities on and players of piobaireachd and the winner of gold medals at Inverness and Oban (after an accident that resulted in the partial loss of three fingers on his left hand); Seumas MacNeill, co-founder and principal of the College of Piping in Glasgow and 1962 Oban gold medal winner; Pipe Major Robert G. Hardie, famous Glasgow bagpipe manufacturer and a former Oban gold medalist; and Ed MacRae, 1982 gold medal winner at Oban and Portree.

In 1972 three schools were established. The California School of Piping, now located in Santa Cruz, is under the direction of Seumas MacNeill. John Burgess, who won the gold medals at both Oban and Inverness when he was 16 years old, shares teaching responsibilities. The Piping School of Dallas was founded by Bob Forbes and features Seumas MacNeill. The North American Academy of Piping was founded by Pipe Major Sandy Jones and John MacFadyen, two notable names in the world of piping. Jones, a native of Idaho, was pipe major of the U.S. Air Force Pipe Band and is now director of piping at The Citadel. Jones became director of piping at the Grandfather Mountain Highland Games in 1971, the year John MacFadyen first went to that Games to judge and perform. Their meeting resulted in the formation of the North American Academy of Piping, with sites at Grandfather Mountain and Accident, Maryland. Until his death in 1979, John MacFadyen was considered one of the top performers of piobaireachd in the world. He was the only piper ever to win the four top piping awards in a single competition season: the gold medals at Oban and Inverness, the Silver Chanter at Dunvegan Castle in Skye, and the Bratach Gorm in London. Since 1979, Hamilton Workman, now of Wellesley, Massachusetts, has been co-director of this workshop. Workman studied under Pipe Major Willie Ross at the Army School of Piping in Edinburgh. When he received his certificate he was the youngest pipe major in the British Army. He was piper to the Earl of Mountbatten and won the silver medal at Oban.

In 1974 an institution with another format was established. The first Delco Scottish Games Workshop was held in King of Prussia, Pennsylvania, and the event has since proved very successful. Prime movers behind the workshop were EUSPBA president Roddy MacDonald and his wife, Gladys, who teaches Highland dancing and is coordinator of Highland dancing at the Delco Games. It was felt that having such a workshop during the Games' off season would give the participants an opportunity to get together for instruction rather than competition, and it indeed has created much harmony among the individuals who attend the event. Top-caliber instructors in piping, drumming, and Highland dancing from the United States, Canada, and Scotland teach at this two-day workshop. In recent years there have been over 500 participants, and the Saturday ceilidh regularly attracts over 1,000 people.

The Rocky Mountain School of Piping in Denver, Colorado, was first held in 1978. Roddy MacDonald is the instructor for this week-long school held just prior to the Rocky Mountain Highland Games. In 1984 Gordon Speirs was added as an instructor.

In 1979 the Ohio Scottish Games began the Ohio Scottish Arts School. This school, which attracts nearly 100 students from throughout the United States and Canada, is held the week after the Games. It offers instruction in piping, drumming, Highland dancing, and the clarsach (Scottish harp).

Two of the more recent piping schools, both established in 1979, were founded by pipers who were students at the Invermark College of Piping. Albert McMullin of Wilmington, Delaware, founded the Balmoral School of Piping and Drumming in Greensboro, North Carolina, and George Balderose of Pittsburgh founded the Balmoral School of Highland Piping in Edinboro, Pennsylvania. McMullin, who went through college on piping scholarships, was pipe major of the Charlotte (North Carolina) Scottish Pipe Band and the Atlanta Pipe Band. He also served as director of the St. Thomas Episcopal School Pipe Band in Houston. He has featured Murray Henderson and Alex Duthart at his school. Balderose was responsible for bringing renowned piper Jim McIntosh to this country to teach, which he did at Edinboro's first two-week school in 1979. In 1980 the school was the recipient of a grant from the National Endowment for the Arts and, since that time, has had McIntosh and Donald Lindsay on its staff. Also in 1980, he was the recipient of the annual Clan Donald grant for further study in Scotland. During his year in Scotland he studied at the College of Piping and took lessons with Jim McIntosh. He was also featured on the BBC.

COMPETITION MUSIC

There are, generally speaking, two types of music for the pipes: light and classical. Both are contested at most Games. The most familiar is the light music or, in Gaelic, Ceol Beag ("small music"). The marches, strathspeys, reels, hornpipes, and jigs fall into this category. These tunes have lively rhythms and are often heard on the fiddle and other instruments as well. Indeed, it was the fiddle that kept some of these tunes in existence when the pipes were banned in Scotland from 1746 to 1782.

Pipe bands play light music only. The band competition is an MSR or timed medley (which is a selection of any bagpipe tunes played within a certain time limit); many Games offer both. The pipes and drums are judged on how well they perform separately and together. The band is judged on its attack (how—and if—they begin together), tone, timing, execution, expression (in the case of the drums, how well they complement the pipes), and transition (the flow from one tune to the next).

According to PCPBA rules, a competing band must have a minimum of nine players: six pipers, two side drummers, and one bass drummer. In the MSR competition, Grades I (when applicable) through III submit one set of four-part tunes, with Grade III allowed to play two-part tunes twice through; Grade IV must play four parts of march music, which may be a two-part tune played twice through. In the timed medley competition, Grade I bands play five to seven minutes; all others play four to six minutes. Scoring is based on a possible maximum of 150 points from three judges, with piping worth 75 points, drumming worth 25, and ensemble worth 50.

Under EUSPBA rules, bands in Grade II (there were no Grade I bands until 1986) must have a minimum of twelve players: eight pipers, three side drummers, and one bass drummer. Grade III bands must have nine players (including six pipers), and Grade IV must have eight players (five pipers). Though not compulsory, some Games offer a Grade V competition for bands that have never won a prize in Grade IV. Grade II bands play either an MSR *or* a medley, the selection being made on the day of the competition. Grade III bands play an MSR. Grades IV and (where applicable) V play either a 2/4 march *or* a medley, the selection being determined for the competition season at the annual general meeting held in November of each year. When a medley is the event, Grade II must play five to seven minutes; Grades III, IV, and V, three to five minutes. Two judges are used in the EUSPBA. A possible score of 100 points is divided 75/25 between the piping and drumming judges, respectively.

Although there are minimum numbers of band players required in each band grade, the size of a band does not necessarily determine its quality. The ability of the members and the effort that they put into their practice sessions account for the band's overall sound. Each additional player increases the possibility that the band's sound will not be unified.

Solo piping light music competitions are usually composed of a 2/4 march or a strathspey and reel. A small number of Games offer competition in jig, hornpipe and jig, or 6/8 march as well. The hornpipe and jig are offered to advanced players only, since this music is quite fast and requires great skill to perform. Light music has a definite tempo, so the piper usually walks in time to the marches or stands and taps his foot in time to the dances.

The judge is considering four elements, much like a band judge, when listening to a solo piper: tuning, timing, execution, and expression. The pipes should be in tune throughout the performance, and the sounds of the chanter and the drones should balance. Proper tuning affects the tone of the pipes and therefore the quality of the sound. In a close competition, pipes that are slightly "off" may make the difference. Timing includes the tempo or speed of the music. The judge also listens for clean breaks in the music; if more than one tune is played, the transition between tunes should be smooth. Execution refers to the fingering of the instrument. A piper's technique in playing the embellishments (grace notes) is judged in this category. The interpretation of the tune—how the piper expresses the intent of the story that the music tells—is the other judging consideration. The judge must weigh all these things in his mind during a two- to three-minute performance, just as the piper must transmit these elements to the best of his ability in that time.

The other class of music is piobaireachd or Ceol Mor (great music). This is the classical music of the pipes. It is for the pipes alone; upon no other instrument can it be played with the same effect. The human voice is the only instrument that can transmit the nuances of expression in a tune with any success. For the serious piper or piping fan, this is the supreme music of the pipes; to the uninitiated, it is incomprehensible. There is no middle ground for the listener; one either hears the profundity of the music or hears a totally alien sound. Gamesgoers have ample opportunities to hear piobaireachd today, because it is competed at nearly every sanctioned Games in the country and is a requirement of the EUSPBA. To gain an appreciation of this unique musical form requires more than exposure; it requires a knowledge of its background.

It is generally accepted that piobaireachd originated on the Isle of Skye in the sixteenth century. The first composers were the MacCrimmons, hereditary pipers to the MacLeods since the early 1500s. The MacCrimmons founded a college of piping at Boreraig that became known as the finishing school of every good piper. A cairn (mound of stones) marks the site of the ruins of the school, which existed from 1570 to 1825. The course of the school is reputed to have been seven years, hence the origin of the saying, "It takes seven years to make a piper." One of the most famous MacCrimmons, Patrick Og, who became hereditary piper around 1670, was celebrated as a player, composer, and teacher. The MacDonalds of Sleat who resided at the opposite end of the Isle of Skye had the MacArthurs as their pipers. Charles MacArthur studied with Patrick Og and became an outstanding piper as well, later founding another piping school on Skye. Each of the schools had its own style of playing, and many tunes today still reflect the two styles in both the method of playing and the setting in which they are taught. Other famous piping families had their start with the MacCrimmons, notably the MacKays and the Campbells.

So inseparable are piobaireachd and the MacCrimmon family that Seumas MacNeill's book *Piobaireachd* divides the history of this music into three periods: pre-history, the era before 1570, comprised of tradition and legends; 1570 to 1825, the MacCrimmon era; and 1825 to the present, the post-MacCrimmon era. According to MacNeill's account, the last two hereditary pipers, the seventh and eighth, were the brothers Ian Dubh MacCrimmon (1730–1822) and Donald Ruadh MacCrimmon (1743–1825). At this point the original purpose and function of the clan system had been decimated; the position of piper was no longer a full-time occupation.

Enter the ninth and tenth hereditary pipers to Clan MacLeod. The son of Donald Ruadh, also named Donald, emigrated to Ontario in 1820. His great-great-grandson, Malcolm Roderick MacCrimmon, was born in Alberta in 1918. Malcolm, inspired by family stories, learned to play the pipes and researched his esteemed lineage. Through correspondence with the seventeenth chief of Clan MacLeod of MacLeod, he was able to complete the missing history between the hereditary pipers and himself.

During World War II Malcolm MacCrimmon was a piper with the Calgary Highlanders, Alberta's only Scottish regiment. He was transferred to the Scots Guards, making him the only Canadian soldier to be transferred to a British regiment. This enabled him to study with Pipe Major Willie Ross at the Army School of Piping. MacCrimmon eventually went to Skye, where Dame Flora MacLeod of MacLeod appointed him ninth hereditary piper to Clan MacLeod at Dunvegan Castle.

MacCrimmon's son Iain, born in 1952, is continuing this tradition. He has studied with some of the top pipers today, including Pipe Majors Donald MacLeod, John MacLellan, Andrew Wright, and Robert Hardie. Iain was a student and is now an instructor at the School of Piping in Idaho. He has judged extensively at Western competitions. He has published three books of pipe music containing his own compositions and those of his friends.

At Malcolm MacCrimmon's suggestion, Chief John MacLeod of MacLeod had papers drawn up in 1979 that would pass the title of hereditary piper to Iain. This was the first time in the history of the clan that a chief had signed a paper naming the hereditary piper. In 1983, tenth Hereditary Piper Iain MacCrimmon played for the MacLeod Parliament in Scotland and went to Skye to pipe for his chief at his ancestral home.

Nearly any emotion or event in the life of a composer could serve as the subject of piobaireachd. Francis Collinson says that the three main types of tunes are salutes, gatherings, and laments. A tune's nature and length—unlike light music, piobaireachd usually lasts five to twenty minutes—was purely a reflection of its composer's mood and expression.

The MacCrimmons are said to have been the first to devise a system of teaching piobaireachd called canntaireachd, in which syllables are assigned to each note of the chanter; the tune is learned first by singing or chanting it and later by playing it on the pipes. Canntaireachd was developed before pipers knew about staff and bar notation (indeed, most were illiterate, but by no means unintelligent); the voice was the most convenient and, as it turned out, the best method for preserving this music. The MacArthurs and the Campbells also developed systems of canntaireachd.

Piobaireachd is composed in phrases. It is not timed; it moves in pulses. This is why the piper walks very slowly and deliberately while playing: there is no beat by which to mark time. Piobaireachd was never meant to be written in the staff and bar notation common to nearly all other forms of music. Grouping notes of music into bars structures its timing and rhythm, and in piobaireachd, the rhythm must flow throughout the tune.

I shall not attempt to undertake to describe the mechanics of piobaireachd; entire works have been devoted to this subject. But to have some appreciation of this very unique cultural product of Scotland, one should have a basic understanding of its form. Piobaireachd can be simply defined as a theme with variations. The theme, called the urlar (which is Gaelic for "ground"), is always played slowly. This is followed by a series of variations, each with its own style and movement and usually more complicated than the last. There are six variations which may be used, and some of these have alternate movements. The urlar is repeated after the variations have been played.

At a recent Delco Scottish Games Workshop, I sat in on a piobaireachd class taught by Jim McIntosh, one of the masters of this form. He said that much, although not all, piobaireachd has been translated from canntaireachd into written music. (This is one of the functions of the Piobaireachd Society.) This allows one to learn the notes of the tune, but not the music; it is virtually impossible to learn piobaireachd without a teacher who understands the interpretation of the music. Learning piobaireachd, McIntosh believes, should teach one to be a musician, not a tactician. McIntosh learned piobaireachd by the canntaireachd method and he also teaches by it. When one learns piobaireachd on the practice chanter instead of by canntaireachd, values are put on the notes, which defeats the purpose of the music. To illustrate the difference, McIntosh distributed a sheet of written music to the students and then had them play along with him as he sang the tune. Those who attempted to read the music in the accustomed manner, dividing it into bars instead of following his phrases, played out of time.

Although it took a long time for piobaireachd to become ingrained in this country, it has now become an important part of the piping tradition here. Proof of this fact is the respected prizes that American pipers are bringing home from Scotland. Competition will keep piobaireachd alive and growing stronger, linking today's pipers with four centuries of Scotland's heart.

DRUMMING

In a pipe band it is the drums that make the volume changes. There is no way to increase or decrease the volume of the pipes; the amount of sound is steady. Drums give the tunes their "peaks and valleys," in the words of drumming expert John Bosworth. The drums are the innovative instruments in a pipe band. Whereas the pipes play tunes as they were written, sometimes hundreds of years ago, the drums have advanced from very basic accompaniments (simple beats) to often complex settings. The drums are given free rein to enhance and complement the pipes. The result is the exciting sound coming from pipe bands today. There are three types of drums in a pipe band: side, tenor, and bass. Side and bass drums are required; tenor drums are common.

John Bosworth of Crofton, Maryland, a professional military drummer who has been playing drums for more than 30 years and judging at the Games for more than 20 years, says that one of the most important members of a pipe band is the bass drummer. His function is to keep the tempo, and in pipe music—as in all music—steady tempo is vital. In competition, the tempo must be exactly the same from the command (initial direction) to the rolls (attack) to the first few bars of the tune, or points are deducted.

After the pipe major sets the tempo, all the other players get their tempo from the bass drum, and its rhythm should be the force that keeps them together. The bass drummer should know the tunes so well that he knows the tempo at which the band sounds best; he should then push, not follow, them along.

Bosworth says it is easy to spot a good bass drummer—he is the one who looks as though he is really enjoying himself.

The side drums play the major drum parts; the settings are written for them. These parts must fit the tune, but once that basic requirement is met, "the sky's the limit," as Bosworth says. The side drums make the tune interesting. The other drums complement the side drums, just as the drums as a unit complement the pipes. Side drums are actually snare drums that have been specially adapted to provide a unique sound. In a pipe band, double snares are used on the drums, which produces an immediate, crisp sound. Also, these drums are very tight; a crank is often used to make the drumhead as tight as possible. This combination of double snares and tight drumheads creates the high-pitched sound of the side drums.

The tenor drums are the drums that provide the flourishes or twirling parts (as the bass drum occasionally does). Not all bands include the flourishes—it does not influence the score in a competition—but some place a lot of emphasis on it, providing an exciting visual display.

Very little competitive drum music *per se* has been written. When the tunes for a competition season are selected, they are given to the bands so that the drum sergeant or other musician can write drum settings to accompany the tunes. Hypothetically, five bands could be playing the same MSR set. However, even though the pipes might be playing the same notes and doing the same fingering (assuming the same pipes setting is used), the drum sections would never sound alike. Bands occasionally request drum settings from the same source, who may have distributed the same setting to all requesting that tune. But you would be highly unlikely to hear the same drum setting at one competition.

The pipes and drums have separate rehearsals during the winter months: the pipers learn the tunes and the drummers the settings written for them. The drummers rehearse on drum pads, then work out the setting on their drums. When both sections have learned the tune, they put the parts together.

In a pipe band competition, the drummers are basically being judged on what they play and how they play it. The first refers to the difficulty of the setting. The latter takes into account phrasing, accents, how the drums move with the pipes (which to a large degree depends on the bass drummer), and cleanness—precision. It takes many hours of practice to meet these standards. For massed bands in which all the drum sections are trying to hold together all the pipe sections, the simplest drum parts are desired. But in band competitions, when drum sections are being judged not only on how well they complement the band but also on how they compare to other drum sections, the most difficult settings are desired.

Competitions called drum corps salutes in which the drum section of a band plays by itself are becoming increasingly popular today. In this form of competition, anything goes! Drum sections often use the drum corps salute as an opportunity to show their versatility and creativity. Brushes (in place of drumsticks), cymbals, and even cowbells have been used in these contests. Many Scottish Games also include solo competitions for side and for tenor and bass drums in which one or two pipers accompany the drummer. In EUSPBA events, the drummers are divided into grades just as the pipers are. Tenor drum competitions test the drummer's ability to combine flourishes with sound enhancement parts. In solo side drumming competitions, the individual exhibits his expertise by playing the most difficult settings possible.

Solo side drumming in the EUSPBA is divided into two classes: open, which has one grade, and amateur, which has four grades. The required competitions are: open—MSR; Grade I—MSR; Grade II—2/4 march in quick time; Grade III—march in any time signature; Grade IV—rudiments of pipe band drumming on drum pad (to attract beginning drummers). The possible total of 100 points covers roll, tone, tempo (and breaks between different timings), execution, rhythm/expansion (how well the drum complements the pipes), quality/variety, and blend (transitions between movements). There are also optional advanced competitions in side drumming and optional competitions in tenor and bass drumming.

At the end of the 1984 EUSPBA competition season, the top competing open side drummers in order of placement were Donald MacLeod, Rick Abrams, Christopher Greenless, Thomas

Part of the massed band at the Caledonian Club of San Francisco Games in Santa Rosa, California.

Malcolm Roderick MacCrimmon upholds a centuries-old tradition: a MacCrimmon playing the pipes at Boreraig. (Courtesy of Malcolm Roderick MacCrimmon)

Tuning the pipes in preparation for competition.

The Manchester Pipe Band competes at the Devon Games.

John Bosworth judges a snare drum competitor.

Duncan McCaskill, Jr., right, a champion drum major, judges a contender in a drum major competition.

Kee, John Keogh, Gordon Bell, Gerry Radford, Oscar Dela Rosa, and William MacNeill. The top open tenor drummers were Matthew Hamilton, Alan Buchanan, Kevin Shannon, Christopher Heller, and Christie Parker, and the top bass drummers were Stewart Hogg, Matthew Hamilton, Kevin Shannon, Tom McGurk, and Roderick Kerr. The top drum majors were Dennis Ducsik, Beth Leeds, David Ricklis, John Riley, Joe Brady, Jr., Roderick Kerr, Stan Jarman, James Engle, Duncan McCaskill, Jr., H. Mallon, and Kevin Shannon.

Solo drummers in the western part of the U.S., like solo pipers, are divided into three classes: novice, amateur, and professional. The novice event is a 2/4 march; amateurs and professionals play an MSR.

Drum majors do not compete with the pipe band but in a separate competition that is a highly popular event at Scottish Highland Games. A drum major in full Highland dress proudly swinging his mace (staff) and marching before the pipes and drums is an impressive sight. A drum major is not a decoration; he leads the band. According to Larry Fullerton, drum major of the highly acclaimed Pipes and Drums and Military Band of the 48th Highlanders of Canada, the key function of the drum major is to direct the band with mace signals. In the British Army, the drum major is senior to the pipe major. (In civilian bands, however, the pipe major is the final authority. Indeed, it is common for bands seen at Games today not to have a drum major.) The drum major sets the tempo at the start of play and gives the tempo changes as needed. He also gives the commands to commence and stop movement and to keep the players' lines straight.

In his book *Scottish Highland Games*, David Webster says that the year 1928 marked the beginning of drum major competitions in Scotland. Although no date has been established for their beginning in the United States, we do know that they have been held for at least 20 years, since they have been an optional EUSPBA competition since the founding of the organization. On the West Coast, the PCPBA does not regulate the contests; the contest sponsors do. A group called the Pacific Coast Alliance of Scottish Drum Majors, which seeks to standardize and clarify rules governing these contests, is in its evolutionary stage. Drum major competitions were begun by civilian bands in an effort to provide a good representation of what a drum major should be. The drum major is highly visible; his appearance and manner are a reflection of the band. Competitions also helped to create consistency among drum majors; inconsistency of style is distracting, as is apparent in massed bands.

According to Larry Fullerton, the purpose of drum major competitions is the same everywhere, but there is wide variation in their components. For instance, in Ireland there is no restriction on when the flourish part of the competition (the manipulation of the mace) is to be performed; in Scotland and North America, however, competitors may flourish only during specific parts of the music. In Canada and the eastern part of the United States, the competition begins with a slow march and moves into a quick march; in Scotland, there is only a quick march. In EUSPBA drum major competitions, a maximum of 100 points is compiled in three areas: dress, 20; deportment or general conduct, 40; and flourish, 40. One band accompanies all the competitors. The most difficult part of the competition seems to be the change from the slow march to the quick march. Few competitors do this well.

PROFILES OF SOLO PIPERS

Impressive changes have occurred in piping in the United States in both solo and band categories during the past two decades. Increased interest has developed into an ardent desire among many musicians for superior performance. Scotland, as is to be expected, has long been the cradle of the best in piping. In 1981 Canada, proud of its proficiency in the Scottish tradition, took the three top prizes at one of the two *crème de la crème* events of solo piping, the Northern Meeting in Inverness (the other being the Argyllshire Gathering in Oban). The United States, a relative newcomer, is eager for recognition and respect in the world of serious piping—and is getting it.

Over the past few years Americans have been making inroads into the upper echelons at Inverness and Oban. Albert McMullin of Wilmington, Delaware, was the first American to win a prize (second) in the Inverness silver medal piobaireachd competition in 1980, and in 1981 was the first American to qualify and compete under the new system for the gold medal competition. Also in 1981 Peter Kent of High Point, North Carolina, took fourth place in the silver medal competition at Inverness and Michael Cusack of Houston won the Grade B strathspey and reel contest. The following year Cusack finished second in the silver medal competition at Oban and James Stack of Pequannock, New Jersey, broke the barrier of tradition by becoming the first piper born in the United States to win the silver medal at Oban. Andrew Berthoff, son of aforementioned historian Rowland Berthoff, followed suit in 1984 by winning the Oban silver medal. Cusack returned to Oban in 1984 and became the first American to win the gold medal there. He was also one of ten invited competitors (and the only American-born competitor) to play in the prestigious Grant's Whisky Championship at Blair Castle.

At the end of each season, the EUSPBA ranks the solo (pipe and drum) and band competitors based on results from sanctioned Games. The method of rating takes many considerations into account so as to be as fair as possible. The total number of points and the number of events entered are figured into a computerized system to obtain a rating. What follows are brief profiles of the top ten EUSPBA open solo pipers according to 1984 rankings.

Burt Mitchell is a mechanical technician who lives in Statesville, North Carolina. He began piping at age eight and has been in the open class 13 years. His father (who has also been his teacher), his brother Bobby (also listed in this section), and his wife are also pipers. His other teachers have been the late John MacFadyen and Roddy MacDonald. Burt competes in about 15 events per year and pipes for Highland dancing.

Mitchell has been a member of the following pipe bands: City of Wilmington, Denny & Dunipace, Midlothian, Savannah Celtic, and the Grandfather Mountain Highlanders (his current band). From 1981–84 he was pipe major of the Charlotte Caledonian Pipe Band, bringing them from a non-competitive to a prize-winning Grade IV band.

A strong advocate of piping as entertainment, he wants the

public to enjoy "piping as music, not as a novelty." He plays the pipes with a folk/ceilidh band called Mad Sweeney.

U.S. championships: EUSPBA overall champion, 1974, 1984; Virginia championship, Alexandria, 1974; Boreraig Trophy, Fair Hill, 1978; piper of the day, many Games.

Foreign championships: at 13, 4th in 18-and-under piobaireachd against 76 competitors, Cowal; 2nd in amateur North American championships, Maxville.

Scott MacAulay of Hamilton, Ontario, is a law student at the University of Ottawa. He began piping at age nine and has been in the open class 11 years. His teachers have been Jack MacFarlane, George Sherriff, Alan Munn, Sandy Keith, Robert G. Hardie, William Livingstone, Sr., Murray Henderson, and Jim McIntosh. He has been involved with six pipe bands, including the Erskine Pipe Band of Hamilton, which was named top overseas Grade II band at the 1974 world championship. In 1977 he moved to Scotland for a year and was a member of Pipe Major Robert Hardie's Muirhead & Son Ltd. Pipe Band, seven-time Grade I winner of the world championship. From 1978–84 he was with Clan MacFarlane Pipe Band of St. Catherine's, Ontario, and became pipe sergeant in 1980. This band was named Grade I North American champion 10 times in 15 years. In 1985 MacAulay, along with Colin MacLellan (also listed in this section), formed the Carloway Pipe Band and served as joint pipe majors. Their goal is for the band to be the first North American band to win the world championship.

MacAulay is on the judges' panel of the PCPBA, MWPBA, and the Pipers' and Pipe Band Society of Ontario. He teaches at workshops and clinics throughout North America, is a composer, and has recorded three albums, including one solo recording. He was awarded a grant by the Canadian government to represent Canada at Inverness in 1985. He calls himself a "hard-core piper"; he has won about 100 North American championships in the past 10 years.

U.S. championships: first winner of the Fair Hill Challenge Charger for MSR, 1984; open jig and piobaireachd, Fair Hill, 1984; Chicago Invitational Solo Competition, 1984; piper of the day, six Games, 1984.

Foreign championships (including Canadian): North American solo piping champion, Maxville, 1984; Ontario championship, supreme solo player, 1984; MSR, hornpipe, and jig, William Livingstone, Sr., Invitational Solo Piping Competition, Hamilton, Ontario, 1984. Best overseas competitor, Braemar, 1984; Perthshire open piping championship, Pitlochry, 1984; 3rd at Oban and Inverness, 1984; Perth; piper of the day, five Canadian Games, 1984.

Donald Alexander Uist MacPhee is a student at St. Petersburg (Florida) Junior College. The Dunedin resident is one of a long line of pipers, including his father, who judges piping in the U.S., Canada, and Scotland, and a cousin, who is pipe sergeant of the famous Strathclyde Police Pipe Band in Scotland. He began piping at age four and has been in the open class 2 years. His father, Sandy MacPhee, is his teacher.

MacPhee was pipe major of both the Dunedin Middle School and High School pipe bands and currently plays with the City of Dunedin Pipe Bands. He spent two summers in Canada playing with the champion McNish Distillery Pipe Band. He hopes to compete at Oban and Inverness and would like to be the first American member of the Strathclyde Police Pipe Band.

U.S. championships: EUSPBA amateur champion in all four grades; amateur piobaireachd quaich, Santa Rosa; piper of the day, most Southern Games.

Foreign championships: many Canadian prizes and trophies, including North American amateur march, Maxville.

James Bell is the manager of a grocery store in his hometown of Parlin, New Jersey. He is the son and student of Pipe Major George Bell (Kenmure Pipe Band), one of the founding members of the EUSPBA. His older brother is a piper and his two younger brothers are drummers. He began piping at age twelve; 1985 marked his 10th year in the open class. He competes at about 10 events annually. He has competed in piobaireachd for 14 years. Since 1975 he has been among the top 10 solo open EUSPBA pipers. Bell is pipe major of the Parlin & District Pipe Band; his brother Gordon is drum major of that band.

He has won many overall championships in this country and several prizes in Canada.

Scott Walker of Nazareth, Pennsylvania, teaches at Warren

Hills Regional High School in Washington, New Jersey. He began studying the pipes at age eight with Donald Leslie, then studied with his grandfather, Robert Walker, who had been a member of the Black Watch. He has also studied with Roddy MacDonald, George Bell, and Jim McIntosh. He has been in the open class 14 years (with a 4-year college break) and competes in 15 to 20 contests per year. He is a member of the Parlin & District Pipe Band.

U.S. championships: EUSPBA march champion, 2nd in piobaireachd, 4th in strathspey and reel; top prizes at several Games.

Colin MacLellan of Brockville, Ontario, is a reedmaker and supplies reeds for many North American pipers and pipe bands. He began piping lessons at age five with Jack Crichton and continued with his father, Captain John A. MacLellan, former director of the Army School of Piping at Edinburgh Castle. He has also studied with William Livingstone, Sr., in Canada and with Donald MacPherson, Ronald MacCallum, and Duncan Johnstone in Scotland. He has competed in the open class for 12 years and in piobaireachd for 16 years. He competes at about 20 Games each year.

MacLellan has been a member of the City of Toronto Pipe Band, which won the Grade I contest in Edinburgh in 1977; the Parlin & District Pipe Band, one of the top EUSPBA bands; and is co-music director with Scott MacAulay of the newly formed Carloway Pipe Band.

MacLellan holds a teacher's certificate from the Institute of Piping in Edinburgh. He has taught at piping schools for 8 years, including the Seaway International School of Piping and the prestigious College of Piping in Glasgow for one year.

U.S. championships: piobaireachd—multiple winner at six East Coast Games; John Wilson Memorial Trophy, Delco, three times; Dame Flora MacLeod of MacLeod Trophy, Dunedin; Iona Trophy, Ligonier; Clan Donald Trophy, Virginia; Boreraig Trophy, Fair Hill; Clan Donald Quaich, 2nd, 1979–81, Fair Hill; light— MSR, Fair Hill, three times; MSR, Loon Mountain, four times; multiple overall champion at eight Games.

Foreign championships (including Canadian): MSR gold medal, Ottawa, 1978; Piobaireachd Society gold medal, Ottawa, 1982; MSR, Toronto, 1982 (first professional championship); Montreal Indoor Championship twice; Scottish Junior Champion, 1975; 2nd in march and silver medal competition, Oban, 1978; gold medal, Inverness, 1982; Strachan Trophy for MSR and 4th in Bratach Gorm competition, London, 1983.

James Stack of Pequannock, New Jersey, is a specialist clerk on the New York Stock Exchange. His father and brother are also pipers. He began playing the pipes at age eight and has been in the open class 10 years. He competes in about 15 competitions per year. He has been a member of the Kenmure Pipe Band and the Parlin & District Pipe Band. He is currently studying with Pipe Major John MacLellan and has studied with John Miller, Duncan McCaskill, Sr., John Sabiston, Donald Lindsay, and Roddy MacDonald.

U.S. championships: EUSPBA champion, 1976; EUSPBA amateur champion, Grades I and II; Boreraig Trophy, Fair Hill, 1976; Clan Donald Quaich, Fair Hill, 1976 and 1978.

Foreign championships: Piobaireachd Society gold medal, Ottawa, 1984; 2nd in under-18 MSR, Cowal, 1976; silver medal, Oban, 1982; piobaireachd, Crieff and Chatsworth, 1982; Grade B march, Inverness, 1982; MSR, Chatsworth, 1984.

Pat Henderson came to the U.S. with her husband, Murray, in 1982 and competed well for two years. Her inclusion on the top solo list of the EUSPBA verifies her ability as a piper. At the end of the 1984 season, she and Murray returned to Scotland.

Bobby Mitchell is a teacher in the Montgomery County (Maryland) public school system. He began piping at age nine and has been in the open class 15 years. He has competed in piobaireachd 19 years. He competes in an average of 10 events per year. Bobby's first teacher was Robert Gilchrist; he has also received instruction from Jim McIntosh and the late John MacFadyen, with whom he lived for a year in Scotland as a teenager.

While at the University of Delaware he started a piping club to keep himself involved in piping. For a while he piped for Highland dancing, first becoming involved by playing for the students of Jamie Jamieson. One of the highlights of his piping career was in 1972 when he was invited to play at Dame Flora

MacLeod's 96th birthday party at the Waldorf-Astoria Hotel in New York City.

Mitchell has been a member of the City of Wilmington Pipe Band and the Denny & Dunipace Pipe Band. In 1980 he started the MacAlpin Pipe Band in Columbia, Maryland. In 1982 this band became the Clan Campbell Pipe Band and advanced to Grade III. He is the band's pipe major.

He is on the board of directors of the Balmoral School in Greensboro, North Carolina. In 1984 he was featured on an album of Scottish hymns. In 1985 he was featured in a solo piper and organ recital in the first such live radio broadcast in his area.

U.S. championships: Clan Donald Quaich, Fair Hill, 1976–82; open piobaireachd, open piping, Virginia, 1981; piper of the day, Grandfather Mountain, 1973–77; British Caledonian Invitational Piobaireachd Competition, Stone Mountain, 1981; Iona Cross for open piobaireachd, Ligonier, 1983.

Foreign championships: open piobaireachd, Maxville, 1969; major amateur events in Scotland, including London Piobaireachd Society, Scottish Pipers' Association, College of Piping, and Boys' Brigade, 1967.

Leslie Jones of West Newton, Massachusetts, is a full-time judge and teacher of piping and Highland dancing. She holds a graduate certificate from the Institute of Piping in Edinburgh. She began piping at age seven and has been in the open class 11 years. She studied in Scotland from 1973–75 and 1976–77. Her Scottish teachers have been Donald MacPherson, John MacFadyen, and Duncan Johnstone; Ed Neigh is her current teacher. She competes at an average of 10 competitions a year and has competed in Scotland annually for the past several years. The Competing Pipers' Society of Scotland recently classified her as Class A.

Jones teaches at workshops and works with area pipe bands; she is a member of the Worcester Kiltie Pipe Band. She performs at concerts, shows, and school assemblies. In the fall of 1985 she and Corporal Iain Massie of the Royal Scots Dragoon Guards opened a full-time piping school in Boston.

U.S. championships: 2nd in piobaireachd, Delco; piper of the day, Loon Mountain and Fort Ticonderoga, 1983; many major awards at several East Coast Games.

Foreign championships: many open prizes in Canada; 2nd, Dunvegan gold medal, 1983.

BANDS

Here follows a description of some of the top bands in the United States today, listed under their respective associations. At the beginning of the 1985 season, there were two Grade I U.S. pipe bands, both members of the MWPBA. In 1986, the EUSPBA upgraded five bands to Grade I: the three listed here, Parlin & District, and Ontario Caledonian.

MWPBA

The Kansas City St. Andrew Pipe Band of Kansas City, Missouri, has been a Grade I band for two years. It was organized in 1963. The 35 members of the band, under the direction of Pipe Major John Higgins, wear the MacDonald of Keppoch tartan. They have competed all over the U.S. and in Canada and Scotland. They play for Burns nights and other events, including bluegrass and folk festivals. They will soon record their first album.

Championships: Grades I and II champion, 1976 Delco Games; Grade II champion, 1982 and 1983 North American Invitational Competitions in Chicago; 3rd in Grade I competition, Chicago, 1984; U.S. Open Championship, Alma, 1984; 2nd, Canadian National Exposition, 1978; 4th, Lesmahagow, 1983.

The Midlothian Scottish Pipe Band of Mundelein, Illinois, was named Grade I in 1985 by the Ontario Pipers and Pipe Band Society. Pipe Major Ian Swinton heads the 23-member band formed in 1975. Midlothian, which wears the New Caledonia tartan, competes in Illinois, Missouri, Michigan, and Minnesota, as well as in Canada and Scotland. The band performs at many public functions and has a junior band that provides experienced pipers and drummers for the adult band.

Championships: MWPBA and North American championships, 1983; 3rd, North American, 1984; supreme champion, Ontario, 1981, 1982, 1984; 2nd at Perth and Rothesay, 3rd at Edinburgh, 8th in world championships, 1983.

EUSPBA

The Worcester (Massachusetts) Kiltie Pipe Band was formed in 1916. Its 20 members wear the Scott tartan. According to Pipe Major James B. Kerr, Worcester was the only Grade I pipe band in the eastern United States in the last 25 years. The band competes in the northeast region and has won every Grade I prize in the region. Until 1986, when Grade I bands were reinstituted in the EUSPBA realm, the band competed in Grade II. In Canada and Scotland, however, Worcester competes in Grade I. Worcester has an annual gala celebration of Burns Night. In recent years they have had some of Scotland's top entertainers as special guests, among them Kenneth McKellar, the Tartan Lads, Alastair McDonald, and Peter Morrison.

Championships: North American championship, five wins, four 2nds; 1st U.S. band to win a prize in Scotland, Lesmahagow, 1969 (over the Glasgow Police Pipe Band and Shotts & Dykehead); 7th, world championship, 1969.

The Manchester Pipe Band of Manchester, Connecticut, is not only one of the top bands on the East Coast, it is one of the oldest, formed in 1914. The 20 members of this band wear the Ancient Sinclair tartan. Manchester, under the direction of Pipe Major Charles C. Murdoch, competes in the northeast region and has won all major Eastern Grade II events. Most of the current members have come up through the band's teaching program for both piping and drumming. The band participates in other Scottish functions, college commencements, and parades. Manchester also has its own dancers.

Championships: EUSPBA Grade II champion, 1976–1980; Grade II champion, North American championship, 1967; best overseas pipe band in Grade II, world championship, 1977.

The Scottish & Irish Imports Pipe Band of Annapolis, Maryland (formerly the Denny & Dunipace Pipe Band) was formed in 1964. The band has 25 members who wear the Black Stewart tartan. Scottish & Irish has won most major prizes on the East Coast. Under its former name the band recorded an album in 1980. It participates in the annual Scottish Christmas Walk in Alexandria, Virginia. The band is under the direction of Pipe Major Timothy Carey.

Championships: Dunvegan Trophy at Eastern U.S. Pipe Band Championship, Fair Hill, 1984; EUSPBA Grade II champion, 1976; Grade II champion, North American championship, 1976;

Grade II champion, Canadian championship (Montreal Games), 1976.

PCPBA

The Prince Charles Pipe Band of Marin County, California, was formed in 1968. The band, whose members wear the Black Stewart tartan, now has a Grade II, Grade III, and juvenile unit. The total number of pipers and drummers is about 70. Prince Charles participates in many civic functions. It is associated with a Boy Scout Explorer Post and a school of Highland dancers. The band also has its own corps of Irish dancers. The senior band is under the direction of Pipe Major Bill Merriman, who, along with fellow former Canadians Jack Sutherland and Jerry Gallante, formed the band. The senior band has competed all over the West Coast of the United States and Canada and has been a consistent winner in its grade. Prince Charles was invited to compete at the 1983 Chicago PipeFest, after which the band competed in Ontario for the first time.

The juvenile band competed in Scotland in 1973 and 1978. During the second trip the band won the juvenile championship at Cowal, becoming the first American band not only to compete, but also to win, in any division at that Games. The band went on to win the best juvenile titles at Edinburgh and Rothesay and placed 8th at the world championship. Also in 1978 the band was invited to play for the Argyllshire Gathering in Oban, which has solo competitions only but annually has a Band for the Day. This appearance made Prince Charles the first American band, the first juvenile band, and the first mixed (both sexes) band to be Band for the Day.

The House of Scotland Pipe Band of San Diego, California, was formed in 1964. This Grade II band, under the direction of Pipe Major Campbell Naismith, is composed of 35 members. The pipers wear Prince Charles Edward Stuart tartan and the drummers wear Campbell of Caudor. House of Scotland played for Queen Elizabeth during the dedication ceremony of a statue of Shakespeare at the Old Globe Theater in San Diego in 1984, and at the East-West Shrine football game. The band performs for various functions, including Burns' dinners and concerts, accompanied by Highland dancers. House of Scotland has made one recording. The band competes in the western United States. Games competitions won include San Diego, Costa Mesa, and Honolulu; PCPBA top band in Grade III.

The Beach Cities Pipe Band of Huntington Beach, California, is a Grade II band formed in 1982. Pipe Major Robert Kelly, a native Scot, heads the 18-member band, whose members wear the Drummond of Perth tartan. Though young, the band is composed of top solo pipers who have been in top West Coast bands. Beach Cities plays for Burns dinners, kirking of tartans, and various other functions. A noticeable point about this band: it tours around in a motor home that broadcasts the band's identity with a mural painted on the vehicle's side. Beach Cities has so far competed only in California; the band has placed 2nd at Santa Rosa and has won other Games.

5

Highland Dancing

When I began to research Highland dancing to learn about the mechanics of the dance, I heard from several sources about a study that was done showing that this activity is more strenuous and more stressful than sports such as football when the two activities are considered in the same time frame. Skeptical and intrigued—and not wishing to write a book by hearsay—I began to search for this study. The more I learned about Highland dancing, the less skeptical I became. I contacted, on various leads, the medical schools at the University of Utah and Harvard University. The Welch Medical Library at Johns Hopkins University ran a computer search for me. I contacted Dr. Richard T. Herrick at the National Strength Research Center in Auburn, Alabama; he put me in touch with Dr. James Sammarco of the Department of Orthopaedics at the University of Cincinnati, who is also physician to the Cincinnati Ballet Company. Dr. Sammarco suggested I request studies that had been published in *The Physician and Sportsmedicine* and contact Dr. James Nicholas, founder and director of the Institute of Sports Medicine and Athletic Trauma and director of Orthopedic Surgery, Lenox Hill Hospital, New York City.

Whew! What I discovered were many studies of ballet. It appears that ethnic dancing, under which category some have suggested Highland dancing falls, had not been deeply investigated from a medical point of view. I have heard from dancers and teachers alike, however, that Highland dancing is probably more strenuous than ballet. This comes from the voice(s) of experience; most serious Highland dancers also study ballet at some time in their dancing careers, as one of its benefits is increased flexibility. Even though ballet involves longer periods of dancing, the dancer does get to put his feet flat on the floor during a performance. Not generally so in the Highland dances (except in one of the Highland steps and in the Irish jig or sailor's hornpipe).

One ballet study that appeared in the November 1982 issue of *The Physician and Sportsmedicine* measured heart rate during actual performances. This study showed that professional ballet dancing may be classified as high-intensity exercise of brief duration (the lively allegro movements are usually preceded and followed by resting intervals). A study done at the Institute of Sports Medicine and Athletic Trauma (*Sports Medicine*, September-October 1975) had an appendix that compared eight performance factors—strength, endurance, body type, flexibility, balance, agility, speed, and coordination—for 61 sports. Only bullfighting and rugby had a combined score higher than ballet, and they were just one point higher. Four sports—basketball, boxing, hockey, and jai alai—scored the same as ballet, and five, including football, were one point lower. When timing, reaction time, rhythm, steadiness, and accuracy were added to the previous factors, ballet, boxing, and hockey scored highest.

So the research does show that dancing is a very strenuous activity. But this only supports what Highland dancers already know. Take a good look at the competitors as they leave the dancing platform: the wet brows, flushed cheeks, and labored breathing should be proof enough. With the exceptions mentioned above, a Highland dancer's heels should not touch the platform. The traditional Highland dances—those for which the kilt is worn—are known for their aggressive and meticulous movements. The national dances are more graceful but also require much energy and precision. It is no wonder that the dances are so short; one must be in top physical condition to be so agile and controlled on the balls of his feet.

HISTORICAL BACKGROUND

The Highland dances seen on the programs of the Scottish Highland Games today are the culmination of influences from the past few centuries. For the most part, the facts surrounding their origin have been passed down verbally, making them subject to the inventiveness or forgetfulness of those whose versions survived. The traditional Highland dances that are still performed were originally male dances. The Highland fling, sword dance, and seann triubhas were connected with war. Not only did the dances evolve from or commemorate martial conflict, but it is also assumed that they were used as exercise to keep warriors physically fit.

The country that has had the biggest stylistic influence on Scottish Highland dancing is France. The histories of Scotland and France are interwoven in many other ways as well. Even before Mary Queen of Scots returned to Scotland from France in 1561 following the death of her French husband, the French influence permeated Scottish dancing. The five basic foot positions used in Highland dancing are almost the same as those used in ballet. Several of the steps and arm movements in Highland dancing are also of French origin. Despite these French refinements, however, Highland dancing remains boldly Scottish. Gaelic Highland step dancing, which can be seen today in a few places in North America such as the Cape Breton area of Nova Scotia, resembles clog dancing; it is done with the arms held at the sides and heavy stamping of the feet. Traditional Irish step dancing is of this nature as well.

There have also been adverse influences on Scottish dances through the centuries. When young Mary Queen of Scots brought her mirthful French court to Scotland's capital, John Knox was already there stoking the fires of the Scottish Reformation. Although he could not condemn dancing outright—the Scriptures do not support this—he condemned it in principle for being, among other things, "not very comely for honest women." The battle against frivolity, in which all music-related activities were easy targets, cut deeply and went on for a long time. Much

God-given creativity and culture were squelched in His name.

A heavier, swifter, and more direct blow was dealt to Scottish culture when the Rebellion of 1745 failed. Another young Scot had come from France to claim the Scottish throne. His reception in some circles was as warm as that afforded Mary, but he brought no lively court. Prince Charles Edward Stuart, better known as Bonnie Prince Charlie, went to Scotland in 1745 to try to do what his father had failed to do 30 years before: regain the British throne for the House of Stuart. Many Highlanders rallied to his cause and helped him score some initial victories. But the tide turned. The young prince managed to escape the massacre on Culloden Moor in 1746 and eventually returned to France, defeated and dejected. The resultant action directed against the Highlanders nearly wiped out their culture. To rid them of future notions of nationalism, outward signs of their society were banned by the Act of Proscription (reproduced in chapter 1). No longer was it permissible to wear the kilt or play the pipes, which was deemed an instrument of war. These restrictions had a concomitant effect on native dancing as well. For the next 35 years, the fiddle kept bagpipe music alive; secret congregating helped the Highland tradition survive. With the repeal of the act in 1782, much Highland culture reappeared, but some had been lost forever. What remained was jealously guarded with high regard for propriety and accuracy.

When the Scottish Games became enclaves for the perpetuation of the Highland tradition, the events were male-dominated, as were the practices from which they were derived. At the first Games of the Highland Society of St. Fillans in 1819, the sword dance was included as a competition. According to the program of their 1826 Games, a prize of a silver "queych" (quaich, or two-handled Scottish drinking cup) was offered to the "Best Dancer of the Ancient Sword Dance," and a set of patent leather sword belts was awarded to the "Best Dancer of Highland Reels." Clearly these were prizes suited to men.

At the Games in Inverness in 1841, Highland piping and dancing in full costume was introduced. The program for the 1893 Highland Gathering at Luss included the Highland fling, sword dance, reel dancing, sailor's hornpipe, Irish jig, and seann triubhas. There was also a Highland fling for boys under 14. In 1908 the Luss Gathering had separate Highland flings for boys and girls under 16 and reel dancing for boys.

The early Games in the United States reflected a similar development. At the Highland Society of New York's first Sportive Meeting in 1836, there was "dancing to bagpipes," but there is no indication that this was Highland dancing. Most likely it referred to the early custom of everyone joining in a reel at the beginning of the day or a ball on the grounds at the end of the day. At all four of the pre-Civil War Games—Boston, New York, Philadelphia, and Newark—dancing was included in the athletic programs.

At our oldest continuous Games, those of the Caledonian Club of San Francisco (first held in 1866), the Highland fling was added to the program of events the second year and the sword dance the fourth year. In 1884 there were 40 boys and girls dancing the Highland fling on the stage at one time; in 1902 the number was 60. Females were getting onto the dancing stages at the Games, liking it, doing well, and staying there.

But changes in tradition occur slowly, and changes in attitudes even more so. In a book entitled *Highland Gatherings* published in 1927, Sir Iain Colquhoun and Hugh Machell wrote, "Highland dancing on the platform, as an exhibition, is best performed by fully grown men, and...they certainly keep it up to a considerable age, to their own evident enjoyment and the benefit of their health. Boys and girls shine best in the ballroom (unless under fourteen)." One must bear in mind that these dances had been performed by men for centuries. They were (and still are) taught in the Highland regiments and were considered manly pursuits.

Girls were expected to compete in the same costume as men and boys: kilt, doublet (jacket), sporran (pouch worn at the waist), and hat. As the girls grew into young ladies and continued to compete, some of the stricter Games committees in Scotland objected to women wearing men's costumes. (The kilt, by the way, is a male garment. Ladies wear kilted skirts, which require only about a third of the fabric that a kilt does and, therefore, have the style but not the appreciated swing of the male garment.) The committee of the Aboyne Games was particularly opposed to the practice and would not allow women to compete in kilts. Something had to be done to appease committees and competitors. A solution was reached in 1953 when the Games introduced a costume for females that has become known as the Aboyne dress. Actually, the costume is a shortened version of a popular seventeenth-century Highland dress with the pattern of a plaid containing white known as arasaid. According to Janet MacLachlan of Ontario, who has done extensive research into the history of Highland dances, photographs exist that show Flora MacDonald wearing this type of dress. Today the Aboyne dress consists of a vested white blouse with plaid over the shoulder and a full, graceful skirt. At Aboyne and a handful of other Games in Scotland, females must dance all the dances in this attire. The costume makes the vigorous, high-stepping traditional Highland dances more difficult to do, but since females compete only against females, no one has an unfair advantage.

With the increasing number of female dancers and the revival of female Highland dress came the revival of some of the lovely national dances performed only by women. The Aboyne dress is particularly suited to the more sedate, elegant movements of the ladies' dances. Among the most familiar of these dances seen at the Games today are "Flora MacDonald's Fancy," "Scottish Lilt," "Village Maid," and "Earl of Errol."

Turnabout is fair play. Deference was made to the men a few years ago (the matter was first discussed in 1979) when the governing body ruled to allow men to dance the national dances. These dances are danced by males in kilts with appropriate hand movements added. (For instance, in "Flora MacDonald's Fancy," where females hold their dresses, males hold their hands as in Highland dancing.) Males can now perform dances never before performed by men.

As the number of females involved in Highland dancing increased, the number of males decreased. It can be safely said that the first factor has had an enormous influence on the second. There are very few male Highland dance competitors in the United States today; Canada and Scotland are experiencing this same reversal of dominance, although not to the same extent. In Scotland there are fewer male dancers competing at the Games today than in previous years, but as might be expected, their number is proportionately higher than in the other Games-celebrating countries. At the Edinburgh Festival each August, there is a separate boys' competition for Highland dancing that attracts many fine dancers.

In the United States the males may not be strong in number, but they make their presence felt. It was just over ten years ago (1973) that Hugh Bigney won the adult world championship in Cowal, the only American ever to win this title. In 1982 and again in 1984 Harry Farrar took both high honors, adult champion and champion of champions, at the U.S. National Highland Dancing Championships. The accomplishments of these two men should serve as an example and a source of encouragement to other American males who are or are considering becoming Highland dancers. Success in Highland dancing is a product of discipline and hard work; gender has nothing to do with it. (It is important, however, that male dancers not be bothered by the fact that they are the minority.) Perhaps there would be more male dancers in the U.S. if more males were aware of the origins and challenges of the art and its popularity among males in other countries.

EVOLUTION OF MODERN COMPETITIONS

Before 1950 dancing competitions at the Games were a source of perplexity in many ways. Each of the competitions was run independently; there was no overseeing organization to offer a framework or advice or to which appeals could be made by disgruntled competitors. There were no standards for technique, which caused a variety of steps and styles to appear. Nor were there standards for judging; local rules and individual preferences were applied. The turning point in this chaotic situation came in January 1950 in Stirling, Scotland. Representatives of Highland dancing associations met with Games sponsors and individuals interested in fostering and promoting the art to consider the establishment of a governing body. At that meeting, the Scottish Official Board of Highland Dancing (SOBHD) was created.

The SOBHD is composed of officers and delegates representing individuals and groups who are devoted to Highland dancing. The examining bodies of the board are the Scottish Dance Teachers' Alliance (which first suggested the establishment of a governing body), the British Association of Teachers of Dancing, and the United Kingdom Alliance of Professional Teachers of Dancing. Affiliated members are individuals or members of Highland dancing organizations in the United States, Canada, Australia, New Zealand, and South Africa.

Thanks to the board's standards for performance and judging, a dancer can compete at any sanctioned competition in the world (and most are sanctioned) secure in the knowledge that the steps he is dancing are the same ones known by the other dancers and by the judges. Along with standardization has come refinement. The board publishes an official textbook that illustrates the basic positions for the feet, arms, and head, the basic movements, and the basic steps for Highland dancing. The traditional Highland dances—the Highland fling, sword dance, seann triubhas, strathspey, and reels—are outlined in the book, as well as basic information on music, competitions, and dress.

Judges for Highland dancing are selected from the board's panel of judges. A judge must have a thorough knowledge of the mechanics of the dances and an understanding of what the dance is trying to convey. Correct steps and movements are, of course, essential, but the attitude and expression of the dancer are also important. The dancer must be able to express the spirit and the story of the dance in his demeanor. To become a judge for the SOBHD, one must pass a comprehensive written examination. The aspirant is then given a mock judging test, after which his scores are compared with those of SOBHD authorities. Judges who are teachers—and most of them are—may not judge their own students. Judges who are competitors—and several of them are—may not judge their own age group in the open class.

The SOBHD requires that a Highland dancing championship have three judges, with each scoring every dancer on the platform independently. A championship is contested in the traditional Highland dances only and must include the Highland fling, sword dance, and seann triubhas. The reel in any of its versions—strathspey and reel of Tulloch, or strathspey and Highland reel *or* reel of Tulloch, or strathspey and Highland reel *and* reel of Tulloch—must also be included. With the exception of the strathspeys and reels, which always have four dancers, a judge usually watches three competitors simultaneously; that seems to be the number of dancers that can be observed at one time most comfortably. However, if there is a large number of competitors or if time is a factor, more than three solo dancers will compete before the judges.

Each year the board announces the championship steps that will be used at all championship events during the calendar year. The board also establishes the order in which they will be danced. This means that in a championship, all competitors will be dancing the same steps at the same time. The championship steps vary from year to year, which assures perpetuation of all the steps. In a regular competition, only the first and last steps of each dance are required to be used as such; the dancer may use any of the steps of the dance in any sequence between these two. This gives the dancer freedom to use his strongest steps when competing, but it also makes the judges' job more difficult. A judge who is also a teacher will have an easier time in such a situation, because an incorrect step or movement is generally spotted quickly by someone who works with the dances constantly.

Each dancer is judged in each dance on technique, general deportment, and timing. There is a total possible score of 100 points, with these areas accounting for 80, 10, and 10 points, respectively. Technique refers to the mechanics of the dance—proper footwork and coordination with correct head, arm, and hand movements. General deportment refers to the dancer's ability to communicate the message of the dance. A dancer should communicate the mood of the dance in a credible manner; facial and bodily expressions should complement and complete what the feet are saying. Strict timing—staying with the beat—is vital in Highland dancing. A dancer who does the steps correctly but who is a bit before or after the beat of the music creates an incongruous effect. A judge is not required to give any points at all to a dancer in the open class who is off the beat. In Scotland the judges are very strict about timing; if an open class dancer is off the beat, he can be eliminated from the dance.

Credit needs to be given here to the dependable and patient dancing pipers who have a symbiotic relationship with the dancers. When a dancer takes his place on the dancing platform and the piper begins to play, it is the responsibility of the dancer to interpret the piper's music; the feet sing what the fingers play. It is the responsibility of the piper to encourage and thereby assist the dancer. The piper sets the tempo of the music; the dancer must dance to the piper's beat. With the exception of the sword dance and seann triubhas, the dances can be accompanied by any of a number of tunes. In class and in practice, dancers use different tunes for the same dance and different settings of the same tune to develop a fundamental feeling for the beat and to learn to adjust to different beats. Regardless of whether the dancer is in the open class and knows most of the music or is a younger dancer still becoming familiar with the tunes, if the dancer starts counting with the piper, he will stay on the beat.

One of the most popular dancing pipers is Jimmy Fee of Weymouth, Massachusetts. Fee pipes for dancers at an average of 18 Games per year. Although he travels mostly to the eastern North American Games, he is known throughout the Highland dancing community. He was born in Dunbarton, Scotland, where he started studying the pipes at the age of eight. His teacher, Pipe Major William Gray, believed that a piper's concentration was heightened if he played for a dancer, so there was usually a dancer present at Fee's lessons. By the time Fee came to this country in 1967, he was used to playing for dancers, so he began playing for dancing competitions at one or two Games per year. He gradually began playing more and more often; now nearly every weekend of the summer finds him at a Scottish Highland Games playing the pipes for the dancers.

The secret of Fee's popularity as a dancing piper is his attitude. He believes that there is more to piping for dancers than just playing the tunes; a piper should try to help the dancer by putting expression into the music and marking the beat. He prefers to be on the platform with the dancers so they can better see and hear him tap his foot in time to the beat. One might think that it would be boring for a piper to have to play the same tune repeatedly, but Fee doesn't think so. He says that a piper has a great responsibility to the dancers; he must concentrate afresh with each new group. He tries not to look at the dancers competing. If they are dancing on the beat, there is no problem, but if even one is off the beat, it is distracting and may affect the tempo of the music.

Fee has two daughters who are former Highland dancers. He once had the pleasure of piping for them as they competed at the Grandfather Mountain Games. His piping expertise is recognized and appreciated beyond the platforms of the Highland Games as well. When not piping for dancers, he pipes in the Worcester Kiltie Pipe Band, one of the oldest and best bands in the eastern United States.

THE ART TODAY

As is true in the other areas of competition at the Games, the quality of Highland dancing in the United States is good and still improving. Although only six Americans have won top titles in the world championships at Cowal, it must be remembered that we are the late entries on the world scene. When Lynn Erbrick, the first American dancer to win at Cowal, captured the junior world championship in 1967, there were only 15 Scottish Highland Games in the United States that are still in existence today. Since then the Games have continued to grow in popularity and number, and the competitors in all the events have become more serious and experienced.

One of the factors contributing to the rise in quality of Highland dancing in this country was the emigration of Scots dancers (like Scots pipers) to the U.S. These successful Highland dancers found eager students here when they came in the 1950s and 1960s. Included in this group is Vera Miller Patterson, now living in St. Augustine, Florida. She has taught and judged in this country for more than 25 years. Among her American successes have been two world champions. Stewart Smith, who died in 1982, spent his adult years in this country teaching Highland dancing on a full-time basis. For many years, he was on the faculty of St. Thomas Episcopal School in Houston, Texas, where Highland dancing and piping are part of the curriculum.

Early in this same period, the 1950s and 1960s, the SOBHD began emphasizing its strict standards for the preservation and perpetuation of the traditional Highland dances. The board was not readily accepted here by all teachers and Games committees. With the help of several "ambassadors," especially the venerable James L. MacKenzie (more on him later), the way was smoothed for the gradual acceptance of the SOBHD. Others like Elspeth Strathern, now living in British Columbia, and Janet MacLachlan, who founded the Western Ontario Highland Dancing Association and runs the largest dancing competition (around 600 competitors) in the eastern part of North America at the Cambridge (Ontario) Games, have been instrumental in pointing American teachers in the right direction. It took about 10 years—until the early 1960s—for the board to become fully instituted in the United States. Now nearly all Games are sanctioned by the board, and the result has been more effective judging, teaching, and dancing.

The constant desire among dancers to learn and improve their technique is evident in the number of workshops and schools they attend across the country. The Delco Scottish Games Workshop is just as popular with dancers as it is with pipers and drummers. Present at nearly all of these workshops since their inception have been two of Scotland's Highland dancing greats, Jessie Stewart and Sheena MacDonald. Jessie Stewart, who started Highland dancing at the age of four, is one of the founders of the SOBHD and the chairman of its technical and judges' panel. She has been teaching Highland dancing at her own school for more than 55 years. Sheena MacDonald is one of only two persons ever to win the adult world championship three times in succession, which she did in 1956–58. (The other was James L. MacKenzie in 1951–53.) She also has her own dancing school.

Because of such positive influences, our dancers are going to Scotland and proving that they are serious, that they have the desire and discipline to compete with the best in the art. And Scotland is taking notice, both of the increasingly intense desire to learn and of the prizes that are leaving her shores. But Scotland has reason to be proud, because the higher quality being displayed among American dancers is the result of her leading and sharing. Something more than technique thrives on the dancing stage; tradition thrives there, too. An enormous sense of pride and joy comes from competing in Scotland, and this is true in all of the competitive events. It comes from the thrill of competing against some of the greatest Games performers in the place where the Games originated and are universally recognized.

AMERICAN SUCCESS STORIES

The most prestigious competition in Highland dancing is that held each August at the Cowal Highland Gathering in Dunoon. There, hundreds of hopefuls vie for the title of world champion. The Cowal Gathering was held intermittently until 1900, when it became an annual event. The trophy presented to the world juvenile champion was first presented in 1910. From this we can assume that world championship competitions have been in existence for more than 75 years. During that time, only six dancers representing the United States have been declared champions, and only one of those winners was in the adult class.

Lynn Erbrick was the first American to win a top prize at Cowal. In 1967, at the age of seventeen, she was declared junior world champion. Her teacher, Marguerite Reid, who usually accompanies her students to competitions, was judging at the Canadian National Exhibition in Ontario that year and couldn't go to Scotland. Reid remembers well the excitement surrounding Erbrick's victory: "When I got into New York from Canada I called home to see if I'd had news from Lynn. She'd telegrammed: 'Won first in world championship.' I wouldn't let myself think that she'd *won* the world championship. For three days I was convinced that she'd gotten a first in one of the dances—probably the seann triubhas, as that was her best one. Finally, her father called—he didn't realize that she'd won either—to tell me he'd heard from a relative in the Washington, D.C., area who had read about Lynn in a newspaper. The headline was 'Yank Wins World Title.' It was not until then that either of us knew she'd won the *whole* thing!"

America's first Cowal winner is now married and living in Stroudsburg, Pennsylvania. She has continued to be absorbed in

Highland dancing through teaching and judging. She and her husband, George Eberz, were heavily involved in the now-defunct Poconos Highland Games, which were held in Stroudsburg. Their daughter Heather competes in Highland dancing.

In 1970, Sandra Scafate, a student of Vera Miller Patterson, was named junior world champion at age seventeen. Scafate continued to compete for a while after winning her Cowal title, but she is now married and living in California and is no longer involved with Highland dancing. The following year Noreen Keros won the junior title at age sixteen. She was a student of Sheila Mittig. Keros also continued competing after Cowal and eventually taught Highland dancing before leaving it. She and her musician husband live in south Florida.

The only American ever to win double honors at Cowal is Mary Beth Miller, who was also a student of Sheila Mittig. She won the juvenile world championship in 1976 at age sixteen and returned in 1977 to win the junior world title. She is now married and living in Oklahoma but is connected with the Kansas City Highland Games. She is writing a book on Highland dancing.

In 1980 Fiona Nash, a student of Catherine Hynd, was named junior world champion at age seventeen. The Nashes are Canadian citizens who were living in California at the time that Fiona competed at Cowal. Since she was studying with an American teacher and living in California, she and her family felt it only fitting that she dance for the United States. She is now living in Ottawa; in 1981 and 1982 she was fourth runner-up and third runner-up, respectively, in the adult world championship representing her homeland, Canada.

An interesting aside concerning Nash. In 1979 she won the British Open Championship in Edinburgh. The trophy she won had been donated several years before by the Southern California Highland Dancing Association, of which Nash's father was president that year. Nash was the first dancer to, as it were, bring the trophy home. Yet another spirit of closeness prevails in the story: John Hynd, Catherine's husband, was the first American to win the title "Best Overseas Dancer" at the Edinburgh Festival, which was bestowed on him in 1958.

Only one American, Hugh Bigney of Lynnfield, Massachusetts, has ever been named the top adult Highland dancer in the
world. The coveted title is certainly prestigious enough, but the
events surrounding his win make it doubly impressive. Just
before Cowal, in mid-August 1973, Bigney had scored another
still-unbroken first for the United States when he was declared
overall best dancer in the dance competition at the Edinburgh
Festival, which includes many styles of dancing (such as Highland, ballet, and tap). This title is awarded to the dancer who
scores the most points in any dance style or combination of
styles. During the festival he won the British overseas and the
boys' championship events and missed winning the British Open
by one-half point. The overall title was awarded to the 17-year-old
for his showing in Scottish dancing only, making him one of the
few persons ever to win it by participating in one dance form
only. Winning the Edinburgh Championship was a complete
surprise to Bigney. "I missed the British Open by one-half of a
point due to my own carelessness. I was enjoying myself so much
doing the seann triubhas that I totally forgot the last setting step
in quick time—my mind totally blanked it out—so I didn't place
in that dance." He had naturally assumed that earning no points
in this dance made the overall title an impossibility.

On August 24, 1973, Bigney celebrated his 18th birthday in
Dunoon, Scotland, making him eligible to compete in the adult
category. The next day, he took advantage of his new status by
winning the title of adult world champion. Within two weeks,
Bigney took the Highland dancing world by storm in an unas-
suming manner, leaving behind a trail of unbroken and noteworthy events. For his country, he became the first dancer to win the
coveted titles of best overall dancer at Edinburgh and adult
world champion at Dunoon. For the Highland dancing world in
general, he became the first person to win both of these titles in
the same year, the youngest-ever adult world champion (at 18
years and 1 day old), and one of a very few to win the Edinburgh
title by dancing in one style only.

To Bigney, being named adult world champion was not only
the culmination of his dancing career; it was the fulfillment of a
lifelong ambition. Recalling his feelings at the moment he learned

of his triumph, Bigney says, "That was one of the high points in my life. I not only had a rush of excitement, but the whole realization of the fact of what was happening to me. Ever since I had begun to dance at the age of five, I had wanted to win the world championship. I had finally achieved this goal. When my number was called last as the winner, I was just overwhelmed; I began to cry. All I remember as I walked around with the cup in the small parade held in the Games area was that I was crying. I didn't care if anybody saw me and I didn't care who took pictures of me crying because I was so happy."

Bigney's first teacher in Saugus, Massachusetts, Judy Thibodeau, was still quite young herself. She attended the Gaelic College in Nova Scotia each summer to take lessons from the great James L. MacKenzie. At Bigney's first lesson, Thibodeau showed him a photograph of MacKenzie and told the boy all about him. Bigney was greatly impressed and wanted to meet and study with him.

When Bigney was nine years old, his wish came true. James L. (as MacKenzie was affectionately known) was judging at the Wilmington (Delaware) Highland Games and Bigney won a scholarship to study with him at the Gaelic College. This experience meant almost as much to the young dancer as winning the world championship did later. Bigney speaks reverently of James L. not just because of his dancing expertise, but because of the deep appreciation and respect for his heritage that he learned from MacKenzie. "I remember that first year at the Gaelic College...James L. sort of took me under his wing. I was always small for my age; I was smaller than the other boys my age who were there to study the pipes with Seumas MacNeill. He would sit me on his lap or put me beside him to pull up my tartan socks and show me how it wasn't right that they didn't line up the way I'd put them on. I'd put them on just like I'd put on socks every day. He showed me that no, the lines needed to line up and this is the way to wear the sporran and couldn't I straighten my kilt? As I reflect back now, I think even more highly of that than studying dancing with him. From that, I gained a respect for the Scottish heritage, for the kilt, for the costume, for the art, for the culture. From James L. saying 'Look, this is how you wear the costume, this is how you should act. As a Scottish dancer you should be proud of your heritage.'

"I can remember that first year watching an exhibition that he did with Seumas MacNeill. James L. danced for about an hour. Between dances he would rest and Seumas would play the pipes.... I remember watching him as a little boy and being amazed at how energetic he was at his age. And I thought, 'If only I could be like that man, as energetic, to have that love of Scottish dancing.' To me, he was the personification of what Scottish dancing was about: the love of the Scottish heritage."

Bigney attended the Gaelic College for two years. The next and last time he saw James L. was during a competition in Scotland in 1970. James L. paid him the high compliment of telling him that he liked his dancing and he was proud to have been a part of his career.

When Bigney was eleven years old, he began to study with Vera Miller Patterson. A native Scot and former junior world champion, she moved to the U.S. in the 1950s. Even though it meant flying from Massachusetts to Ohio whenever he could for lessons, Bigney was committed to her as a teacher and to himself as a Scottish dancer. In her small kitchen in Lorain, Ohio, he spent hours trying to perfect details: "To Mrs. Patterson it wasn't okay just to have something almost right; you needed to be right no matter what." She brought him back to the basics of Scottish dancing and drilled and developed him into a world champion. Bigney credits Patterson's knowledge of the mechanics of the body as one of the most important reasons for her effectiveness as a teacher. She has a great command of Scottish technique and understands ballet technique; she knows how the body should work and respond to the demands of dancing.

Patterson instilled a deeper love of Scottish dancing in Bigney; he found the joy and excitement she derived from it real and infectious. "Sometimes she would talk to me and say, 'Be happy; doesn't this dancing make you feel happy?' Once in Scotland she said, 'Look at the mountains, the hills. This is what we're dancing for. This is what it is all about.'" From James L. and from Patterson he learned the importance not only of knowing how to do the Scottish dances, but also of knowing why one does them.

The first United States championship Bigney won was the Atlantic International when it was held in Ocean City, Maryland. (It is now held at the Grandfather Mountain Games.) He was twelve years old then and went on to win the title the next two years. He won numerous other U.S. championships and won the Eastern Canadian championship twice. When he first won the latter, he tied with Sandra Scafate, another of Vera Patterson's champion students, for the most aggregate points.

The 1973 world championship at Cowal was the last Highland dancing competition in which Bigney participated. He felt he had done what he wanted to do in Scottish dancing and even convinced himself that his entire dancing career was finished. "I had studied Highland dancing for thirteen years and I had had ballet training on and off during that time. But Scottish dancing was my first love.... I *cared* about Scottish dancing. I worked hard for that world championship; I wanted it. It was on the airplane returning from Cowal that I realized I wanted a rest. At that time I deluded myself into thinking that dancing was over for me as a serious thing." That fall he enrolled in Brigham Young University as an English major. After one semester, he knew that a short rest from dancing was all he really wanted; he would remain a serious dancer. Shortly after making that decision, he went abroad to serve the two-year missionary ministry required of all young men of the Mormon faith. Upon completion of his assignment, he returned to BYU but left after a semester to pursue a professional dance career.

Bigney went to Salt Lake City to study with William Christianson, founder of Ballet West and one of the fathers of ballet in America. He joined Ballet West as a full-time company member, studying also with Bruce Marks, the artistic director, and Toni Lander, former ballerina of the American Ballet Theater, the Royal Danish Ballet, and the London Festival Ballet. Bigney learned much from Lander. "She is a great adherent to the fact that our bodies can only do certain things and that sometimes when we try to force them, we are doing damage; we must try to use our bodies naturally. I began examining my Scottish background and realized how much that is true. You can stretch its limitations, but you should never force the body."

In 1982 Bigney joined Pacific Northwest Ballet. The Seattle company does a lot of choreography by George Balanchine, which suits Bigney well; Balanchine's work makes heavy use of petite allegro movements, and Bigney's Scottish training has made him very strong in this style. The company's management has encouraged Bigney's interest in choreography. Bigney has choreographed a ballet called *Celtic Dances*, based on the Scottish technique. It is a piece based on the strathspey and reel for two men and two women, set to music written by Paganini.

Bigney's love affair with Scottish dancing has continued and even intensified through his involvement with choreography. "In examining Scottish dancing from a choreographer's standpoint, I discovered new things about it. I discovered in fact what a fine technique it really is and how much can be said for it. I think that Scottish dancing is truly one of the, if not *the,* hardest techniques that exists. I think its difficulty lies in the fact that it is so strict in some ways and yet needs to be so free and loose in others. It is finding that balance that is so difficult."

He has done much solo work for Pacific Northwest Ballet and has danced many character roles, including Dr. Coppelius in *Coppelia* and Jester in *Swan Lake*. He has been a soloist in two Balanchine ballets, *La Valse* and *Western Symphony*. For the past few years he has performed as Herr Drosselmeyer in the Stowell-Sendak version of *The Nutcracker*. He has performed throughout the United States and has toured in Canada and Taiwan. In addition to a full performing schedule, he is a guest teacher of ballet.

Although Bigney no longer competes in Scottish Highland Games, he frequently attends Games in his area as a spectator and has performed Scottish Highland dancing upon request at various functions. He readily acknowledges the significance of Scottish dancing in his life. "Highland dancing was my life. I don't know what it means not to dance. Dancing *is* my life. My Highland dancing was my means of entertainment and the way I grew up. I had most of my life experiences through my experience in Highland dancing. I learned how to win and how to lose gracefully. I learned the meaning of hard work and dedication. I still draw upon those experiences. Sometimes now when I get up and I'm sore and dead tired and I don't want to go to ballet class or to rehearsal, I think on my Highland dancing days—how I needed to persevere and the struggles and the payoff—and I say, 'I can do it!' "

Bigney has earned the British Association of Teachers of Dancing certificate and in 1982 and 1984 coached one of the finalists in the U.S. Inter-Regional Dancing Championships. His future plans include opening a studio to teach ballet and Scottish Highland dancing.

Bigney is married to an American of Scottish descent, the former Kenda Stuart, and they have two children, Chaundra and Hugh, Jr. His 7-year-old daughter studies at the professional school of Pacific Northwest Ballet; she has performed in *The Nutcracker* and *A Midsummer Night's Dream*. His son, who turned four in the summer of 1985, began studying ballet a few months after his birthday.

THE DANCES

As previously stated, the history of the various dances seen at the Games today is incomplete. A few facts and the best-loved fancy have survived to present some semblance of origin. But whatever their true inspiration, we know that each of the dances was created to tell a story. Knowing what each dance conveys will enable the viewer to appreciate more fully the dancer and the dance.

The Highland Fling

This best-known of the Highland dances is said to depict the antics of a stag on a mountainside. The dancer's raised arms represent the stag's antlers. This is the only dance done in one spot with no traveling steps; the reason for this is another legend, unrelated to the stag story. The Highland fling was supposedly danced by victorious warriors, and the steps were performed on a targe (shield). This limited the dancer's movement and demanded meticulous footwork as well: most targes had a sharp metal spike protruding from the center.

The Highland fling is danced to a strathspey tune and is the only traditional Highland dance in which the tempo of the music does not change. It requires the highest degree of control, poise, skill, and exact timing. Hence it is said to be the most basic of the dances. Because of its precise nature, it is often used in dance-offs to determine the best dancer of the day.

In this dance, watch particularly for a good turning-out of the legs. When the legs are properly turned out, well to the side, the front of the kilt lies perfectly flat. Watch also for the fling, the step that gave the dance its name. In this step, the dancer hops on one foot while moving the other foot in front and back of the calf.

The Sword Dance
(Gillie Chalium)

This dance has roots that may stretch as far back as 77 A.D. during the reign of Agricola, the Roman emperor of Britain. Over the emperor's five-year rule, his son-in-law, the renowned historian Tacitus, chronicled many interesting occurrences, including, it is said, the Caledonian practice of dancing on upturned swords.

In 1054 Malcolm Canmore, crusading to gain the Scottish throne, slew one of MacBeth's chiefs at Dunsinane. Legend has it that Malcolm, full of the joy of victory, laid his sword—most likely the mighty claymore—over that of his late adversary and danced in triumph. The dance then became a ritual performed by warriors on the eve of battle. If the dancers' feet did not touch the swords during the dance, good fortune was expected in the ensuing battle. Touching the swords, however, was a bad omen.

Gillie Chalium or Calum is translated "servant [of God] Columba." The name Malcolm is from the Old Gaelic *mael Coluim*, which is translated "servant of Columba." St. Columba is credited with bringing Christianity to Scotland in the sixth century.

Janet MacLachlan of Ontario has done extensive research into the history of Highland dances, and her studies have not produced direct evidence for the Canmore legend. She supports the theory that the Gillie Chalium is more closely associated with St. Columba, as it is a representation of the victory of good over evil. The sword of the victor, held in the right hand, is symbolically

Hugh Bigney, left, is congratulated by Angus Morrison on his 1973 clean sweep of the Cowal and Edinburgh competitions. (Courtesy of Vera Miller Patterson)

Hugh Bigney today as a member of Pacific Northwest Ballet. (Photo by David McNutt)

Kitty Hart performs the sword dance to piper Jimmy Fee's accompaniment.

Tracey Fairlee exhibits fine form in the seann triubhas.

The reel is danced by a team of four, but each dancer is judged individually.

Dancers in the sailor's hornpipe demonstrate common shipboard activities in uniforms similar to those worn in the Royal Navy.

Sandra Weyman vents her contempt as the put-upon wife in the Irish jig.

crossed over the sword of the vanquished, held in the left hand.

There is only one tune for this dance, and it is also called "Gillie Chalium." Two Highland broadswords are used: the hilt of the bottom sword is placed to the dancer's left and that of the top sword is placed directly in front of the dancer. The dancer moves counter-clockwise, dancing outside and inside the four imaginary squares formed by the crossing of the swords. One must be nimble and precise to avoid touching or displacing the blades; touching them causes a loss of points, and displacing them causes disqualification from the dance. This is especially difficult at the end of the dance, when the tempo is faster.

A few Games in the United States have a separate competition called broadswords. In this dance, a cross is formed by four swords with the points touching. A team of four dancers dances over them at the same time. Thousands of Americans have thrilled to performances of the Argyll Broadswords by the dancers who accompany the Royal Scots Dragoons military unit on its U.S. tours. According to Janet MacLachan, this dance is said to have been first danced by the soldiers marching south with Bonnie Prince Charlie in 1745.

The Seann Triubhas

The name of this dance is Gaelic for "old [or without] trousers." The movements in this dance supposedly express abhorrence at the Act of Proscription banning Highland customs pronounced after the defeat of Bonnie Prince Charlie. The decline in fortunes suffered by the prince after his defeat in battle is reflected in this dance just as the hopeful exuberance of preparing for battle is reflected in the sword dance. The free-moving kilt of the Scots was replaced by the tight-fitting trousers of the English as part of the ban. Although the seann triubhas is composed of beautiful and graceful body movements, its quick and haughty hand movements suggest the hatred of repression. The shaking movement of the legs represents the act of unshackling both the oppressors' garb and bondage. The freedom of action afforded by the kilt is demonstrated with the faster music in the last part of the dance.

In her book *The Story of Scottish Country Dancing*, Evelyn Hood says that the story above cannot be accepted, as trousers were in common use in the Highlands before the 1745 uprising. She believes that the seann triubhas was a merry dance more of the pantomine tradition.

Janet MacLachlan writes that another common interpretation of this dance is the symbolic brushing away of evil, similar to Scottish women's practice of sweeping their houses clean on Hogmanay (New Year's Eve) in preparation for the New Year.

An additional note on the seann triubhas. In an article from the 1981 program of the Ohio Scottish Games, Timothy J. Crouch states that the brush step that appears at the beginning of the dance comes from the Scottish-themed ballet *La Sylphide*. This ballet, which marked the beginning of the Romantic movement in ballet, was written by Jean Schneitzhoffer and choreographed by Phillipe Taglioni and was first performed in Paris in 1832. D. G. MacLennan added the brush step to the seann triubhas in 1908.

Reels

Unlike the three dances already discussed, reels are group dances. Four dancers participate, but each is judged individually. Reels have always been associated with recreational, rather than martial, activity.

Reels are usually preceded by a strathspey (see chapter 6) done in the same formation but in a different musical tempo: reel time is faster than strathspey time. The basic step, the *pas de basque* (which is the same as the setting step done in Scottish country dancing), was brought to Scotland by the French court of Mary Queen of Scots in the mid-sixteenth century. The figure-eight movement is said to represent the interlacing patterns commonly used by the Celts to symbolize eternal life. This pattern is apparent on their great stone crosses.

Perhaps the most common reel seen at American Games is the reel of Tulloch (also known as the Hullachan). The dance is supposed to have originated at a church in the village of Tulloch. It seems the minister was late in arriving one cold Sunday morning and the congregation was left waiting outside the locked doors. In order to keep warm, they began to move about, clapping their hands and stamping their feet. Someone began to hum or whistle a tune and the movements got more lively. Eventually these brisk steps were fashioned into a dance.

National Dances

Although still a part of the Highland dancing legacy, the national dances are not considered traditional Highland dances, the vigorous, high-stepping dances originally performed by kilt-clad males as part of the athletic competitions at Scottish Games. The steps of the national dances are similar to the steps in the Highland dances, but since many of them are women's dances, they are more flowing and graceful in nature and, when danced by women, are performed in the more accommodating Aboyne dress.

Among the dances seen at the Games that were written specifically for women are "Village Maid," "Earl of Errol," "Blue Bonnets Over the Border," "Scottish Lilt," and "Flora MacDonald's Fancy." The latter is one of the oldest and most famous of these dances. It was written in honor of Flora MacDonald, the brave young woman who helped Bonnie Prince Charlie (here he is again!) escape to the Isle of Skye and eventual safety in France after his crushing defeat at the Battle of Culloden. National dances seen at the Games that are danced in the kilt are "Wilt Thou Go to Barracks, Johnny" and "Highland Laddie."

The sailor's hornpipe is so called because it is an ancient dance that was accompanied by the music of the horn pipe (similar to the modern tin flute), which eventually became a highly popular instrument among seafaring men. Its movements depict shipboard activities from the days of the sail: hauling ropes, climbing shroud lines, splicing the mainbrace, and serving as lookout. Its English origin is reflected in the costume worn for this dance, which is based on the uniform of a sailor in the Royal Navy.

The Scottish version of the Irish jig that is danced at the Games is a parody of the real dance. In the Irish style of step dancing, the hands are held stiffly at the sides. In the Scottish version, the controlled abandon with which it is danced is apparent throughout. When danced by females, the Irish jig portrays an angered Irish washerwoman whose husband has obviously stopped at a pub on the way home. She taps her foot in fury awaiting his late arrival, and her motions show how he will be welcomed home. When performed by males, the dance is said to tell the story of the tune "Paddy's Leather Breeches." The breeches in question were washed by an Irish washerwoman and shrank to a most uncomfortable fit. The dancer's actions illustrate his rage at her carelessness.

The dress for the Irish jig is usually bright green or red with white (or some other combination thereof). Men often wear pants, jacket, bow tie, and hat and may carry a shillelagh. This is the only dance in which different shoes are worn. These shoes are Highland dance pumps (red or green in color) that have a hard sole at the front, a soft sole at the arch, and a stacked hard heel with a "jingler" inserted in the heel to make the characteristic noise. The sharp sound helps to accent and convey the perturbation revealed in the dance.

DANCE TRAINING

Learning Highland dancing is a gradual process. The first thing that must be drilled into a new student is the basic foot position, which is similar to the first position in ballet: standing with the heels together and the toes apart, making a 90-degree angle. (The ballet dancer strives for a perfect 180-degree turnout.) The feet do not want to do this, as it is an unnatural way to stand, but it is essential to Highland dancing.

Most teachers make their students work on strengthening their legs and building up their stamina before introducing the steps of the dances. Since the dances are vigorous and precise and are done on the balls of the feet, they require a great deal of control. I have watched students in baby classes (under age six), holding my breath all the while for fear one or two might dance off a platform. It is no easy task to try to dance on one's toes (with the feet always turned outwards whether on the floor or in the air) and combine the correct foot positions with the correct movements and positions of the arms, hands, and head, all in time to the music. In the Highland fling, there is the added complication of staying in one spot. Of course, experience is a great refiner. Even though these little ones are bouncing all around, they are nevertheless bouncing, and the more they bounce, the more agile and graceful they become.

Desire, discipline, persistence, perseverance, and practice, practice, practice make an able dancer. To encourage mastering the steps and excelling in the dances, dancers follow a grading system similar to that of pipers. There are five classifications (six if one begins in the baby class) through which all dancers must advance: beginner, novice, intermediate, advanced intermediate, and open. A beginner must place first, second, or third in six competitions before becoming a novice. After placing in three novice competitions, a dancer moves to the intermediate class. For one year after the date of the third competition in which a dancer places as an intermediate, he dances as an advanced intermediate. During this period the dancer must try to dance in as many competitions as possible, because at the end of that year he is automatically moved into the open class. The advanced intermediate class has the same purpose as the EUSPBA open Grade II class in piping: to give newly progressed competitors breathing space before meeting seasoned competitors. With the exception of the advanced intermediate class, progression through the classes depends upon the amount of time and effort a dancer puts into his practice.

There is also considerable expense involved if one wishes to become an accomplished Highland dancer. Traveling from Games to Games, especially by air, is expensive. On top of that, the current cost of a good new outfit for an adult dancer is about $500. Fortunately, given proper care, a kilt is nearly indestructible. A pair of gillies (dancing shoes) costs $25–$30 and, depending on the individual dancer, may have to be replaced several times a year. Irish jig shoes cost about $45.

The time and cost factors may be great, but the rewards that come from dancing are greater still. Much satisfaction comes from competing and knowing that one has mastered a difficult skill. I have queried many dancers about what it means to be involved in Highland dancing. The most common answer given had nothing to do with personal accomplishments; the dancers mentioned the camaraderie among dancers here and abroad prominently.

Sandra Weyman, who was one of the top dancers in the eastern part of the United States for several years, expressed her experience in these words: "It is difficult to put into words what dancing means to a person who has been involved in it for as long as I have. It becomes a very definite and important part of your life. The self-discipline learned from dancing extends to other areas of life. This is a real plus that children gain from this activity.

"Highland dancing is certainly the most strenuous activity in which I have participated. Dancing has made me more aware of myself; I find that I am happiest as a person when I am in good dancing shape. Because of this, I have become very interested in other sports and in fitness training. During the last few years, this interest has extended to learning more about injury prevention and balanced ways of training. Because of injuries, I have stopped dancing for a period of time on two occasions. During these layoffs I have tried other forms of dancing, including ballet and jazz. However, I have found that absolutely *nothing* gives me the self-satisfaction of Highland dancing.

"Competition has provided a wonderful opportunity for travel and a chance to see parts of the country that I might never have seen. A great deal of group fun is involved when traveling to competitions with fellow dancers and friends. There is a real sense of belonging when you attend a competition, knowing that you are part of a unique group—including all other competitors as well—joined by a common bond. Even if you fly hundreds of miles by yourself to a competition, you feel at home once you arrive.

"We have always said that dancers must be slightly crazy to travel great distances to dance in all kind of conditions. There are sometimes heartaches to contend with when competing or teaching, but something always draws you back and picks you up again. Knowing that you have practiced *all* that you could, put *all* of yourself into it, and are now standing on a platform in the sunny South or among the misty hills of Scotland gives a feeling of satisfaction, of belonging to something greater than yourself, that is truly hard to describe even when you have experienced it. It is a quality that simply cannot be put into words; it just compares with nothing else."

THE CHAMPIONSHIPS

There are many Highland dancing competitions in the United States, most of which are found at Scottish Highland Games. Depending on a dancer's desire, time, and resources, he could travel nearly every weekend in the summer and many weekends during the rest of the year to compete in Highland dancing. But there are relatively few championships, which must be authorized by the Scottish Official Board of Highland Dancing. The board has authorized 12 United States championships: Western United States (Santa Rosa, CA), Lakes and Prairie Closed (Minneapolis, MN), Midwest Open (Kansas City, MO), Great Lakes Open (Detroit), Southwestern (Houston), Atlantic International (Grandfather Mountain), Florida (Dunedin), Eastern United States Closed (Fair Hill, MD), Southern Regional Closed (Savannah, GA), Ohio Open (Oberlin), Texas/Oklahoma Closed (Houston), and the United States Inter-Regional (site varies).

The history of the United States Inter-Regional Championship is a short one. During the past few years several persons involved in Highland dancing in the U.S. saw the need to organize a national championship, one that would draw representatives from every part of the country. This was the only country in which Highland dancing was performed that did not have a national Highland dancing championship. Nor did the U.S. have a national Highland dancing organization.

By the end of the 1970s Highland dancing activity, which before had been found mainly in the northeastern and Great Lakes regions and in parts of California, was established in all areas of the United States. An organization was needed that would be representative of the entire country. Christie Freestone of Alma, Michigan, headed up a group of teachers of Highland dancing that laid the groundwork for what would be a functional national organization. A precursory meeting was held at the 1980 Grandfather Mountain Games to share ideas. At the National Conference of Highland Dancing held in Las Vegas, Nevada, in October 1980, the Federation of United States Teachers and Adjudicators (FUSTA) was introduced. The founding officers were: president, Christie Freestone; vice president, Jeanne

Roberts of Michigan; secretary, Janis Burkhardt of Michigan; and treasurer, Diana Krugh of Texas. Various Highland dancing organizations in this country promote the art in their respective areas, but FUSTA is the first truly national as well as the first professional organization of teachers and judges of Highland dancing.

The purpose of FUSTA is twofold: to sponsor a national Highland dancing championship and to unify the country so that teachers and dancers may get to know each other. Its founders believed that the national standard of dancing would rise if dancers from across the country could see each other perform, and in the short history of the FUSTA, this has already proven to be so.

To implement its goal of a national Highland dancing championship, in 1981 the FUSTA divided the United States into six regions. A preliminary championship was held at a designated site in each of these regions to determine the top dancers in each area. Eight dancers, two from each of four age groups, were selected from each region to be that region's representatives at the national championship. (In 1983 the by-laws were revised to include the top three dancers from each of four age groups, making a total of 72 dancers competing at the national championships beginning that year.) The Virginia Scottish Games in Alexandria was selected as host to the first United States Inter-Regional Highland Dancing Championships, held on July 26, 1981.

Judges for the premiere event were Elspeth Strathern and Adeline Duncan of British Columbia and Vera Miller Patterson, then of San Francisco. Dancing pipers were Jimmy Fee of Weymouth, Massachusetts, and John Recknagel of Toledo, Ohio. Catherine Fisher, director of Highland dancing for the Virginia Scottish Games, was the dance organizer for the first event.

Here follow the names of the 48 dancers from 22 states who represented their regions at the inaugural United States Inter-Regional Championships. The Games that hosted the preliminary championships at which these regional finalists were selected are given in parentheses.

Eastern region (Colonial Highland Gathering, Fair Hill, Maryland): 12 and under, Kim Ann Demsey, Elizabeth Regan; 13–15, Cheryl Fisher, Moira Campbell; 16–17, Gail Houston, Karen Munro; 18 and over, Sandra Weyman, Kathleen Campbell.

Midwestern region (Alma Highland Games, Alma, Michigan): 12 and under, Kathleen Rayburn, Kathleen Swanson; 13–15, Kitty Hart, Leslie Grover; 16–17, Shirlee Finch, Mary Jo Rohrer; 18 and over, Tracey Fairlee, Elaine McKeller.

Northwestern region (Northwestern Regional Competition, Seattle): 12 and under, Christine Burrows, Kristine McSkimming; 13–15, Holly MacKenzie, Heather Galloway; 16–17, Cindy Aspitarte, Laurie Snygg; 18 and over, Robin Hegge, Liza Tewell.

Southern region (Tidewater Scottish Festival, Virginia Beach, Virginia): 12 and under, Andrea Rouzie, Alison Cormack; 13–15, Wendy Teer, Megan Grant; 16–17, Elaine Burgin, Tracey Teer; 18 and over, Elizabeth McLeod, Margaret Morrison.

Southwestern region (Kansas City Highland Games, Kansas City, Missouri): 12 and under, Susan McKee, Evelyn Hwang; 13–15, Michelle Powell, Martha Butler; 16–17, Roxanna James, Dora Russell; 18 and over, Tomi Crain, Marsha Young.

Western region (Western Regional Competition, Northridge, California): 12 and under, Mary Hokeness, Penny Bruce; 13–15, Linda Esslinger, Sandra Esslinger; 16–17, Rosemary Simpson, Janice Jones; 18 and over, Kay Shofner, Harry Farrar.

At the end of the day the top three dancers in four events were named from each group. The top finishers in the four age groups—Susan McKee of Texas, Cheryl Fisher of Maryland, Shirlee Finch of Michigan, and Kathleen Campbell of Pennsylvania—danced for the title "Champion of Champions," with Kathleen Campbell emerging as the victor.

The pride and sense of accomplishment that champion dancers feel is also felt by their teachers. At the first national championship, Florence Hart of Minneapolis, Minnesota, had two of her students, Kitty Hart (her daughter) and Shirlee Finch, among the 12 winners. Marguerite Reid, who as Lynn Erbrick's teacher shared the excitement of the first American to win at Cowal, saw three of her students win top honors at Alexandria: Kathleen Campbell, Cheryl Fisher, and Sandra Weyman. The following month, Campbell and Fisher won the British Overseas Championships for their respective age groups at the Edinburgh Festival, creating the rare phenomenon of multiple winners from the same school of dance.

The second national event was held at the 1982 Portland Games. In 1983 the site was the Ohio Games; in 1984, the San Diego Games; in 1985, the Grandfather Mountain Games. The 1986 event will be held at the Games in Chicago. At each national championship, host Games are selected for the next two years. The six-year rotation of sites shifts the burden of expense for the participants from year to year and from region to region. It also gives the competitors an opportunity to travel more widely and gives dance aficionados in the various areas an opportunity to see the top dancers in the United States every six years.

The fame and worth of the national championships were acknowledged quickly both here and abroad. At the 1982 Portland Games, Lynne Dickson Abbott, a well-known Australian teacher and judge who won the adult world championship title in 1970, was a judge for the regular dancing competition on Saturday. She was so impressed with what the FUSTA and the national championships were doing that she donated a special award. The Australian Achievement Award, presented to the dancer who earns the highest number of points for the day, is a plaque on which is affixed an Australian opal. In addition, the winner and the winner's teacher each receive an opal ring. The first recipient was Cheryl Fisher.

Profiles of the winners of the 1985 national Highland dancing championship conclude this chapter on Highland dancing in the United States. Thanks to the enterprising efforts of the FUSTA, the United States can now name the dancers who best represent the Highland dancing tradition.

12 and Under

Trophy winner **Laura Carruthers** is a student at First Lutheran Elementary School in Burbank, California. Her Highland dancing teacher is Catherine Hynd. Laura's mother, Connie, teaches Highland dancing and is on the board of the Southern California Highland Dancing Association. Her father Walt is treasurer of the Scottish-American Athletic Association; he began competing in heavy events before Laura was born. For her 7th birthday, Laura asked for Highland dancing lessons; now she and her father compete at Games together. She has been in the open class 3 years and has accumulated six dance-off or best dancer awards. She does Highland dancing demonstrations for Masonic groups and clan gatherings. Her family belongs to Clan Cameron.

U.S. medals/trophies: over 100/over 30

Other U.S. championships: Western (trophy), national (trophy, 1984)

Foreign competitions: Vancouver (trophy, under 11, under 12; Mallard Memorial Shield Award)

First runner-up **Kristina Gilbertson** is a student at Rolling Hills Junior High School in Los Gatos, California. Along with Highland dancing, she also plays the bagpipe and is a member of the Prince Charles Junior Pipe Band.

Kristina's mother, Mary, is a former Highland dancer and currently teaches piping. Kristina, who began Highland dancing lessons at age three, studies with Norine Vujovich. She has been in the open class 6 years. She dances at many public functions; in 1984 she and fellow students/FUSTA winners Rebecca Rugg and Mary Hokeness danced for Queen Elizabeth in San Francisco.

U.S. medals/trophies: several hundred/80

Other U.S. championships: Western, national (1982; 2nd runner-up, 1983; 1st runner-up, 1984)

Heather Campbell of Philadelphia, Pennsylvania, was named second runner-up at her first national championship in 1985. At that time she had been in the open class 5 months. A student at St. Catherine School, Heather has had a lifelong interest in Highland dancing. Four of her sisters share her love of the art; two of them, Kathleen and Moira, also competed in the 1985 national championship. Heather, who began Highland dancing at the age of five, and her sisters are students of Marguerite Reid.

15 and Under

Trophy winner **Susan McKee** of Houston, Texas, has represented the Southwest region at all five national championships.

She was the recipient of the Australian Achievement Award at the 1985 championship. A student at Bellaire Senior High School, she got involved in Highland dancing at her previous school, St. Thomas, which is one of the few below-college-level schools in the United States to include the Scottish arts as part of its curriculum. She began dancing at age nine and has been in the open class 6 years. Her Highland dancing teacher is Diane MacPhee.

U.S. medals/trophies: over 800/over 150

Other U.S. championships: national (trophy, 1981, 1983; 2nd runner-up, 1982; 1st runner-up, 1984)

Foreign competitions: British Overseas (1st runner-up), Cowal (6th overall, 1983; 1st runner-up, 1984)

First runner-up **Karen Fisher** of Bowie, Maryland, is a student at Benjamin Tasker Middle School. She started Highland dancing lessons at the age of five and has been in the open class 5 years. Karen and her older sister, Cheryl, study with Marguerite Reid in Philadelphia. Their mother Catherine also studied with Marguerite and now has her own Highland dancing school in Bowie. Karen competed in Scotland in 1983.

Other U.S. championships: Atlantic International (trophy), Rocky Mountain (trophy), Eastern Regional (trophy)

Second runner-up **Penny Bruce** is a student at Presentation High School in San Jose, California. She is a member of Bruce Clan International and is a Highland dancer with the Prince Charles Pipe Band. She also studies ballet. Penny became interested in Highland dancing through her uncle, who was a Highland dancer. She began studying dancing when she was eight and has danced in the open class 5 years. Norine Vujovich is her teacher.

Other U.S. championships: Western (trophy, 1st runner-up, 2nd runner-up), Southern California (trophy), Western Regional (trophy twice), national (trophy, 1982; 1st runner-up, 1983)

17 and Under

Trophy winner **Valerie Ann Langston** lives in Stone Mountain, Georgia, and attends Redan High School. She has studied Highland dancing since the age of four and has competed in the open class 4 years. She is a student of Anne Burgin. Valerie praises the art of Highland dancing for its discipline-building and says that what she gains by being a serious dancer far outweighs all that she has to give up to dance.

U.S. medals/trophies: over 200/45

Other U.S. championships: Atlantic International, Southern Regional (twice)

First runner-up **Kathleen Rayburn** of Sterling Heights, Michigan, is a student at Sterling Heights High School. She started studying Highland dancing at age five with her aunt, Pat Kelman, who was a champion dancer in Toronto before moving to the United States. Kathleen has danced in the open class for 9 years. She has danced at ethnic festivals and concerts and has appeared on cable television. She also studies ballet.

U.S. medals/trophies: over 400/over 90

Other U.S. championships: Ohio Open (twice), U.S. Highland Dancing Association District 3 Closed (five times), national (1981; 2nd runner-up, 1984)

Foreign competitions: Ontario Open Championship (trophy), Canadian National Exhibition (trophy, twice)

Second runner-up **Thomas Kaspick** lives in Cambridge Springs, Pennsylvania. He is a student at Saegertown High School. A member of Clan MacPherson, he began studying Highland dancing at age twelve. A student of Jane Porter, he has competed in the open class for 2 years. In 1985 he became an associate teacher of Highland dancing.

Other U.S. championships: Eastern Regional, Atlantic International (trophy)

Foreign competitions: Canada (12 trophies); Braemar (1984)

18 and Over

Trophy winner **Cheryl Fisher** of Bowie, Maryland, is a student at Ursinus College in Southeastern, Pennsylvania. She has competed in all five national championships and was trophy winner in the first three. She was "Champion of Champions" in 1983 and 1985 and the recipient of the Australian Achievement Award in 1982 and 1983. She began studying Highland dancing at age five. She has danced in the open class for 12 years and is a student of Marguerite Reid. Cheryl has participated in the Delco Scottish Games Workshop choreography competitions. She also studies ballet and was a member of City Dance in Washington, D.C. She has performed at the annual Maryland Renaissance Festival and for the National Capital Area Scottish Festival, the Scottish Choir of Philadelphia, the Daughters of Scotia—Philadelphia branch, the Robert Burns Society of Annapolis, Maryland, and the U.S. Naval Academy in Annapolis.

U.S. medals/trophies: over 250/over 100

Other U.S. championships: national (see above), Ohio Open (trophy, 1980, 1981, 1983), Great Lakes (trophy, 1983), Atlantic International (trophy, 1976, 1977, 1979–84)

Foreign competitions: British Overseas (trophy, 1981), British Open, other Edinburgh Festival events, Perth Commonwealth Championships, Cowal (5th runner-up, 1982, 1983; 2nd runner-up, 1985)

First runner-up **Kathleen Campbell Drummond** was a dance major at Temple University in Philadelphia. She is now doing graduate work toward a master's degree in dance therapy at Goucher College in Towson, Maryland. She began studying Highland dancing at the age of six and has been in the open class 16 years. Kathleen is a student of Marguerite Reid. She has participated in various choreography competitions.

Other U.S. championships: Atlantic International, Midwest/Great Lakes, Eastern Regional, Southeastern, national (trophy, 1981; first runner-up, 1982)

Foreign competitions: Canadian National Exhibition; Cowal (4th, junior; 6th, adult), Edinburgh Festival, British Overseas, British Open, World Pipe Band Championships, various Games in Scotland (Perth, Campbelltown, Montrose)

Second runner-up in this category was **Elaine Burgin.** (See Introduction to Part 1.)

6

Scottish Fiddling

When asked to name a musical instrument associated with Scotland, most people would reply, "The bagpipe." But another instrument is equally important as a means of capturing and conveying the spirit of the Scottish people: the fiddle, another in the trio—along with the pipes and the harp—of the national instruments of Scotland. For the past 20 years the fiddle has been enjoying a rebirth of popularity in Scotland, and for the past decade Scottish-style fiddling has also been growing in popularity in the United States. In order to understand the reason for and significance of this revival of Scottish-style fiddle music today, we must take a brief look at its history.

From early Scottish fiddle manuscript collections (of which there are many), historians have concluded that the fiddle as we know it today was an established part of Scottish music by the mid-1600s or early 1700s. Robert Bremmer's *Scots Reels or Country Dances,* published in Edinburgh in the late 1750s (see the Scottish country dancing section in chapter 7), was the first collection of true Scottish fiddle music and the first to include Scots reels in its title. Thirty years later in Edinburgh, Angus Cumming of Strathspey published the first collection of fiddle music from that district, *A Collection of Strathspeys or Old Highland Reels.* During the time following the Act of Proscription in 1746, when the playing of bagpipes was banned, the fiddle kept the traditional pipe tunes alive adroitly and with an amazing similarity of sound.

THE SCOTTISH STYLE

One of Scotland's two contributions to the music world was a musical form called the strathspey, named for the geographical district from which it originated. (The other contribution is piobaireachd.) The Strathspey district is famous for its fiddlers, and one must understand the strathspey form in order to understand the fiddlers and their music. In his book *The Traditional and National Music of Scotland,* Francis Collinson writes:

> In its own particular territory of northeast Scotland, and particularly in the Strathspey district which gave the characteristic music of that title its name, the fiddle holds supremacy over the pipes. The strathspey, it should be added, though played now as often on the pipes, is essentially *fiddle music,* depending for its full effect upon the characteristic up-bow stroke of the Scottish traditional fiddler, and the capacity of the instrument to stop the sound abruptly after the essential reversed dotted rhythm figure, particularly in the old "slow strathspey."

The up-bow stroke Collinson refers to that is used with this dotted rhythm figure (which, when played, sounds like a sixteenth note followed by an accented dotted eighth note) is called the Scottish snap. The Scottish snap has also been described as a driven note. In other styles of fiddle and violin playing, the bow is brought down to accent a note, but in the heavily accented strathspey style, the bow is driven up and into the string with a quick flick of the wrist, resulting in a unique sound. Much Scottish fiddle music was composed or adapted for Scottish country dancing, which requires strong rhythmic beats. The fiddle was the main accompaniment to Scottish country dancing for many years. The Scottish snap evolved to add energy to the music and give lift to the dancer.

This irregular rhythm, this strathspey idiom, is not only found in all forms of Scottish fiddling music—even slow airs and marches—but in all Scottish music. The soul of the music reflects the soul of the Scottish people, captures their emotions and energy, and reveals their vitality. If one unfamiliar with the Scottish style plays a Scottish tune, though the correct notes are played at the correct time, without this feel for the spirit of the music that portrays the spirit of the people it is merely correct notes at the correct time, nothing more.

FIDDLING'S GOLDEN AGE

The fiddle entered a new era under the influence of Niel Gow, who was born in the Strathspey district in 1727. Gow began playing the fiddle at age nine. When he was eighteen, he won a fiddling competition open to all players in Scotland—all the more remarkable when you consider that he was self-taught except for a few lessons when he was thirteen. It has been said that Niel Gow was such an expert at the Scottish snap that when he played, people could dance hours longer than usual because of the energy he put into the dance; he seemed to lift them off the floor. Accordingly, he was in great demand at dances throughout Scotland. A blind fiddling judge claimed that he could recognize Gow's bowing even if he had listened to 100 fiddlers. Gow was also a composer, authoring approximately 70 tunes for dancing and listening.

Niel Gow's sons, especially Nathaniel, and later descendants kept the great Gow fiddling tradition alive for nearly 100 years. Nathaniel was even better known as a composer and in greater demand as a fiddler than his father. Nathaniel's son Neil Gow, Jr., chose the medical profession but also composed tunes for the fiddle. Though he died at the age of 28, he left a legacy that includes two well-known tunes for which James Hogg wrote the words: "Bonny Prince Charlie" and "Flora MacDonald's Lament."

There were other fiddler/composers of note before and after the Gows. The one who is called the last of the great composers was the prolific James Scott Skinner (1843–1927). At least 600 of his tunes are known today.

A tradition of excellence in the Scottish fiddling style extends from the generations of students of Niel Gow to the present day. Many fiddling experts feel that the top fiddler in Scotland today is Douglas Lawrence, a violinist with the Scottish National Orchestra. He is a protégé of the late Hector MacAndrew and a proponent of his style. MacAndrew's great-grandfather was a student of one of Niel Gow's students, so it can be said that his style is directly descended from that of Niel Gow. It was Hector

MacAndrew who was enlisted by Yehudi Menuhin in 1974 to help bring Scottish fiddling to the world's classical audiences by hosting a BBC-TV performance from Blair Castle.

The period from Niel Gow's birth (1727) to Scott Skinner's death (1927) has been called the golden age of Scottish fiddling; some say Hector MacAndrew extended it. That age is now being revived and given renewed recognition. Besides Douglas Lawrence, there are several outstanding fiddlers in Scotland today: Angus Grant, Bill Hardie, Angus Cameron, Willie Hunter, and Ron Gonnella, to name a few. It is interesting to note that these great fiddlers all have fiddling in their backgrounds, often going back five or six generations. In several cases there is a connection between fiddling and piping.

The familial correlation between fiddlers and pipers is not surprising when one considers how the fiddle and the pipes are linked—not only in their history and purpose, if you will, but in their very sound. It has been said that a good piper makes the pipes sound like a fiddle and a good fiddler makes the fiddle sound like the pipes. Many musicians are skilled on both instruments. In addition, many pipe tunes heard today were originally fiddle tunes and vice versa.

THE CURRENT REVIVAL

As mentioned earlier, Scottish-style fiddling is today enjoying a new wave of popularity on both sides of the Atlantic Ocean. In Scotland there are several reel and strathspey societies that geographically cover the entire country. Many of these have over 100 members and present concerts with that many fiddlers on stage at once. In 1976 Scotland's national newspaper, *The Daily Record*, began sponsoring the annual Golden Fiddle Awards. This competition to find the finest player of traditional Scottish fiddle music attracts fiddlers from all over Scotland and elsewhere. A concert that follows the competition brings the contestants together with other fiddlers to form the Golden Fiddle Orchestra. At one recent concert in Glasgow's Kelvin Hall, more than 550 fiddlers accompanied a massed Scottish choir to make a total of over 1500 performers on stage at the same time.

Until the promotion of Scottish fiddling began in the United

States, fiddling activities were very limited here. John Turner of Virginia was playing Scottish tunes in Colonial Williamsburg; Scottish-born Robin Williamson was playing and recording under the name "Robin and His Merry Band" in California; and Ron Gonnella made occasional concert tours of the United States, as did Shetland fiddler Aly Bain. Beginning in 1972, Turner and Gonnella gave concerts together in Williamsburg. Barbara McOwen and the Berkeley Scottish Players were just getting together and starting to play for dances, but the group did not record until the mid-1970s. In the Northeast, Canadian fiddlers, especially those from the Cape Breton area of Nova Scotia, paid occasional visits. Obviously, opportunities to hear this style of fiddling were few and irregular, to say the least.

Major credit for accelerating the revival of Scottish fiddling in the United States through organized efforts goes to Paul and Nancy Brockman of Falls Church, Virginia. Though neither of them plays the fiddle, both are avid Scottish country dancers and fiddling aficionados. While attending the Old Fiddlers' Convention in Galax, Virginia, in 1973, they heard a fiddler named Guy Faust from Coadington, Ohio, playing Scottish dance tunes. He did not know the traditional names of the tunes, and his style had been Americanized, since the tunes had been passed down unwritten in his family for generations. The Brockmans realized the superiority of the fiddle over the widely used accordion as an instrument to accompany Scottish country dancing. They shared Faust's concern that the Scottish style of playing for dancing and listening pleasure be continued.

To increase awareness of the art among American Scotiaphiles, the Brockmans worked through the Virginia Scottish Games to find a way to stimulate a revival. A workshop led by Helen Stokoe Phillips, a fiddler and a friend of Aly Bain, was held at that Games in 1975. The following year the Brockmans founded an organization called the U.S. Scottish Fiddling Revival, Ltd. (Scottish FIRE); it was incorporated in 1978. FIRE was to be to fiddling what the piping and dancing associations were to those arts: a regulatory group to standardize and unify the ancient practice in the historic tradition.

To encourage people to learn the Scottish style of fiddling, the

Brockmans and their Virginia associates decided to hold competitions similar to those held in Scotland. They received encouragement and support from the Virginia Scottish Games in Alexandria and the Brockmans' clansmen in Clan Donald, U.S.A. Rules for playing and judging were based on those of the Eastern Scottish Fiddling Championships at Kinross, which were supplied by Aly Bain. Since the Brockmans and their friends did not know any Americans practicing the art of Scottish fiddling, a general invitation was extended to all fiddlers for what would be the first fiddling competition in the United States. The first judge was, again, Helen Stokoe Phillips. Phillips is the daughter of Professor William Stokoe of Gallaudet College in Washington, D.C., who had taken up the bagpipe when he was 40 years old and was instrumental in the revival of piping in the mid-Atlantic area in the 1950s. Phillips has judged many Scottish fiddling competitions throughout the country since that first contest in 1976, including the first seven national championships.

The results of the first U.S. National Fiddling Championship were as follows. John Turner of Chesterfield, Virginia, who is still considered the top American-born Scottish fiddler in the U.S., won the championship. Steve Hickman, an Irish-style fiddler from the Washington, D.C., area who has his own Scottish country dance band called Findhorn Ceilidh, was second. Stuart Ian Duncan, a 12-year-old from Vista, California, who fiddled in his father's bluegrass band, was third.

As FIRE and interest in Scottish fiddling grew, the national championships were able to broaden their appeal and allow neophyte American fiddlers to be exposed to some of the greatest names in Scottish fiddle music. At the third competition, Andrew Bathgate, a Scot who is considered an expert on Scottish country dance music, served as honorary judge and participated in a day-long workshop on fiddling for Scottish country dancing that was led by John Turner. The fifth national championship, judged by Ron Gonnella, Helen Phillips, and Paul Brockman, was dedicated to Hector MacAndrew, who had died shortly before. At the 1985 National Championship, the title of National Scottish Fiddling Champion was again won by John Turner; Alasdair Fraser placed second; and Ed Perlman of West Newton, Massachusetts, finished third. The junior champion was Jon Fricke of Owings, Maryland, followed by Shawn MacDonald of Ironville, Nova Scotia.

Paul and Nancy Brockman stepped down as executive director and secretary/treasurer, respectively, of FIRE in 1981. Paul served as chairman of fiddling and Nancy as fiddling steward for the Virginia Scottish Games, the Games that gave life to their vision, until 1985. FIRE has grown in size and scope and is now run by officers who are themselves Scottish fiddlers.

The main method of exposure to Scottish fiddling in the United States today is through competitions or demonstrations held at the Games. Games now hosting fiddling competitions, listed alphabetically by city, are: Alexandria, Virginia (Potomac Valley Championship and the U.S. National Championship); Alma, Michigan (Great Lakes Championship); Altamont, New York (Northeastern U.S. Championship); Chino, California (Pacific Coast Championship); Costa Mesa, California; Essex Junction, Vermont (Vermont International Championship); Fair Hill, Maryland (Eastern U.S. Championship); Huntingtown, Maryland (Southern Maryland Championship); Ligonier, Pennsylvania (Allegheny Mountain Championship); Linville, North Carolina; Loon Mountain, New Hampshire (New England Regional Championship); Norfolk, Virginia; Northridge, California; Santa Rosa, California (Niel Gow Competition); and Stone Mountain, Georgia (Southeastern U.S. Championship). To compete in the national championship, a fiddler must have placed first, second, or third in a previous national event or have won at least one FIRE-sanctioned competition (including the preliminary competition held just prior to the national championship). In the competitions, the participants are required to show their dexterity on the fiddle and their understanding of the Scottish style by playing a variety of tunes. There are three classes of competitors. A novice is a beginning fiddler (no age restriction). When a novice wins three competitions, he moves into the open class or, if he prefers and is qualified, the junior class, which is any fiddler under the age of eighteen. The open and junior competitions require an air followed by a medley of a march, strathspey, and reel (in that order). A novice plays three tunes, either an

John Turner, America's greatest contribution to the world of Scottish fiddling.

John Turner, left, and Bill White lead the Montgomery clan in the 1981 Grandfather Mountain parade of tartans.

Jonathan Fricke, former national junior Scottish fiddling champion, tunes up.

MSR or an air followed by a strathspey and reel. At some Games, other tunes may be added as separate, supplemental competitions. The contestants are graded on a system of 100 points per tune, with timing worth 30 points, execution or command of the instrument worth 30, and expression/interpretation worth 40.

There is now a solid core of devotion to this unique form in the U.S. At present, approximately 75 to 100 persons participate in the various Scottish fiddling competitions. The interest seems to be centered in the East and along the Pacific Coast and in adults, although some fine young fiddlers are making impressive showings. (In Scotland it is the younger fiddlers who are beginning to dominate the Scottish fiddling scene.) In 1981 Colin Gordon, a native Scot who lives in Los Angeles, formed the Scottish Fiddlers of Los Angeles, a group of about 30 fiddlers that has performed in several concerts and recorded an album. The Boston Scottish Fiddling Club, also formed in 1981, has over 50 members who meet regularly to learn more about fiddling and have a jam session. They sponsor workshops and special fiddling events. This increased exposure can only benefit the art of Scottish fiddling; more and more people are being drawn to it every year.

Because of the increasing interest in the Scottish style of fiddling, two week-long schools were established in 1984. The Jink and Diddle School, under the direction of John Turner, was held in Valle Crucis, North Carolina, the week preceding the Grandfather Mountain Games. The Valley of the Moon School was held near Santa Rosa, California, the week preceding the Games held at that site. Instructors for the latter school were Buddy MacMaster of Cape Breton, Nova Scotia, Alastair Hardie of Edinburgh, and Alasdair Fraser. Both schools were deemed a success and will continue.

Also in 1984, FIRE and the Scottish Fiddlers of Los Angeles sponsored the first Scottish fiddling composition competition in this country. The judges were Alastair Hardie and John Mason of Ayr, Scotland. Nineteen composers submitted 71 tunes. Winners in the best overall category were: first, Shauna Pickett-Gordon of Highland Park, California; second, Alasdair Fraser; and third, John Turner. The winning tunes from all categories—

best overall, airs, hornpipes, jigs, marches, strathspeys, and reels—were played at the Niel Gow Scottish Fiddling Competition at the Santa Rosa Games in September.

Over the past few years, what former FIRE newsletter editor Bill White has called the "closet fiddlers" (those who had never played in a competition) have come out into the public view. White, of Williamsburg, Virginia, has competed in fiddling himself. Competitive performances have also been heard from Eric Tweedy of Decatur, Georgia, Mary Ann Sereth of Los Angeles, Sharon Kerr of Virginia Beach, Virginia, Vivi Fuchs of Swanzey, New Hampshire, Jan, Stacey, and Christina Tappan of Pasadena, California, Sharon Newcomb of Rancho Palos Verdes, California, Valerie Wilcox of North Babylon, New York, Hazel Stewart of Rochester, New York, Charles Glendinning of Tacoma Park, Maryland, Calum Mackinnon of Seattle, and Mary Ellen Endo of Chicago—all of American birth—as well as Scottish-born American residents Colin Gordon of Los Angeles, Bill Eddie of Port Ewan, New York, and Nan Gibson of Alexandria, Virginia. The 1983 and 1984 national championships were won by Alasdair Fraser, a native of Scotland now living in Sausalito, California. He has won fiddling competitions in Scotland and is a teacher, competitor, and judge in the U.S. For Scottish country dancers, the Berkeley Scottish Players continue to perform in the San Francisco Bay area, Barbara McOwen has a new fiddle band going in Boston, Steve Hickman's Findhorn Ceilidh Band is still active in Washington, D.C., the Thistle Band of Los Angeles features Colin Gordon's lead fiddle, and Tidewater Virginia dancers delight to the music of John Turner and his friends.

JOHN TURNER: FIDDLING'S BEST

Without a doubt the best American-born Scottish-style fiddler and one of the most ardent promoters of the art of Scottish fiddling in the United States today is John Turner, chairman of the board of FIRE. Turner has won eight of the ten U.S. National Fiddling Championships and in the first few years of the development of fiddling here competed in every competition held in the U.S. From 1976 until 1983, when Alasdair Fraser of California won the nationals, Turner was undefeated in Scottish fiddling competitions in this country. He has also made an impact on Scottish fiddling on the other side of the Atlantic; he won the Banchory Cup Competition in Scotland in 1979. Banchory is the birthplace of Scott Skinner and has a very strong reel and strathspey society, which made his victory even more meaningful. Also in 1979, he placed fourth at the Golden Fiddle Awards and was named one of the four top Scottish fiddlers by *The Daily Record*. In 1981 he was again a finalist and again took fourth place in these world championships of Scottish fiddling. He returned to Scotland in 1984 and was again named a finalist in the Golden Fiddle awards. He also won the open competition at the Aberdeen Music Festival.

Turner's spot among the top Scottish fiddlers in the world is the culmination of a lifetime association with this idiom. He began his fiddling involvement at age two, imitating his father on a toy fiddle purchased by his parents. His interest in music in general was natural: music was all around him. A get-together with his family was an opportunity to hear and play all kinds of music, as most of his relatives played some type of instrument.

The music he was surrounded by was often Scottish music. Turner's family is of Scottish descent, as are many families in the rural area of Virginia where he was born. Though he has played a variety of musical styles (including rock music on violin, saxophone, and guitar), during the past few years he has been playing Scottish style almost exclusively. He plays no other folk style. When the opportunity permits, he does enjoy playing baroque music.

Many of the recent Scottish fiddling experts had a foundation in classical music, and John Turner is no exception. At the age of five, he began studying with an Italian-American violin teacher; about six years later, he switched to a German-American teacher. Both of these instructors were first-generation Americans whose heritages figured significantly in their playing and teaching styles. Since Turner is also a former student of Hector MacAndrew, he is able to link his own musical heritage to the great Niel Gow.

Turner currently judges several fiddling competitions annually and teachers privately and in fiddling workshops. He enjoys teaching and believes that his strength lies in getting across the feeling of Scottish music to people—as he says, "helping them express their own heritage through their playing."

He is intensely interested in the development of Scottish fiddling in the United States; he hopes to build upon the existing foundation and establish this idiom in its rightful place in American folk art and in the Scottish tradition. Indeed, it is his desire someday to devote his full career time to this end. Turner is a graduate of the College of William and Mary, has done graduate work in education at the University of Virginia, and has a doctor of ministry degree from Union Theological Seminary in Virginia. He serves as associate minister of Grace Covenant Presbyterian Church in Richmond. At present he leads the worship services at the Games at Grandfather Mountain and Loon Mountain.

Turner sees the Games as the best method of increasing awareness and appreciation of Scottish fiddling today. In his official role with FIRE, he hopes to see fiddling on the programs of more Games along with its partners in tradition: piping, dancing, and athletics. He hopes to reach areas not covered by Games as well; one way he hopes to do this is through lecture-performances on Scottish culture and Scottish music across the country.

Turner's work in expanding Scottish fiddling also includes recording and publishing. He has made nine records, including a two-volume anthology of fiddler/composers called "Fiddling Rogues and Rascals" done for historical purposes. Some of Turner's tunes are included in his book *Fiddletree Manuscript*. In 1984 he published *Turner's Melodies,* a collection of 68 original tunes. He hopes to publish a series of books that will give the musical notations for all of his records, particularly the anthology. The combination of records and books would be an excellent resource for persons wishing to learn Scottish fiddling or present Scottish fiddling programs.

Music may be a universal language, but the very nature of any given tune bespeaks its origin. The fiddle is a versatile instrument that, put into proper hands governed by a proper frame of mind, can emit strains that capture and convey the very soul of the musician and of the Scottish people. A tragic incident that occurred in March of 1982 illustrates this special function of Scottish fiddle music.

John Turner, his wife, Chris, and their 20-month-old daughter Allison were involved in a car accident that proved fatal to Chris; John and Allison survived. John gave voice to his grief two weeks after Chris's death by composing "John Turner's Lament for the Death of His Wife." This tune, a slow air, is now well known among fiddlers. John has written other tunes for and about Chris, as have others. In the spring of 1983, John released an album entitled "The Graceful Young Woman," which includes the title tune, the previously mentioned lament, and others such as "The Lass of New Kent" and "Allison Was Her Delight," which were composed by him.

John and Chris had met through music. Chris was also a violinist who had studied the Scottish style of fiddling and often played the bass fiddle in groups John organized to play for Scottish music engagements. She was a Highland dancer as well and often danced as part of John's Scottish programs. John began teaching fiddling to Allison when she was 11 months old, beginning with basic lessons on how to handle and respect the violin and how to move the bow across the strings. Allison, now 5 years old, is continuing to study both the violin and Highland dancing. If she continues in her interest in fiddling, she will be a fourth-generation fiddler and be able to claim a link to the great Niel Gow.

One month after the accident, John and Allison were at the Celtic Festival of Southern Maryland so that he could compete in the fiddling competition there. When John's turn came, he announced that his performance would be dedicated "to Chris, who will always be 28." While he was playing, Allison went to his side and danced. The memory of Chris Turner has indeed become a part of the Scottish fiddling tradition.

John Turner married Moira Paulson in Richmond in August of 1983. Moira is no stranger to Scottish activities: a native of Edinburgh, she teaches Scottish country dancing, assists in running Fiddletree Music Company, and is former treasurer of the Council of Scottish Clan Associations.

John Turner's words will serve as a postscript to this section on Scottish fiddling.

"To me [fiddling is] a paradigm of what's important in the

Games in general. When people in this country put on kilts and toss the caber or compete in a Highland dancing competition or do a Scottish country dancing demonstration or play the pipes or play the fiddle, they are continuing a tradition....Fiddling continues and encapsulates the story that is told through the athletics, through the dancing, through the piping. An important part of life, after all, is telling one's story. Scottish fiddling is one of the most beautiful ways any of the world's countries has of telling its story."

7

Other Components
of the Games

Sheepdogs have been used to help in the management of livestock for thousands of years. (Dogs minding flocks are mentioned in the Book of Job in the Bible.) Of the more than 50 types of working dogs in the world today, the border collie is held in the highest regard. This breed originated in and took its name from Scotland around the year 1600.

Sheepdog trials—programs of everyday herding tasks run over a course to test dogs' working ability—were first held in 1873 in Bala, Wales. Rules and events varied until the formation of the International Sheep Dog Society of Great Britain in 1922. In Great Britain today there are over 400 annual sheepdog trials. Open trials are held from April through September; nursery trials, which give young sheepdogs their first taste of competition, are held in the winter. These trials attract huge crowds of spectators, and millions more watch on television as the well-trained animals prove that border collies are among the wisest—if not *the* wisest—dogs in the world.

Watching a sheepdog trial in Scotland is a special treat. Past spectators have said that it is fascinating to watch a small dog respond to the command of his shepherd and go speeding off out of sight over crags and through heather, only to reappear momentarily behind his charges. The native Scot might regard such an event with the nonchalance born of familiarity, but the "displaced Scot" is gripped by a feeling of romance and nostalgia and finds it difficult to be so detached. This sheepdog, the gallant and faithful breed known as the top class of working livestock dog, was bred in the British Isles specifically to contribute to the vital sheep industry. Especially in the Scottish Highlands, the border collie is prized for his ability to navigate even steep and narrow sheep paths with ease. Watching a dog work so well with a shepherd in the homeland is an understandable thrill for the visitor of Scottish descent.

Many of the Scottish Highland Games in the United States include sheepdog demonstrations where the remarkable talents of the border collie can be seen. Though the voice of the shepherd may not have a charming Scottish brogue and the terrain may be flat and green, the dog is the same. He still displays an uncanny bond with his master, a clear understanding of his duty, and an intense desire to complete his task. Whether he is alone with the shepherd in an open area or must work his way through a crowd of onlookers, he is diligent in his work.

Years of selective breeding have made the border collie ideally suited in temperament to his designated role: the expert herding of sheep and other types of livestock, including cattle and fowl, in close accord with man. The border collie works primarily in response to signals, but his natural initiative and judgment enable him to know when to be more forceful and when to remain still while working. The same dog that must be courageous enough to subdue an unruly sheep is innately gentle with lambs. (This trait also makes them excellent dogs for families with children.)

The border collie was bred to work hard: one dog can handle several hundred sheep. He is very intelligent and eager to learn, which makes him easy to train. Of the eight breeds in the American Kennel Club's miscellaneous class, the border collie is rated highest in obedience.

Another highly desirable trait of this dog is that he can be trained to work quietly. A good sheepdog does not bark unnecessarily, because the noise may frighten the sheep and cause them to scatter. Also, a good dog is calm and works stealthily; he creeps up on the sheep to direct them rather than bolting into the herd and frightening them. This creeping movement is very absorbing to watch. The dog crawls along close to the ground, then drops down on his stomach (a maneuver called clapping), repeating this action until the sheep begin to move. When the dog does run, he runs low to the ground, giving him a flowing, graceful appearance. Incidentally, one must not assume that the dog is cowering when he has his tail between his legs; that is merely a common style of carriage.

Many of the border collies seen at Games here are imported from Scotland, but the dogs are also bred and available in the U.S. The lineage of most of the finest border collies (a good dog may cost around $4000) can be traced to a dog named Old Hemp who was born in Northumberland in 1893. A superior specimen, his stud services were used heavily, and his offspring are considered today's dominant breeding line. The first of his line arrived in America in 1923 when Sam Stoddart, a Scot who had emigrated to New Hampshire, bought Spot, one of Old Hemp's descendants. Spot was named supreme champion, the highest sheepdog honor in the world, by the International Sheep Dog Society in 1923. Sam Stoddart became the first president of the North American Sheep Dog Society at its formation in 1940, and Spot was the first entry in its register.

The border collie has one unusual characteristic found in no other breed of dog: the "eye," which is the inborn power to control the sheep by staring at them. The dog fixes a gaze upon a sheep as he quietly and determinedly approaches; the sheep becomes transfixed and obediently heads in the desired direction. Even the most stubborn sheep becomes unnerved under this unflinching maneuver. The dog's relatively small size (30–40 pounds on the average) does not hinder the confidence with which the dog exhibits this trait.

The importance of the bond between sheepdog and shepherd cannot be overemphasized. Dog and man must work as one. One of the finest displays of this harmony that I have ever seen was at the now-defunct Celtic-Scandinavian Festival at Baltimore's Inner Harbor in 1980. Dr. Gib McLaughlin of Indiana, Pennsylvania, brought some of his Scottish black-faced sheep and his two faithful companions, Glen and Hemp, to demonstrate why border collies are so highly regarded as herding dogs.

Since the dogs are always a popular attraction, spectators had completely lined the sides of the working area to get a good view. I was eager to see if the crowds would have any effect on the dogs, but they were absolutely oblivious. During the cast—the initial action of running to the right or left and behind the sheep in a large semi-circle—the dogs ran right through the legs of the surprised spectators. One of the dogs nearly clapped right on one onlooker's foot. Their main concern was not the crowd, but the sheep they had been commanded to work.

I later visited Dr. McLaughlin's farm, Burnhead, to watch the dogs in a working situation. The self-control of these animals is incredible. On one occasion, with four dogs eager to do the work at hand, one was sent to round up a group of ewes; the other three were commanded to lie down. Each did so with head up, eyes alert, and ears perked, often looking at Dr. McLaughlin with great expectancy and inching forward in the direction of the work in progress. It was obvious that they could barely contain their desire to work, but their obedience to their master was more important.

On the morning of my visit, a thick fog hung just above the ground. Although the sheep were completely hidden from view, the flock was known to be on the side of a hill. Dr. McLaughlin merely faced the direction he wished the dog to go and directed him accordingly. The dog scurried off and, soon after, the muffled sound of a few distant bells could be heard, signaling the approach of the flock.

Short of watching a dog actually working, the best way to see the talent of shepherd-sheepdog teams on display is at sheepdog trials. The first sheepdog trial in the U.S. was held in conjunction with Philadelphia's centennial in 1880, and trials as regular events began in 1928. Today there are approximately fifteen international sheepdog trials held annually in this country.

The first trial held in conjunction with a Games was held at the Colonial Highland Gathering in Fair Hill, Maryland, in 1969. Two other Games—those at Quechee, Vermont and Salado, Texas—also have sheepdog trials. The Fair Hill event, now called the International Open Sheep Dog Trials, is the largest of the Games trials and has instituted many firsts. In 1971 the Fair Hill trials began using a point system for grading developed by John Shropshire, course director there for several years. The first world championship trials were held at Fair Hill in 1973; two years later, the Games hosted the first brace trials (two dogs working together) ever held in the United States.

In the trial at Fair Hill, each shepherd-and-dog team is given five sheep and twelve minutes to complete the course. They are scored on the number of sheep successfully put through a series of nine obstacles. The last obstacle is a pen, and the shepherd shuts the gate after the dog has herded the sheep through. The objective of the trial is to determine the dog's ability to control the sheep over the course. Many of the dogs's skills are tested, including gathering (a combination of the cast and the dog's initial attempts to move the sheep toward the shepherd), driving (the most difficult action, as the dog must move the sheep away from the shepherd, going against his natural instincts), and penning. He may be penalized or disqualified for going off the course, running excessively, or biting the sheep.

The trials also test the working relationship of man and dog. The shepherd must remain in a designated area at the foot of the course and may only direct the dog by whistle or verbal signals. Most verbal signals have equivalent whistle commands that are used to direct the dog at the top of the course, some 300 yards away. (The dog can hear the whistle at far greater distances than this.)

At the beginning of the trial, the shepherd and border collie are placed at the foot of the course. The sheep are enclosed in a pen with collapsible sides at the top of the course. At the signal to begin, the sheep are released from the pen and begin moving about freely. Using an almost indiscernible signal, the shepherd sends the dog to gather the sheep. The dog is cast and approaches the sheep from behind. The shepherd commands the dog through each of the obstacles, hoping to end up with the five sheep in the pen at the foot of the course within the prescribed time limit.

In demonstrations and trials, the Scottish black-faced sheep is often used because it adds tremendously to the atmosphere of the whole affair. In most cases, the role of the sheep is merely to play the adorable herdee. On occasion, however, they abandon their role, much to the chagrin of shepherd and dog alike. If the day is particularly hot or if the sheep are tired, they may refuse to be herded anywhere. They become stubborn or pugnacious, literally lying down on the job or even being so bold as to defy the hapless sheepdog. Such behavior is not uncommon when the sheep are expected to fit into a Games timetable, but it is less likely to occur on a farm where the shepherd works the sheep around their timetable. Even if the sheep behave themselves, they do not always clear the obstacles fast enough. If the sheep run wild, it is almost impossible for the dog to regain control and get them back on the course in time, although the faithful sheepdog will surely try his best. This is where the innate ability and expert training of the border collie shine.

To observe a shepherd and a dog in confident control of a flock is to observe traces of centuries of Scottish history. It is to witness the longstanding legacy of the loyal, hard-working border collie—the best working sheepdog in the world.

SCOTTISH COUNTRY DANCING

A form of Scottish dancing demonstrated at many Games in the United States today is Scottish country dancing. This is the social or ballroom dancing of Scotland as opposed to the competitive, individual Highland dancing. A strong French influence is apparent in both forms of dancing, but so are the spirited movements characteristic of the Scottish spirit.

Scottish country dancing was developed by Lowland Scots and was originally accompanied by the fiddle. Country dancing is dancing done in rows with the partners facing each other. This type of longways dancing was known in fifteenth-century Italy. By the end of the seventeenth century, longways country dancing was highly popular in England, where the dances of the country folk had been incorporated into court dancing. In 1650 John Playford published *The English Dancing Master,* which included many tunes and the dances accompanying them as well as illustrations of figures (combinations of movements) used in the dances. This book was so popular that there were 18 editions. Playford's eighteenth edition, published in 1728, includes 900 country dances. Country dancing was popular at this time in

Scotland, too. Whereas in England footwork was not emphasized (as evidenced by Playford's inclusion of figures instead of steps to illustrate the dance movements), in Scotland the footwork was very intricate and precise. Also, the Scottish style was based on native tunes that had very strong rhythm and, therefore, appeared more energetic.

Particularly from the sixteenth century on, whatever was the dance rage in one country's court soon caught on in others, and since what was current at court was of interest to the populace, the latest rage was quickly adopted and adapted throughout the land. France's influence on Scottish country dancing is evidenced today by the names of some of the steps and figures: *pas de basque, poussette,* and *allemande,* to mention a few. Notice that when a Scottish country dancer or a Highland dancer prepares to dance, he stands in a variation of the balletic first position.

Robert Bremner published his *Collection of Scots Reels or Country Dances* in Edinburgh in the late 1750s. This was the first compilation of native Scottish tunes. The popularity of these tunes was illustrated by their influence in the dancing manuals of other countries. By the end of the century, such indigenous dances as the threesome and foursome reels were among the most popular in Europe and America. Bremner's book came out at a time when Scotland was producing some of the most influential men of the day. The arts were flourishing in Edinburgh. Public dance assemblies fashioned after those popularized in Bath, England, in the early 1700s were in vogue, and country dancing was the favorite form of dance at these assemblies, judging by the large amounts of time set aside for them.

The waltz and quadrille became the rages in Edinburgh, London, and other European cities in the early nineteenth century. At that time it was fashionable to have small, private quadrille parties. Country dancing was still popular in the ballroom and at public dance assemblies and, thanks to Sir Walter Scott, became entrenched in the popular tradition of the day. In 1822 he arranged the festivities for a visit to Scotland by King George IV, an event which endeared the king to many Scots and made them aware of their heritage. Edinburgh hosted a continual succession of events bringing the monarch together with

Highlanders and their chiefs, all—even the king—outfitted in kilted costumes of newly created tartans. All aspects of the Scottish tradition, including native dancing, became fashionable again.

In the nineteenth century and early twentieth centuries, dancing masters were popular and important in Scotland. These teachers taught new and old Lowland and Highland dances. One of the most influential of these dancing masters was Francis Peacock, the official town dancing master of Aberdeen from 1747 until his death in 1807. In 1805 he published *Sketches Relative to the History, Theory, But More Especially the Practices of Dancing*, still considered one of the best dance manuals ever published. He was the first dance writer to give detailed instructions for the steps of the Scottish reel.

A dancing master's influence on Scottish social life was enormous. He traveled to towns and villages teaching not just steps, but social graces as well. Several dancing masters were musicians in their own right, such as renowned fiddler James Neill of Forfar. His teaching career lasted from 1855 until his death in 1918 at the age of 84. One of his pupils was Lady Elizabeth Bowes-Lyon, the present queen mother. If not for the dancing masters, many of the old country dances might have been lost. In the late 1800s and early 1900s, other types of dances were gaining popularity, especially in the cities. Although the dancing masters did teach these fashionable dances, they always included native dances in their repertoires.

The concern of many Scots about the disappearance of the old dances led them to establish an organization to ensure their preservation. The Beltane Society was formed in the early 1900s in Glasgow for the express purpose of learning the old country dances. Jean Milligan was the chief instructor. In order to standardize the dances, Milligan co-founded the Scottish Country Dance Society with Ysabel Stewart in 1923. Its purpose was to collect, revive, and publish the old country dances. The ladies were surprised and encouraged at the response to their initial invitation to interested participants. A book of twelve dances was published and the search for others began. Two branches were formed, in Edinburgh and in Glasgow, during the society's first year.

Very early in the history of the Scottish Country Dance Society, teachers were trained to teach only the approved steps and dances to assure their uniformity. Nowadays, teachers must be certified by the society. Rules for timing (the best tempo fitted to the revived steps) that were of particular benefit to bands were established in 1934. Soon demonstration teams were performing at every possible opportunity. In 1937 the BBC first televised a program on Scottish country dancing; it later carried a series on the subject entitled "The Kilt Was My Delight." The society's summer school at St. Andrews, established in 1927, is still in operation. The teaching staff of this popular and famous school was headed by Jean Milligan until her death in 1978, when she was well into her nineties. The summer school is now divided into two two-week sessions and has an average attendance of over 700 international students per year.

In 1951 the society was granted the title of Royal Scottish Country Dance Society by King George VI. Queen Elizabeth, whom the society reports is "a beautiful dancer," has been patron of the society since 1947.

Today there are thousands of Scottish country dancers all over the world. The society's 1984 membership numbered over 26,000 in the United Kingdom and ten other countries. So standardized are the steps that they allow a dancer to feel at home on dance floors in any city. When one joins a Scottish country dance class, part of his dues goes toward membership in the International Royal Scottish Country Dance Society, which annually publishes a bulletin and a book of dances.

There are two types of dances: the fast reels and jigs and the slower strathspeys. The music of the strathspeys, as you will recall from the chapter on fiddling, is distinguished by the up-bow accenting stroke known as the Scottish snap. The origin of this dance form is uncertain but there are early documented traces of it. There was a popular couples dance in sixteenth-century France called the *branle d'Ecosse*, the step for which was similar to that of the modern-day strathspey. A branle was an around-the-room couples dance, as opposed to longways dancing; d'Ecosse indicated that the steps were of the Scottish persuasion.

A room full of couples—the men in full Highland evening

dress, the women in long white dresses adorned with tartan sashes—organized into sets (groupings of three or four couples) and moving together smoothly, yet with spirit, is an entrancing sight. It looked like so much fun that I had to try it. I found Scottish country dancing to be more difficult at the beginning than it appears. The dancing is done on the balls of the feet in gillies—the same soft-soled, laced dancing shoes worn by Highland dancers. The first thing one must master is the ability to stand, walk, and dance with the heels turned in and the toes pointing out at all times. There are five basic steps, but there are also a number of figures (step sequences) to learn. Proper etiquette is important: the gentlemen lead the ladies most politely onto the dance floor, and the partners always bow and curtsey to each other at the beginning and end of each dance. The dances usually begin with the first couple progressing down the set dancing with the opposite-sex partner in each couple. When couples are not actively involved in the dancing, they remain in position, ready to join in at the appropriate time.

Students of Scottish country dancing are encouraged to show that they enjoy the dancing. Eye contact is stressed so that one's partner, the others in the set, and anyone watching know that it is fun—a lot of fun. The more you relax and enjoy it, the easier it is to learn Scottish country dancing. It is a Scottish tradition in which almost everyone can participate.

THE CLARSACH

As mentioned earlier, there are three traditional Scottish instruments: the bagpipe, fiddle, and harp. The Scottish harp, or clarsach, is a Celtic harp. It is the oldest of these three instruments, having been in Scotland for over 1,200 years. As clan chiefs had their own pipers, so did they have their harpers. The harpers held a place of high honor—they sat at the right hand of the chiefs—in the clan establishment. They performed instrumental or vocal selections accompanying and sometimes serving as the bard, who recited epic poems for entertainment and enlightenment.

According to Francis Collinson, there are two examples of the earliest clarsachs in the National Museum of Antiquities of

Scotland. The Caledonian or Lamont harp is believed to date back to 1464, and the Queen Mary harp dates back to about 1564. Mary Queen of Scots was an ardent clarsach player, as was King James I.

The clarsach was popular in Scotland until the middle of the eighteenth century, when the destruction of the clan system had its concurrent effect on this instrument. It was not until the early 1890s that the clarsach was heard from again. Thanks to the first president of the Gaelic Association, Lord Archibald Campbell, who commissioned nine clarsachs to be made at this time, the instrument was revived. In 1892 Campbell began a clarsach competition at the first Gaelic Mod, a week-long series of competitions in various Gaelic arts. The clarsach was assured a permanent comeback in 1931 when the Clarsach Society was formed in Scotland with Hilda Campbell of Airds, an enthusiastic proponent of the instrument, as president. Today there are annual competitions for the clarsach in Scotland, and it is offered in the music curriculum of some school systems.

The clarsach is inspiring interest in this country as well. Dr. Herbert P. MacNeal, who founded the Council of Scottish Clan Associations, has been a leading proponent of this instrument in the United States over the past few years. He was one of the founders of the Scottish Harp Society of America in 1982. The goals of this society, presided over by Christina Tourin, a harp teacher and maker from Waterbury, Vermont, are to promote interest in the clarsach to people of all ages, research the ancient music of Scotland, encourage instruction of the instrument in schools, be a part of all Scottish functions, and encourage clans to once again support a clan harper.

The Scottish harp is a small instrument; it is less than 45 inches in height and has about 30 strings. It produces a warm and lovely tone and is an excellent accompaniment to the voice.

The clarsach has been used at many Scottish functions around the country, and its emergence at the Games will make it better known. Harp demonstrations have been given at various Games for the past few years. The instrument first appeared at Grandfather Mountain in 1982. At those Games in 1983 a clarsach was presented by the Council of Scottish Clan Associations to Chris-

Border collies in action. The dog on the left serves as a hindrance while the dog on the right encourages the sheep to turn around and enter the pen guarded by his master.

Even when relaxed, the border collie's ears are perked in alertness and his eyes are ready to respond to his master's signals.

Competitors at the 1985 national clarsach competition: from left, Darcy Fair, Diane Proulx, Sue Richards (kneeling), and Mary Tooke.

Scottish country dancing at the Southern Maryland Games.

The lighter side of competition: a bonniest knees contest.

tie Saunders, a blind harper. (It is interesting to note that one of the few harp heroes, if you will, whose history has survived to this day is Roderick Morison, better known as Rory Dall or Blind Rory, born around 1660.) In 1983 the clarsach was also heard at a few other Games, including Delco, Ohio, and Virginia. In 1984 it expanded to Vermont, Red Springs (North Carolina), Santa Rosa, and Stone Mountain, Georgia. Also in 1984 the first annual Scottish Harp Week was held in conjunction with the Ohio Scottish Arts School the week following the Games in Oberlin.

The Virginia Scottish Games in Alexandria hosted the first U.S. National Scottish Harp Competition in 1984. There were no applicants in the junior (under 16) class, but winners in the other categories were: senior beginner—first, Mary Tooke (Ardmore, Pennsylvania); second, Joan Weiss (Chevy Chase, Maryland); third, Gareth McKenzie (Alexandria, Virginia); senior solo—Angus Fallon-MacGregor (Milwaukee); second, Kasha Breau (Forestville, Connecticut); third, Ann Rose Borden (Winston-Salem, North Carolina). Sue Richards (Rockville, Maryland) was named most promising player and Angus Fallon-MacGregor was declared national champion. Fallon-MacGregor received the Herbert P. MacNeal Cup as national champion and the Ellice McDonald, Jr., award as senior solo winner. The latter award is a two-week trip to Scotland to study the clarsach at Stirling University. The award for best senior beginner was the use of a harp for one year donated by Salvi Harp Company of Genoa, Italy. Judges for the first event were Lucille Jennings of Athens, Ohio, and Christina Tourin.

In 1985 Sue Richards fulfilled the promise she showed the year before by being named national champion. Winners in other categories included: senior beginner—first, Martha Clancy (Philadelphia), second, Joan Weiss, third, Gareth McKenzie; senior solo—first, Sue Richards, second, Dianne Proulx (Durham, New Hampshire), third, Darcy Fair (Doylestown, Pennsylvania).

In a competition a contestant receives a score of a possible 100 points, based on his technical mastery of the instrument (30 points); his musical mastery, including rhythm, tempo, and timing (30 points); and expression and interpretation of the music

(40 points). There are three categories of competition: junior, senior, and open. The junior and senior categories are divided into beginners—those who have played the instrument less than three years—and solo. Only solo competitors—those who have played for more than three years—may play in an open competition. Beginners play two tunes and may sing if desired; solo players play three tunes, one of which must be for harp and voice. If the contestant does not wish to sing (vocal ability is not judged, however), the competition committee supplies a vocalist. Open competitors must play four tunes: one is specified by the competition committee, one is a contrasting tune of the contestant's choice, one is a selection for harp and voice specified by the competition committee, and one is a selection for harp and voice of the contestant's own choice. Singing in Gaelic is encouraged.

The foundation has been laid and the roots are spreading. Seven clarsach competitions were held in 1985, at the Ohio, Essex Junction (Vermont), Alexandria, Waterville (Maine), Loon Mountain (New Hampshire), Stone Mountain (Georgia), and Santa Rosa and Chino (California) Games. We should see the clarsach at many more Games soon.

OTHER EVENTS AND ACTIVITIES

A number of miscellaneous events are offered at the Games. Common ones include races such as the kilted mile; the tossing of such implements as rolling pins, beer kegs, and frying pans; and the tug-of-war. Many Games also offer special events for children that are mock heavy events or versions of those novelty events found at the Games in Scotland. These include egg-and-spoon races, three-legged races, and pillow fights.

A recent innovation growing in popularity is the bonniest knees contest, in which female judges are asked to rate that portion of the male leg that has been covered for years because of the infamous Sassenach (British) practice of wearing trousers. Several of these contests also include other categories such as boniest and most dimpled knees. To guarantee objectivity, some contests require that the judges be blindfolded.

Another recent Games development, this one from Scotland, is haggis hurling. (Professor Rowland Berthoff has delicately described haggis as an old peasant dish of highly seasoned meat scraps; nothing, however, can dilute the fact that the ingredients should be cooked in a sheep's stomach.) The "official" rules of this sport have been established by the World Haggis Hurling Association in Edinburgh. This group has developed a fanciful history and quite a set of regulations for the event—among them specifications for the weight of the haggis, the proper hurling style (the hurler must rub his hands in peat and stand atop a barrel), the titles for officials (hagarian) and throwing area (hurling heather). Some Games use a real haggis for the event; others improvise, a creative event in itself.

A few Games have displays of Scottish dog breeds other than the border collie. The Tidewater Scottish Festival in Norfolk, Virginia, has an exhibition and a parade of several Scottish dog breeds. The Virginia Scottish Games in Alexandria offers exhibitions of deerhound coursing and cairn terrier trials. The Scottish deerhound, considered the "Royal Dog of Scotland," originated in the Highlands over 1,000 years ago. Their keen sense of smell and the combination of strength (the dogs average 30 inches in height and weigh around 100 pounds) and speed made them superb hunters of the Scottish red deer. Quiet and dignified, they are excellent companions as well. Though seldom used for their original purpose, in coursing demonstrations the dogs display their innate hunting ability by chasing mechanical lures. The cairn terrier originated in the Isle of Skye and was used in hunting to flush out small burrowing or climbing animals. In the trials, a tunnel is dug and covered over, and prey, often a raccoon, is placed in a pen at the end of the tunnel. The dog is given scent of the prey and then is timed on his run through the tunnel to the prey.

Several Games today offer a kirking of the tartans, either at a worship service at the Games site or at a local church. This is an American institution, and a relatively recent one at that. It was originated by the St. Andrew's Society of Washington, D.C., in 1941 as a war relief service. The first service was conducted by Dr. Peter Marshall, a Presbyterian minister who was born in Coatbridge, Scotland, and emigrated to the United States in 1927. In 1947 he was elected chaplain of the U.S. Senate. He was president of the Washington St. Andrew's Society from 1944–48. (Dr. Marshall was the subject of the 1951 book *A Man Called Peter,* which was written by his wife, Catherine, and made into a movie in 1955.) The kirking of tartans has developed into an annual event for many Scottish clubs and organizations. During this moving service, pieces of tartan are piped into the church or service site to be blessed. The blessing praises the faith and fortitude of the fathers of the clans and honors the noble tradition which all Scots proudly share.

Almost all Games have a ceilidh (a gathering featuring music and dancing) in the evening. Some ceilidhs, such as those held at the Grandfather Mountain Games, are structured and feature professional entertainment; others depend to a large degree upon the talent in the audience. Both types, however, provide a fun evening of Scottish folk songs, piping, fiddling, dancing, and other types of entertainment. Participation is encouraged at these casual affairs, whether it be in community singing, joining in a Scottish country dance, telling a Scottish tale—whatever one may contribute to the enjoyment of all. One sees babes in arms, the most senior of citizens, and all ages in between at these gatherings. A ceilidh is an opportunity for people to get together in a relaxed and friendly atmosphere after a day of competition, working in a tent or booth, or managing a Games.

A much more formal evening of entertainment offered by some Games is the tartan ball. Highland evening dress is usually required, which makes a gala spectacle in itself. Scottish country dancing is featured at these occasions to the accompaniment of live Scottish music.

CLAN SOCIETIES

The many clan tents at Scottish Highland Games in the United States cause most Gamesgoers to assume that tents are common at Games in Scotland as well. But from what I have been told, there are no clan tents at the Games in Scotland, unless this American practice has been instituted of late. (The same is true of the wearing of the kilt, which is so popular at American Games. At Games in Scotland, kilts are worn by competitors and American visitors, but by very few Scots. The exception to this rule is the Lonach Games, which features the March of the Clansmen. This march around the stately homes in the area and the Games site totals six miles—a bit farther than the clan parades held at many American Games.)

Clan societies and Games are, to a large degree, dependent upon each other for growth and support. Many clans are involved in the sponsorship of Games. For example, the Ligonier Games in Pennsylvania began as a Clan Donald picnic; Old Westbury, New York, is the site of a Games sponsored by the Long Island Scottish Clans Association; Clan Douglas and the Syracuse Scottish Pipe Band offer the Central New York Games in Liverpool; and Clans of the Highlands, Inc., sponsors the Pacific Highland Clan Gathering in Chino, California. The clans give other support to the Games through donations, advertisements, trophy sponsorship, and other means. The clan troupes with their decorated tents and tables add to the color and festivities of a Games.

But the relationship works both ways. The Games provide the clan societies with one of the most effective means possible of keeping old members and acquiring new ones. Clan representatives—armed with the tentworkers' bible, *Scots Kith and Kin,* published by Albyn Press Ltd. for Clan House in Edinburgh—can impress and intrigue a curious neophyte. Some clans go even further and have their appointed genealogists on hand prepared to assist those who have begun the fascinating unraveling of lineage. A prospective member can peruse a collection of books, pamphlets, newsletters, maps, photographs, and other items to get an indication of the activities of his Scottish family. He can purchase an array of items emblazoned with the clan crest and/or name so that he becomes immediately identified with the clan.

Clan societies provide a place for non-competitors (though competitors are often clan members as well) to become involved and really feel as though they are a part of the Games. Clan tents are places to share refreshments, shade, and stories. Once a person becomes involved, he usually gets hooked on clan activities. Volunteer work in the clan tent can lead to an office in the clan. The only limits to involvement are self-imposed.

Those who have worked in clan tents will appreciate an observation (playfully attributed to "Somerled, circa 1152") that appears on a handout generated by Clan Donald: "The three most important ingredients of a successful clan tent are an understanding spouse, a station wagon, and masking tape!" The hours are long, the labor often heavy, but the compensation in terms of enjoyment and a feeling of contribution are great.

The appearance of clan tents at the Games can be traced, like so many other Games traditions, to Grandfather Mountain. Royce McNeill of Charlotte, North Carolina, has never missed a Games at Grandfather Mountain and has been involved in clan activities since the Games' inception, and he recalls that there were no clan tents at the first gathering. Since it rains almost every day in the mountains and most of the folks who were at Grandfather Mountain in the beginning were campers who were familiar with the area, they brought their tent awnings to the second Games for protection against the weather. Banners were strung from the tent poles to beckon fellow clan members to join with them in breaking bread and discussing kinship. The practice was so popular that the participants decided to continue it on a regular basis, and it soon spread to other Games. Now clan tents are almost universal at U.S. Games, and there are over 100 at Grandfather Mountain.

The word *clan* comes from a Gaelic word meaning "children," which denotes "family." That is precisely what clan societies in the United States and elsewhere offer: a feeling of family. When the clan system originated in the Highlands, it was a feudal system with the chief offering protection to fellow clan members. Under the new and revitalized system in the United States, there is a high commissioner or president or chairman (the term varies) who serves as leader of his "family." His superior is the high chief or chief (a blood title) or commander (an appointed title) of the clan. The Lord Lyon, King of Arms, in Scotland is the only person in the world who can decide who is a rightful clan chief, as well as who can have and use a particular coat of arms. With the increased interest in clan activities, many clan organizations and societies that have been without a leader for perhaps generations are petitioning the Lord Lyon to find their true chief or, if the blood line is broken, to assign a clan commander.

This resurgence of clan activity is a fairly recent development. According to the research of Professor Rowland Berthoff (see chapter 4), the three earliest American clan societies were the Macleans and MacBeans, dating from the 1890s, and the Macneills, dating from 1921. History shows that the MacBean society disintegrated before World War I and lay dormant for about 40 years. Renewed interest led to reinstitution of the society in 1963, and six years later the clan literally got a big boost when astronaut Alan L. Bean of the Apollo 12 crew carried a piece of MacBean tartan with him as he walked on the moon on November 19, 1969. (A piece of that tartan is now on display at the Museum of Scottish Tartans in Comrie, Scotland.) The rest of the American clan societies appeared after 1950, with most of them forming in the 1970s. Only about one-third of these clans were branches of parent societies in Scotland.

Although many of the clan societies do not have a large national membership, clan interest is always on the rise. The three largest clan societies in the United States are Donald, Campbell, and MacLeod. Clan Donald has twelve regions and a membership of almost 3,500; the actual number of individual members is much larger because family units are only counted as one in the total number. Clan Campbell has ten regions and Clan MacLeod has eight; each of these has approximately 2,000 family unit members.

The effects of this renewed family enthusiasm are also felt in Scotland. Heads of clans descended from generations-ago chiefs find themselves held in esteem by devoted clansmen throughout the world. A clan chief or commander as guest of honor is a frequent sight at Games in the United States today.

In 1974 Dr. Herbert P. MacNeal of Convent Station, New Jersey, founded an organization called the Council of Scottish Clan Associations, Inc., to provide better communication within the ever-increasing Scottish community. He and his wife, Ethel, have devoted many hours working and traveling throughout the country to strengthen the organization. The 1984 directory issue of the *Claymore*, the council's newsletter, lists more than 135 Highland clan and Lowland family organizations in North America. The council has an audio-visual library and extensive reference material, and it offers assistance in answering almost any type of Scottish-related question imaginable. There are eleven regional commissioners and numerous state commissioners who assist in the functioning of the council.

In 1982 Dr. Herbert MacNeal was succeeded as president by the late Ronald Carr of Houston. The council honored Dr. MacNeal's contribution to the Scottish community by establishing the Herbert P. MacNeal Scholarship Fund to aid students in the Scottish arts. Alexander Marshall of New York City is the council's current president.

Along with the act of identifying one's self with one's clan usually comes the acquisition of the ultimate sign of unity, the one that shows your colors from afar—the tartan.

Research has dispelled the romantic myth that, from antiquity, clan members went about their daily tasks clad in garments of tartan cloth, the precise setts (patterns) of which distinguished them from their neighbors. Actually, tartan originally referred to a kind of cloth with or without a pattern. It is known that various regions and clans had developed local tartans before the Rebellion of 1745. The wearing of these tartans was banned under the Act of Proscription in an attempt to quash the clan system.

Although there were other contributors—including Scotland's national poet, Robert Burns—to the renewed spirit of nationalism that became so prevalent in Scotland in the early nineteenth century, Sir Walter Scott did the most to instill the Highland system with a sense of romance through his writings such as *Rob Roy, Waverly,* and "The Lady of the Lake." He was, as mentioned before, instrumental in planning King George IV's 1822 visit to Edinburgh, which placed a royal sanction on all things Scottish. The seal of approval was permanently affixed when another monarch, Queen Victoria, began her annual visits to Balmoral in 1848. Her love of Scotland and her contribution to the spirit of nationalism through the decor and dress at Balmoral and the support of the Braemar Gathering evoked a far better response than did the efforts of her Stuart ancestor, Bonnie Prince Charlie, 200 years earlier. The tartan boom was on. Wearing the tartan was a tangible link with the proud and dauntless clan spirit of old.

Today many clan tartans and variations of those tartans—dress, hunting, and clan setts done in reproduction (the very muted tones similar to those produced by vegetable dyes of old) and in ancient and modern colors—are seen at U.S. Games and other Scottish events. Books have been written describing the tartans and their histories as well as how and when to wear them.

In May 1963 the Scottish Tartans Society was inaugurated to study tartans and Highland dress and to educate the public in such matters. The society is headquartered in Comrie, Scotland, and has established the Museum of Scottish Tartans. The meticulous work of collecting and preserving authentic tartans has culminated in the recording of nearly 200 designs. Dr. Micheil MacDonald, director of the Scottish Tartans Society and curator of the Museum of Scottish Tartans, has traveled extensively to promote the cause of the society. He frequently attends the Games in the United States, where the society's tent and attendant lectures give Scotiaphiles the opportunity to learn about the society's ongoing work firsthand.

SOMETHING FOR EVERYONE

Besides clan societies, which cater to members of the same Scottish family, there are many other Scottish organizations in the U.S. that people of Scottish descent can join. Many of these organizations also send representatives to the Games to encourage participation in their activities. In these broader-based organizations, usually the only requirement for membership is a desire to affiliate one's self with the purpose and benefits (cultural, educational, and/or social) of the organization. Many St. Andrew's Societies follow the original rule of offering membership only to males of Scottish descent, but an increasing number are permitting female membership as well.

The largest and oldest Games in the United States today continue to be sponsored by the Caledonian Club of San Francisco. The second oldest Games are sponsored by the Detroit St. Andrew's Society, and several of the newer Games such as those in Waterville, Maine, and Modesto, California, are sponsored by St. Andrew's societies. Other Scottish clubs are also involved in the sponsorship of Games. The United Scottish Society in California held its first Games in 1927; more recently, Scottish clubs in Miami and Anchorage, Alaska, have joined in the promotion of Scottish traditions by hosting Games.

Among the other Scottish clubs and organizations represented at the Games are Scottish cultural clubs, heritage and genealogy groups, Robert Burns clubs, and groups specializing in various musical instruments and music. The Council of Scottish Clan Associations is represented at the majority of Games. Not all groups appear at all Games, of course, but any number of these may be represented.

There are many Scottish import and specialty shops in the United States today catering to the rising interest in things Scottish. At almost any Games in this country, one may purchase anything from Scottish confections to complete Scottish outfits from representatives of these shops. The vendors are an integral part of the Games scene today. Most of these shops have mail-order services, of course, but the convenience of having the vendors at the Games is a welcome benefit to many. General shops offer an assortment of souvenir-type articles that thrill first-time visitors to the Games, and specialty shops make available the particulars such as bagpipe reeds and dancing gillies. If an item is not available, one can even order it to be picked up at the next Games where the shop will appear.

Along with these goods, many food vendors offer such delights as meat pies, bridies (meat-filled pastries), fish and chips, scones, shortbread, and a variety of other tempting goodies.

I dare not single out specific vendors for fear of appearing to be advertising, but suffice it to say that there are numerous vendors seen at the Games and established throughout the United States. In one directory I found 89 U.S. listings, which in itself bespeaks the Scottish interest in this country.

There are two major publications covering Scottish news and events in the United States: *The Scottish-American* (which originated in 1983 as *the Scottish Merchant*) and *The Highlander,* now in its 24th year. *The Scottish-American* is published by Dr. W. Reynolds ("Renny") McLeod and edited by Don Bond in West Virginia. *The Highlander* is published and edited by Angus Ray in Illinois.

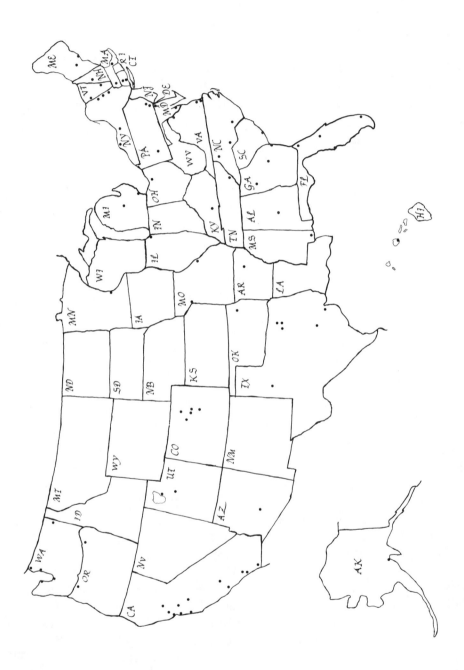

8

Listings of Games
in the United States

As of the October 1985 publishing deadline for this book, there were, to the best of my knowledge, 82 Scottish Highland Games in the United States either actually being held or in the planning stages. The map accompanying this chapter shows the dispersal of the established Games throughout thirty-three states. Though the summer months are generally considered to be the Games season, Games now cover nearly the entire calendar year, beginning in January in Orlando, Florida, and ending in November in Salado, Texas.

This chapter lists the Games alphabetically by state and town or city. I have included as much information as possible to show the scope of each Games. The data for these entries was obtained from questionnaires sent to all of the Games, from the brochures and programs supplied by the Games, or from personal experience. I have also collected information from people who have attended or helped to run Games. Some of the events at individual Games may have expanded since this was written, an indication of the continual growth of the Games.

Please note that only Games and events under a Games format are included in these synopses and on the map. There are many more Scottish festivals, fairs, and clan picnics in the U.S., as well as individual piping, drumming, and dance events. In addition, Scottish activities are often included in folk festivals covering several nations. These other Scottish events are diverse and widespread and, since I do not wish to single out or risk over-looking any of them, let me simply say that Scots in the United States are constantly gathering and making themselves known.

We are indeed in the midst of, as Donald Francis MacDonald says, a "Games explosion." This happy fact has its accompanying frustrations. I have tried to pursue every lead I've been given or have discovered in order to have a good grasp of the Games scene in the United States today. It has not always been easy to keep track of Games that are far away from me, spring up suddenly, or have been going on for years but intentionally keep themselves local. For instance, I just discovered a Games that started in September 1984 in Brockton, Massachusetts. Besides the Games listed in this chapter Games commenced in 1985 in Fort Worth, Texas (May); Paso Robles, California (June); Amherst, New York (September); and Biloxi, Mississippi (November). In 1986 Games will take place in Glasgow, Kentucky, at the end of May and in Austin, Texas, in mid-November in conjunction with the two-week International Gathering of the Scots. I have tried to the best of my ability to find out where Games are being celebrated so that we can all share, even vicariously, in the activities of our fellow Scots.

The Scottish Games tend to follow a more or less standard format, with competition in athletics, dancing, piping, drum-ming, bands, and (in many cases) fiddling. The first U.S. Nation-al Scottish Harp Competition was held in 1984 at the Virginia Scottish Games in Alexandria, and the rapidly increasing interest in this instrument will undoubtedly lead to the establishment of Scottish harp (clarsach) competitions at other Games. Most Games have at least two competitions that are sanctioned by the governing bodies of the events. All the Games offer various trimmings that celebrate and promote our heritage. Though not explicitly mentioned in the individual accounts here, nearly all Games have opening and/or closing ceremonies in which guests of honor are introduced and massed bands presented—still one of the most stirring sights at any Games for the Gamesgoer.

These entries are as concise, yet as detailed, as possible. Each lists the usual location, date, competitions, demonstrations, other events, clan/organization/vendor attendance, evening activities, and contact person. Where possible, I have listed the address of the Games rather than that of the current presiding officer, since the officers change frequently. I have also included my brief impressions of Games I have attended and those of other Games attended by friends and acquaintances.

A few explanations are in order concerning the specifics of the listings. Whenever dancing is mentioned by itself as a competition, it refers to both Highland and national events. The sanctioning bodies for the competitions are: heavy events, North American Scottish Games Association (NASGA); dancing, Scottish Official Board of Highland Dancing (SOBHD); piping, either the Eastern United States Pipe Band Association (EUSPBA), Pacific Coast Pipe Band Association (PCPBA), or Midwest Pipe Band Association (MWPBA); and fiddling, U.S. Scottish Fiddling Revival, Ltd. (FIRE). "Member ASGF" denotes a member of the Association of Scottish Games and Festivals. The abbreviations used are: (s), sanctioned; 28d, 28-pound weight throw; 28h, 28-pound weight toss; 56d, 56-pound weight throw; 56h, 56-pound weight toss; and MSR, march, strathspey, and reel.

ALABAMA

Selma—Alabama Scottish Festival; two days; mid-June. Established 1983. Heavy events: stone, caber, sheaf. Highland dancing demonstrations. Band competition. Other events: tug-of-war; kilted mile; foot races; children's games; ladies' rolling pin toss; kirking of tartans. Clans and Scottish organizations. Vendors. Barbecue. Ceilidh. Contact: Alabama Scottish Heritage Society, Rt. 7, Box 543, Selma, AL 36701. Member ASGF.

This festival grew from a family reunion into a popular Scottish event. In 1984 Duncan Clark of New Zealand, former heavy events champion in Scotland, and Larry Satchwell demonstrated the heavy events. Clark's wife Joan, a Highland dancing teacher, led Scottish country dancing. The master of ceremonies and soloist was Forrest Warren, soloist at Madison Avenue Presbyterian Church in New York City. This Games was not held in 1985 because a permanent location could not be found; they plan to be back in 1986. Watch for site and date announcements.

ALASKA

Eagle River—Alaskan Scottish Highland Games and Gathering of the Clans; two days; first weekend in August. Established 1982. Heavy events: open and amateur; caber, stone, 56d, 56h, 28d. Dancing (s). Solo piping (s) and drumming (s); drum major. Pipe bands for performance; trio and medley competitions. Fiddling. Other events: tug-of-war; kilted mile; women's and children's caber and stone. Clans. Vendors. Ceilidh. Contact: Alaskan Scottish Club, P.O. Box 3471, Anchorage, AK 99510.

The first Scottish Highland Games in Alaska were sponsored by the Alaskan Scottish Club. The inaugural Games was heartily accepted by the community—the mayor of Anchorage proclaimed the opening day Scottish American Day—and enjoyed by attendees.

ARIZONA

Phoenix—Caledonian Society of Arizona Annual Gathering and Games; one day; third or fourth Saturday in March. Established 1966. Heavy events: caber and all weights for distance and height. Dancing: all classes. Solo piping: open and amateur MSR and piobaireachd. Drumming; drum major. Bands: MSR and time limit. Clans. Vendors. Ceilidh. Contact: David R. Logan, president, Caledonian Society of Arizona, 5219 S. 44th Pl., Phoenix, AZ 85040.

ARKANSAS

Batesville—Arkansas College Ozark Scottish Festival; one day; mid-April. Established 1980. Heavy events: amateur; lightweight and heavyweight men's divisions. Dancing (s). Solo piping: open and amateur. Bands (s). Other events: women's and children's events (including caber, sheaf, and stone); track events; kilted mile. Clans. Ozark crafts. Scottish feast. Ceilidh. Contact: Arkansas College, Batesville, AR 72501. Member ASGF.

The Batesville gathering was started to help introduce Scottish traditions to the campus. This small liberal arts college was founded by Scottish Presbyterians in 1872 and is still affiliated with the Presbyterian Church. It now has its own pipe band and

Highland dancers and offers scholarships in the Scottish arts. In addition to the Games, the college has a Burns Night and a kirking of the tartans. The Games also emphasize the Scottish influence on Ozark traditions by including demonstrations of Ozark arts and crafts. Arkansas College is fulfilling the purpose of its Games, as evidenced by the increasing participation of the campus and community—all the more satisfying considering the previous lack of exposure in the area to such events.

CALIFORNIA

Campbell—Campbell Highland Games; one day; mid-August. Established 1979. Held at Campbell Stadium. Heavy events (s): stone, hammer, 28d, 56h, caber. Dancing (s). Solo piping (s): novice and amateur. Drumming (s); drum major, open. Bands for performance. Clans and Scottish organizations. Vendors. Contact: Campbell Chamber of Commerce, 328 E. Campbell Ave., Campbell, CA 95008.

These games honor Ben Campbell, who purchased what became Campbell Ranch in 1851. That ranch site is now the city of Campbell.

Chino—Pacific Highland Clan Gathering and Games; two days; third weekend in October. Established 1979. Heavy events (s): professional and amateur; two stones, two hammers, 28d, 56d, 56h, caber. Dancing (s): solo and team choreography competition. Solo piping (s): novice and amateur. Drumming; drum major (s). Bands for performance. Fiddling (s); Pacific Coast Fiddling Championships. Other events: tug-of-war; Scottish fiddling workshop; parade of clans; church service at Games. Demonstrations: Scottish country dancing; folk music; Gaelic singing; harp; Northumberland piping; mouth music. Clans and Scottish organizations. Vendors. Ceilidh. Contact: John MacRae, president, Clans of the Highlands, Inc., 2308 Shady Hills Dr., Diamond Bar, CA 91765.

Clans of the Highlands, Inc., sponsor of this Games, was also the host of the first World Heavy Events Championships in Pomona in 1980.

Corte Madera—Marin County Highland Gathering; one day; end of May. Established 1974. Held at Marin County Day School under auspices of Prince Charles Pipe Bands. Heavy events demonstrations. Dancing under direction of Northern California Highland Dancing Association. Solo piping (s): novice and amateur. Drumming (s): novice and amateur. Bands for performance. Fiddling. Clans. Vendors. Contact: Jack Sutherland, 230 Chapman Dr., Corte Madera, CA 95401.

Costa Mesa—United Scottish Society's Highland Gathering and Games; two days; Memorial Day weekend. Fourth oldest existing U.S. Games; established 1927. Heavy event (s): professional and amateur; stone, two hammers, 28d, 56d, 56h, caber. Dancing (s): competition for City of Edinburgh Medal, highest dancing award, donated in 1950 by the Lord Provost of Edinburgh to encourage Highland dancing in Southern California. Solo piping (s): novice, amateur, professional, all events; drum major. Bands (s): Grades II–III. Other events: ladies' and children's athletics; men's lightweight events; tug-of-war; kilted mile; soccer; rugby; tartan drum toss; drumhead memorial service, including kirking of tartans. Demonstrations: wrestling; fiddling; sheepdogs; Scottish country dancing. Clans. Vendors. Dinnerdance. Contact: Thomas W. Smith, secretary, United Scottish Society, Inc., 3309 Vail Ave., Redondo Beach, CA 90278.

The year 1982 marked the 50th anniversary of this Games along with the inauguration of a two-day schedule and a new site, the Orange County Fairgrounds. This facility can accommodate 500 motor homes or trailers. The grounds also have many shade trees; picnicking is encouraged. The parent organization of this Games boasts over 900 members who represent and promote the Southern California Scottish element.

Fresno—Central California Highland Gathering and Games; one day; end of September. Established 1978. Heavy events (s): professional and amateur; all except sheaf. Dancing (s). Solo piping (s): Grade III. Drumming. Bands for performance. Other events: women's athletics. Clans. Vendors. Ceilidh. Contact: Keith Tice, 5891 N. Fairbanks, Clovis, CA 93612.

Keith Tice, a top American Scottish athlete, is heavily involved in this Games. He considers this Games site, Coombs River Ranch, to be one of the most beautiful he has seen—and he has seen a lot of Games sites.

Modesto—Highland Games and Gathering of the Clans, sponsored by the St. Andrew's Society of Modesto; one day; first Saturday in June. Established 1982. Heavy events. Solo piping and drumming; drum major. Band competitions, plus mini-bands. Demonstrations: Highland and Scottish country dancing. Other events: foot races; children's games. Clans and Scottish organizations. Vendors. Contact: P.O. Box 2545, Modesto, CA 95351.

Monterey Peninsula—Scottish Highland Games; one day; first Saturday in August. Established 1970. Heavy events (s): stone, hammer, 56d, 56h, caber. Northern California Caber Tossing Championship. Dancing (s). Solo piping (s): novice and amateur. Drumming (s): novice and amateur. Other events: 100-yard dash; tug-of-war; hole-in-one contest. Sheepdog and Scottish country dancing demonstrations. Clans and Scottish organizations. Vendors. Ceilidh. Contact: The Scottish Society of Monterey Peninsula, P.O. Box 1633, Carmel, CA 93921.

A ceremony unique to this country is held to draw attention to and drum up enthusiasm for this Games. The championship caber, which was selected in Scotland by Charlie Allan, one of the Games' former champions, hangs from the ceiling of the Red Lion Pub in Carmel throughout the year. Brass plaques denoting each year's winner are attached to the caber. (The carpet in the pub is a reproduction of the Wallace tartan.) The Saturday before the Games, the caber is taken down and toasted, then carried through the streets of Carmel behind the Monterey Scottish Pipe Band. Kilted citizens and plainsfolks join in the parade, which eventually returns to the pub. The caber is piped into the pub, and a ceilidh is held there. Gordon Varnedoe suggested the idea of the caber parade, which is done on occasion in Scotland, to the Scottish Society of Monterey Peninsula. Varnedoe was also responsible for having Charlie Allan make the caber selection.

Sacramento—Scottish Highland Gathering, sponsored by the Sacramento Caledonian Club, California State University at Sacramento, and the city of Sacramento; one day; second Saturday in June. Established 1960. Held at the university campus. Heavy events: stone (Braemar style), hammer, 28d, 56h, caber. Dancing (s). Solo piping (s): novice, amateur, trio. Drumming (s): novice, amateur. Bands (s): five-minute medley. Other events: tug-of-war; children's games. Scottish country dancing demonstrations. Clans and Scottish organizations. Ceilidh. Contact: P.O. Box 1444, Fair Oaks, CA 95628.

San Diego—San Diego Scottish Highland Games; one day; first weekend in August. Established 1974. Held at Helix High School Stadium. Heavy events (s): professional and amateur; stone, two hammers, 28d, 28h, 56d, 56h, caber. Dancing (s): Pacific Coast Dance Championships. Hosted 1984 U.S. Inter-Regional Highland Dancing Championship. Solo piping (s): all events. Drumming; drum major (s). Bands (s): Grades I–III; time limit. Other events: Scottie dog show. Clans and Scottish organizations. Vendors. Highland dinner/ball. Contact: P.O. Box 3662, San Diego, CA 92103.

San Diego is the sister city to Edinburgh. When this event started, the Royal Braemar Society in Scotland presented a caber to the Games. The Braemar Challenge Caber Toss is now an annual event.

San Fernando—San Fernando Valley-Greater Los Angeles Scottish Heritage Highland Games; two days; first weekend in May. Established 1981. Held at California State University-Northridge (North Campus). Piping. Drumming. Fiddling. Other events: bicycle race; tug-of-war. Demonstrations: heavy events; sheepdogs; Scottish country dancing. Clans. Vendors. Contact: P.O. Box 844, Arleta, CA 91331.

Santa Rosa—Caledonian Club of San Francisco Annual Scottish Gathering and Games; three days; Labor Day weekend. Oldest existing Games in U.S.; established 1866. Sanctioned competitions in all Games events (including both styles of stones in athletics). U.S. Heavy Events Championships; U.S. Caber Toss Championships. Dancing (s); Western United States Open Championships; City of Dundee Shield dancing award. Piping (s): MacCrimmon Quaich awarded to top amateur piobaireachd piper; invitational piping contest. Fiddling (s): Niel Gow Scottish Fiddling Championship. Clarsach. Other events: five-a-side soccer. Clans and Scottish organizations. Vendors. Contact: John Dickson, Caledonian Club of San Francisco, 1310 Merced St., Richmond, CA 94804.

This Games site—the Sonoma County Fairgrounds in the heart of the Sonoma-Napa-Mendocino wine country—is huge; it has to be to accommodate the more than 30,000 people who flock to this gathering. The grandstand seats about 5,600 (grandstand admission is extra) and is packed throughout the competition. One can witness most of the events without ever having to leave the grandstand.

The pipe band competition is indicative of the precision with which the Games is run in general. There are three-minute intervals between bands, and if a band does not appear in time, it loses its travel money. This kind of enticement, plus the placement of clocks throughout the grounds, enforces the tight scheduling. Participants are treated well; there is a reception for out-of-area bands, and the bands are also treated to a day trip in San Francisco or the wine country. (A popular practice is to record the performances of the top bands on Saturday and have the tapes available on Sunday.) The heavy events competitors have a picnic on Sunday evening. At the closing ceremonies each pipe band is led into the grandstand area by a dancer, and dancers on the platform perform to the music of the ceremony. Proceeds from the Games go to local charities.

COLORADO

Aurora—Aurora Scottish Games; one day; third Saturday in May. Established 1983. Heavy events: heptathlon (Braemar-style stone). Other events: farmer's walk; women's heavy events. Contact: Greg Bradshaw, 14426 E. Wyoming Pl., Aurora, CO 80012.

This Games was started by Greg Bradshaw to help develop the

heavy events circuit in Colorado. Other competitions will be added in the future.

Colorado Springs—Pike's Peak Scottish Games; one day; third Saturday in July. Established 1983. Heavy events: heptathlon (Braemar-style stone). Women's heavy events. Dancing. Solo piping. Contact: Greg Bradshaw, 14426 E. Wyoming Pl., Aurora, CO 80012.

Estes Park—Long's Peak Scottish Highland Festival; two days; first weekend after Labor Day. Established 1978. Heavy events (s): heptathlon (Braemar-style stone). Dancing (s). Solo piping (s): Grades I–V; trios (s). Drumming. Bands (s). Fiddling. Competitions in Celtic harp, dulcimer, tin whistle, Irish step dancing. Other events: women's and juniors' heavy events; rolling pin toss; keg toss; tomahawk throw; black powder shoot; farmer's walk; kilted mile; tug-of-war; children's games. Scottish country, Welsh, and Morris dancing demonstrations. Scottish dog breeds exhibition. Clans. Vendors. Ceilidh. Contact: P.O. Box 1820, Estes Park, CO 80517.

This Games begins with a parade through the resort town of Estes Park, which is located at the main entrance to Rocky Mountain National Park. The events are held next to Lake Estes in the shadow of Long's Peak (elevation 14,256').

Ft. Collins—Ft. Collins Scottish Gathering; one day; first Saturday in June. Established 1982. Heavy events: heptathlon (Braemar-style stone). Women's and juniors' heavy events. Solo piping. Contact: Greg Bradshaw, 14426 E. Wyoming Pl., Aurora, CO 80012.

Golden—Rocky Mountain Highland Games; two days; second weekend in August. Established 1963. Heavy events: Braemar-style stone, 28d, 56d, 56h, Rocky Mountain caber, sheaf. Dancing (s); choreography; Sword of the Rockies awarded for best sword dance in any class. Rocky Mountain Highland Dancing Championships. Solo piping (s): amateur and open; trios; quartets. Drumming (s): amateur I and II and open; drum major.

Bands (s): all grades. Other events: Cumberland wrestling; tug-of-war; manhood stone; women's heavy events; children's games. Exhibits of Scottish Highland cattle and MG automobiles. Clans and Scottish organizations. Vendors. Ceilidh. Highland dancing workshops periodically. Contact: St. Andrew's Society, c/o Charles Todd, 3606 E. Hinsdale Pl., Littleton, CO 80122.

The first ten years of the Rocky Mountain Highland Games were more like a family picnic. The Games then changed in format and moved from a park to Brooks Field on the campus of the Colorado School of Mines. Accommodations are available to all who wish to stay in the campus dormitories. The Rocky Mountain School of Piping, under the direction of Roddy MacDonald, is held on campus the week preceding the Games.

CONNECTICUT

Litchfield—Scottish Festival of the St. Andrew's Society of Connecticut; one day; third Saturday in September. Established 1984. Heavy events. Dancing. Solo piping. Bands. Contact: St. Andrew's Society of Connecticut, P. O. Box 1195, Litchfield, CT 06759. Member ASGF.

Norwalk—Round Hill Scottish Games; one day; the Fourth of July. Third oldest existing Games; established 1924. Heavy events: amateur caber. Solo piping (s) and solo drumming (s). Bands (s). Other events: foot races; shot put; eleven-a-side soccer; children's games. Clans and Scottish organizations. Vendors. Contact: P.O. Box 261, Belden Station, Norwalk, CT 06850. Member ASGF.

These Games, which are called "the Cowal Games of the U.S.A.," have been held on the Fourth of July since 1923. If the Fourth falls on a Sunday, the Games are held the next day.

FLORIDA

Dunedin—Dunedin Highland Games and Festival; three days (tattoo Friday night); last weekend in March. Established 1966. Heavy events (s): invitational professional heptathlon; four amateur events. Dancing (s): Florida Championships; broadswords team competition. Solo piping (s) and drumming (s); drum major. Bands (s): Grades II and IV; Florida Pipe Band Championships (in conjunction with other Florida Games). Other events: tug-of-war; kilted mile; parade of tartans. Clans and Scottish organizations. Vendors. Two ceilidhs. Tartan ball. Contact: Dunedin Highland Games and Festival Committee, Inc., P.O. Box 507, Dunedin, FL 33528-0507. Member ASGF.

Dunedin is a very Scots-oriented town; it is named for Edinburgh (Dunedin is Gaelic for "castle on the rock") and is the sister city of Stirling, Scotland. Its middle school and high school have pipe bands (the school mascot is the Highlander), and there is an adult pipe band, the Dunedin City Pipe and Drum Corps, as well. According to my sources, Dunedin is a good place for Americans to compete against Canadians in all events without venturing up north; at Games time, the town is inundated with our northern neighbors seeking relief from the winter doldrums. There are many baseball spring training camps in the area, including another group of Canadian hibernators, the Toronto Blue Jays—giving visitors the chance to experience both Scottish and American Games.

Jacksonville—Jacksonville Scottish Highland Games and Gathering of the Clans; one day; second weekend in April. Established 1977. Heavy events (s): professional heptathlon; amateur. Dancing (s). Solo piping (s) and drumming (s); drum major; drum salute. Bands (s): Grade IV; Florida Pipe Band Championships (in conjunction with other Florida Games); all-state pipe band selection. Fiddling demonstration. Other events: children's games; kirking of tartans at a local church; parade of tartans; medieval battle; military tug-of-war; bonniest knees contest (with blindfolded judges); haggis hurl. Clans and Scottish organizations. Vendors. Competitors' ceilidh. Tartan ball with buffet. Contact: St. Andrew's Society of Jacksonville, P.O. Box 2105, Jacksonville, FL 32203. Member ASGF.

The St. Andrew's Society of Jacksonville was formed in 1977 and held its first Games the same year. One of the features of this Games is the release of racing pigeons during the opening ceremonies. (Pigeon racing is considered a national sport in Scotland.) The event was not held in 1985 but will return in 1986.

Miami—Southeast Florida Scottish Festival; one day; second Saturday in February. Established 1984. Heavy events: amateur. Dancing (s). Solo piping (s) and drumming (s). Bands for performance. Demonstrations: Scottish country dancing; sheepdogs. Other events: tug-of-war; children's games; kirking of tartans; eighteenth-century military encampment. Clans. Ceilidh. Tartan ball. Contact: Scottish American Society of South Florida, P.O. Box 633, Miami Shores, FL 33158. Member ASGF.

Orlando—Orlando Scottish Highland Games; one day; third weekend in January. Established 1978. Heavy events (s): professional heptathlon; amateur. Dancing (s). Solo piping (s): Grades I-V amateur; open piobaireachd, MSR. Drumming (s): all classes; drum major; drum salute. Bands (s): Grades III and IV; Florida Pipe Band Championships (in conjunction with other Florida Games). Other events: inter-clan athletics; tug-of-war; kilted mile; Florida Championship Haggis Hurl; parade of tartans; kirking of tartans. Demonstrations: Scottish country dancing; sheepdogs. Clans and Scottish organizations. Vendors. Tartan ball. Contact: Orlando Scottish Highland Games, P.O. Box 2948, Orlando, FL 32802. Member ASGF.

This Games, held at the Central Florida Fairgrounds, kicks off the Games year. A bit of Scotland pours over into nearby Disney World because of this event, as the dancers and pipe bands are usually invited to give a performance and march in the midday parade there on the Sunday after the Games. In 1983 a kilted skydiver descended from an aircraft in front of the reviewing stand during the opening ceremonies.

GEORGIA

Mount Vernon—Brewton-Parker Scottish Festival and Games; one day; mid-April. Established 1985. Heavy events: heptathlon. Bands for performance. Demonstrations: solo piping and drumming; Scottish country dancing; fiddling; harp. Contact: Brewton-Parker College, Hwy. 280, Mt. Vernon, GA 30445.

The mascot of this college near Vidalia, the Baron, was selected over 50 years ago to reflect the Scottish heritage of the area. The Scottish connection lay dormant until a couple of years ago when it was revitalized to develop campus and community spirit. To further the cause, Games were begun to be the focal point of the annual Founder's Week. Students donned kilts representing clans of the earliest Scottish settlers in the area to compete in the heavy events. Pipers and drummers were at the first event; Highland dancers will be added in the future. A juried arts and crafts show is held along with the Games.

Savannah—Savannah Scottish Games; one day; first Saturday in May. Established 1978. Heavy events (s): professional heptathlon. Dancing (s): Southern Regional Closed Championships. Solo piping (s) and drumming (s); drum major; drum corps. Bands (s): Grades III and IV. Other events: kirking of tartans at a local church; parade of tartans; military tug-of-war. Clans and Scottish organizations. Vendors. Competitors' river cruise. Ceilidh. Tartan ball. Contact: Savannah Scottish Games, P.O. Box 1611, Savannah, GA 31401. Member ASGF.

Spring in Savannah has a lot more in common with Scotland than just her sons and daughters: the new air brings the midges, reminiscent of visits to the Isle of Skye and other Highland places. This is the only Games site I know of where the dancers must cross a moat into a fortress to compete. The Games are held at Fort Jackson, which was built beginning in 1809 and was used in the War of 1812 and the Civil War. The fort flanks the Savannah River about three miles from this lovely Southern city with its ample charm and history. Robert Louis Stevenson was a visitor to Savannah and frequently mentions the city in *Treasure Island*. To share a common moment with a famous fellow Scot, one may dine in the Pirate's House Restaurant, where events in that book take place.

Stone Mountain—Stone Mountain Scottish Festival and Highland Games; two days; mid-October. Established 1973. Heavy events (s): professional heptathlon; amateur. Southern United States 16-Pound Hammer Throw Championship. Dancing (s): Southeastern Regional Competition. Solo piping (s) and drumming (s); drum major. Invitational piobaireachd competition; awarding of MacCrimmon Quaich. Bands (s): Grades III and IV: dress and deportment. Fiddling (s): Southeastern U.S. Scottish Fiddling Championships. Other events: clan challenge athletics; parade of tartans; worship service at Games site with kirking of tartans; tattoo. Demonstrations: Scottish country dancing; sheepdogs. Clans. Vendors. Ceilidh. Contact: Stone Mountain Highland Games, P.O. Box 14023, Atlanta, GA 30324. Member ASGF.

Stone Mountain is an 825-foot bulbous oddity—the largest granite monolith in the world—in a most unlikely setting. It has been turned into a monument to the Confederate States of America. Carved into the side of the mountain are the likenesses of Confederate President Jefferson Davis and Generals Robert E. Lee and "Stonewall" Jackson. So huge a sculpture (about a city block long) demands to be viewed from a distance; the wooded park at the base of the mountain serves this purpose and also serves as the Games site. Stone Mountain is one of the fastest-growing Games in the country. It is a favorite with many competitors, as it traditionally marks the end of the Games season and one last opportunity for camaraderie. It was the first American site of the International Gathering of the Scots in 1982.

HAWAII

Honolulu—Highland Gathering; one day; end of March. Established 1982. Heavy events: professional; amateur; stone, sheaf, caber, hammer, 22d, 56d, 56h. Dancing (s); five special trophies. Solo piping (s): amateur and open. Drumming (s): novice and open. Bands (s). Other events: 5K and 10K races; tug-of-war; kilted mile; junior athletics; children's games; Hawaiian events (lawn bowling, spear throwing). Vendors. Contact: Hawaiian Scottish Association, 2615 S. King St., Suite 206, Honolulu, HI 96826.

ILLINOIS

Chicago—Chicago Highland Games; one day; last weekend in July. Established 1982. Held in Grant Park on the city's lakefront. Heavy events (s): invitational professional; amateur. Dancing (s).

Solo piping (s). Bands (s): all classes. Other events: farmer's walk. Clans and Scottish organizations. Vendors. Ceilidh. Contact: Bill Currie, president, PipeFest USA, Inc., 1728 N. Wells St., Chicago, IL 60614.

The first North American Invitational Bagpipe, Drum and Dance competitions attracted over 500 competitors. The emphasis was on pipe bands, and the travel and prize monies attested to the city's desire to draw the best. And it did: six Grade I Canadian bands performed at the inaugural ceilidh. In 1984 20 bands competed for prize monies totaling over $30,000. This is the premiere MWPBA event.

MAINE

Trenton—Acadian Scottish Festival; two days; third weekend in July. Established 1980. Held near Acadia National Park. Heavy events: amateur; caber, hammer, sheaf. Bands for concert. Other events: tug-of-war; tomahawk event; piping and drumming workshops. Demonstrations: dancing; solo piping; drumming; fiddling; sheepdogs; eighteenth-century encampment. Clans and Scottish organizations. Vendors. Ceilidh. Tartan ball. Contact: Thom J. White, Rte. 3, Box 169, Trenton, ME 04605.

Waterville—Highland Games and Gathering of the Clans; one day; second weekend in August. Established 1979. Heavy events: amateur; stone, sheaf, caber. Dancing (s). Solo piping: amateur. Pipe bands for performance. Clarsach. Other events: tug-of-war; children's games; women's and juniors' heavy events. Demonstrations: Scottish country dancing; fiddling; sheepdogs; eighteenth-century encampment. Scottish animals on view. Clans and Scottish organizations. Vendors. Contact: John D. Murray, president, "Am Fasgadh," R.F.D. 3, Box 39, Saco, ME 04072. Member ASGF.

MARYLAND

Fair Hill—Colonial Highland Gathering and International Open Sheep Dog Trials; two days; third Friday and Saturday in May. Established 1960. Heavy events (s): invitational professional heptathlon. Dancing (s): Eastern U.S. Closed Championships.

Solo piping (s). Special Friday evening competitions: Boreraig piobaireachd, Clan Donald Silver Quaich piobaireachd (invitational), and St. Andrew's Society of Baltimore Silver Charger MSR. Solo drumming and drum major (s). Bands (s): Eastern U.S. Pipe Band Championships. Fiddling (s): Eastern U.S. Fiddling Championship. Other events: International Sheep Dog Trials; sheep to shawl contest. Clans and Scottish organizations. Vendors. Contact: Colonial Highland Gathering, 20 Wakefield Dr., Newark, DE 19711. Member ASGF.

Looking out across the gently sloping, mist-hung fields of Fair Hill in the morning puts one in mind of the hills of bonnie Scotland. Hearing the pipes on every side and seeing black-faced sheep being rounded up by border collies adds to the illusion. This Games is held at DuPont Steeplechase Race Course, which provides ample grandstand seating in front of the dancing and heavy events area.

Huntingtown—Celtic Festival of Southern Maryland; one day; last Saturday in April. Established 1979. Heavy events (s): professional heptathlon. Highland, Irish step, and Scottish country dancing demonstrations. Solo piping (s). Drumming: all grades, beginner. Pipe bands for performance. Fiddling (s): Southern Maryland Scottish Fiddling Championship. Other events: children's games; kilted mile; Celtic two-mile footrace; parade of tartans; folk music. Clans and Scottish organizations. Vendors. Ceilidh. Contact: P.O. Box 209, Prince Frederick, MD 20678. Member ASGF.

The Games site is an open field at King's Landing YMCA Camp, about an hour south of Washington, D.C., nestled on the Patuxent River. Ospreys and hawks circle above, seemingly oblivious to the intruding sounds of the pipes, drums, fiddles, and numerous other musical devices. This is truly a homey, local affair; something is always happening on the performing stage, and there are all sorts of Scottish—as well as other Celtic—goodies to sample.

MASSACHUSETTS

Pittsfield—Berkshire Indoor Highland Games; one day; second Saturday in May. Established 1984. Heavy events. Dancing (s). Solo piping (s) and drumming (s); drum major. Bands (s). Other events: children's games (including caber). Ceilidh. Contact: Berkshire Indoor Highland Games, Inc., 78 Northumberland Rd., Pittsfield, MA 01201. Member ASGF.

This Games, held at Berkshire Community College, was formed at the merging of the Williamstown Gathering, a piping competition that was started in 1978, and the Scotia Highland Dancing Association competition, started in 1966.

MICHIGAN

Alma—Alma Highland Festival and Games; two days; last weekend in May. Established 1968. Heavy events: amateur; caber, light stone, sheaf (using 25-pound bag of Michigan beans). Dancing (s): broadsword team competition; Midwestern U.S. Closed Regional Championships. Dance workshops held in July and November. Solo piping (s): amateur and open jig, MSR, piobaireachd. Drumming (s); drum major. U.S. Open Pipe Band Championships. Fiddling (s): Great Lakes Scottish Fiddling Championship. Other events: soccer; road run; farmer's walk; sheepdog demonstrations. Clans. Vendors. Ceilidh. Teen dance. Scottish pub and dance. Contact: P.O. Box 506, Alma, MI 48801.

Alma calls itself "Scotland USA," and on the Games weekend the population of 10,000 is far outnumbered by those of Scottish descent or design who gather for the event. The Games are held at Alma College, which has a pipe band and offers courses in Highland dancing, piping, and drumming. Use of the dormitories is available for a nominal fee during the weekend. As a prelude to the opening ceremonies, a large parade of pipe bands, marching bands, floats, and honored guests (including such regulars as the governor of Michigan, Alma's Queen of Scots, Miss Michigan, and Miss Dominion of Canada) winds its way through the town to the Games site. Because of its location, Alma attracts both U.S. and Canadian competitors, including several Grade I Canadian bands. A crafts fair and a juried art fair are held at the college during the Games weekend, which closes a statewide promotional effort called Michigan Week.

Detroit—St. Andrew's Highland Gathering; one day; second Saturday in June. Second oldest current Games in the United States; established 1867. Held on Bob-Lo Island. Heavy events demonstrations. Dancing (s): Great Lakes Open Championships (not held during Games). Solo piping and drumming (s). Bands (s). Contact: Alec Bryce, 18044 Santa Barbara, Detroit, MI 48221.

My grandparents came to this country from Dundee and settled in Mount Clemens, near Detroit. My father recalls going to the Games on Bob-Lo Island when he was a young boy. The crowds were still rather large then. This Games experienced a decline in participation and attendance and lived through changes of site, but refused to die.

MINNESOTA

St. Paul—Scottish Country Fair; one day; first Saturday in May. Established 1972. Heavy events: amateur; caber, sheaf, hammer, stone. Dancing (s): Lakes and Prairie Closed Championships; separate competition for Macalester students. Solo piping (s) and drumming (s). Bands (s): Grades I-IV. Other events: tug-of-war; parade of tartans. Sheepdog demonstrations. Clans and Scottish organizations. Vendors. Contact: Madison Sheely, coordinator, Macalester College, 1600 Grand Ave., St. Paul, MN 55105.

Macalester College, site of this Games, offers courses in piping, drumming, and Highland dancing. The Games attracts local artisans who sell their wares—everything from Indian beads to oil paintings. As part of a Minnesota Scottish weekend, the St. Andrew's Society of Minnesota and the Twin Cities Scottish Club sponsor a golf tournament on Friday morning, a Heather and Thistle Ball on Friday evening, and a kirking of tartans on Sunday.

MISSOURI

Kansas City—Kansas City Highland Games; one day; third weekend in April. Established 1968. Heavy events: amateur; caber, stone, stone over bar, ball and chain, sheaf. Dancing (s): Midwest Open Championships; Midwest Regional Competition.

Solo piping: open and amateur; Grades I–V; quartet competition. Drumming: amateur and open; drum major; drum corps. Shrine bands: Grades I–IV. Fiddling demonstration. Other events: 10K run; tug-of-war. Clans. Vendors. Ceilidh. Contact: Kansas City Highland Games, P.O. Box 1112, Shawnee Mission, KS 66222.

St. Louis—Gateway Highland Games; one day; third Saturday in June. Established 1984. Heavy events (s). Dancing (s). Solo piping (s) and drumming (s). Bands (s). Other events: bicycle race. Clans and Scottish organizations. Vendors. Contact: David Campbell, chairman, 304 LeChateau Village, 10411 Clayton Rd., St. Louis, MO 63131.

Games were held in St. Louis in 1976 and 1977. Proceeds from this Games benefit the St. Louis Variety Club, an international organization that benefits children's charities. Wooed by the contagious enthusiasm of chairman David Campbell, major corporations and businesses have rallied to help this Games succeed in its philanthropic mission. This gathering attracts major competitors in all events. Bicycle racing, a traditional event at Games in Scotland, is held, and local professional athletes are featured as amateur competitors.

NEW HAMPSHIRE

Loon Mountain—New Hampshire Highland Games; two days; second weekend after Labor Day. Established 1976. Heavy events: amateur; all except hammer; Loon Mountain Stone Carry (240 pounds). Dancing (s). Solo piping (s): awarding of MacCrimmon Quaich. Drumming (s); drum major; drum corps. Bands (s): Grades II–IV. Fiddling (s): New England Scottish Fiddling Championship. Clarsach. Other events: children's games; haggis hurling; tug-of-war; kilted mile on a mountain course; eighteenth-century reenactment by the 74th Regiment of Foot, Argyll Highlanders; Sunday worship service with pipe band and kirking of tartans. Scottish country dancing demonstrations. Clans and Scottish organizations. Vendors. Ceilidh. Scottish country dance ball with Scottish country dance band. Contact: P.O. Box 130, Cambridge, MA 02238-0130. Member ASGF.

New England in the fall is ecstasy, and this gathering is held in the White Mountain National Forest at the Loon Mountain Recreational Center off the Kancamagus Highway, said to be one of the most beautiful roadways in the country. Loon Mountain boasts New Hampshire's longest aerial tramway ride—7,000 feet—which affords breathtaking views of the area. All ski lodge facilities are used by the Games—even the fireplace. There is a country store in the facility where one may buy local crafts and pure maple syrup. The logistics of the Games separate the events, but everyone seems to find his way to the lodge eventually.

NEW YORK

Altamont—Capital District Scottish Games; one day; Saturday before Labor Day weekend. Established 1978 (original Games held 1946–69). Heavy events (s): professional; all but hammer. Dancing (s): hosted 1983 Northeastern U.S. Regional Championships. Solo piping (s) and drumming (s); drum major. Bands (s): Grades II–IV; Northeastern U.S. Pipe Band Championships. Fiddling (s): Northeastern U.S. Scottish Fiddling Championships. Other events: children's games; tug-of-war; Irish step dancing; bonniest knees contest (with blindfolded judges); sheepdog demonstration; Scottie dog contest; parade of tartans; U.S. finals of World Haggis Hurl Championship. Clans and Scottish organizations. Vendors. Competitors' ceilidh. Contact: 40 Terrace Ave., Albany, NY 12203. Member ASGF.

Altamont is a small town near New York's capital, Albany, in the expanse that separates the Adirondacks from the Catskill Mountains. The site of this Games, Altamont Fairgrounds, provides a lovely rural setting. In the morning, the surrounding hills are nearly hidden by low-hanging mist. From the large grandstand one may take in most of the activities of the day. There is a large, tree-covered picnic area. The pipe band championships attract many excellent bands.

Fort Ticonderoga—Memorial Scottish Gathering; two days; second weekend in July. Established 1978. Heavy events: professional heptathlon. Dancing (s). Solo piping (s) and drumming (s). Bands (s): Grades III and IV. Other events: tug-of-war; Mt.

Defiance Hillclimb; children's games; torchlite military tattoo. Contact: Star Rte. 197, Schuyler Falls, NY 12985.

Glens Falls—Glens Falls Gaelic Festival; one day; last Saturday in July. Established 1977. Piping and drumming workshops held throughout the year by the sponsor, Glens Falls Academy of Gaelic Art. Heavy events: amateur; caber, hammer, stone, sheaf, 28d. Dancing (s). Solo piping (s) and drumming (s); drum major. Bands (s): Grades II–IV. Other events: children's games; foot races; Irish step dancing; parade of tartans. Clans and Scottish organizations. Vendors. Ceilidh. Contact: Harold Kirkpatrick, 492 Glen St., Glens Falls, NY 12801.

Liverpool—Central New York Scottish Games; one day; second Saturday in August. Established 1934. Heavy events: professional and amateur; all but hammer. Dancing (s). Solo piping (s) and drumming (s); drum major. Bands (s): Grades II–IV. Other events: tug-of-war; children's games. Clans and Scottish organizations. Vendors. Ceilidh. Contact: James D. Engle, chairman, 133 Weymouth Rd., Syracuse, NY 13205. Member ASGF.

Sponsored by Clan Douglas #232, Order of Scottish Clans, and the Syracuse Pipe Band, this Games is the fifth oldest current Games in the United States. It attracts a large number of major dancing and piping competitors despite the fact that it is held on the same day as the Fergus, Ontario, Games. The village of Liverpool is adjacent to Syracuse. The Games site is a large park, Griffin Field, on Lake Onondaga. There are plenty of bleachers from which to survey the field. The year I was there— and I hope this is a tradition—the spectators all joined hands for the singing of "Auld Lang Syne" at the end of the closing ceremony.

Old Westbury—Long Island Scottish Clans Association Scottish Games; one day; fourth Saturday in August. Established 1961. Heavy events: amateur; caber, stone. Dancing (s). Solo piping (s). Pipe bands for performance. Other events: day-long soccer; foot races; tug-of-war; eighteenth-century encampment demonstration by the 42nd Royal Highland Regiment of Foot. Clans and

Scottish organizations. Vendors. Contact: Hamish A. Cowie, Games secretary, 132 Cowie Rd., Commack, NY 11725. Member ASGF.

The setting of this Games, like that of the Charleston (South Carolina) Games, is an old manor home with exquisite gardens. Westbury Gardens is listed on the National Register of Historic Places; the gardens are formal, fashioned after those popular in eighteenth-century English manor houses. In the early 1920s the Prince of Wales was entertained here while in the area for a polo meet. This landscape provides a beautiful backdrop for the Long Island Games. All of the Games activities take place on the vast front lawn of the house. Picnic tables abound and piping platforms are interspersed in the shade of the huge linden and beech trees that cover parts of the lawn.

NORTH CAROLINA

Linville—Grandfather Mountain Highland Games and Gathering of the Scottish Clans; two days; first full weekend after the Fourth of July. Established 1956. Sponsored by Scottish Heritage USA, Inc. Heavy events (s): professional heptathlon; amateur. Dancing (s): Atlantic International Championships. Solo piping (s) and drumming (s). Fiddling (s). Pipe bands for performance. Other events: kilted mile; tug-of-war; mountain marathon; sheepdog demonstration; only U.S. Games with AAU track and field events; Sunday worship service with kirking of tartans; parade of clans (over 100 represented); torch procession. Clans and Scottish organizations. Vendors. Two ceilidhs. Tartan ball. Contact: Martha B. Chase, Box 1676, Johnson City, TN 37605. Member ASGF.

Grandfather Mountain offers the largest assemblage of tartans in this country. The setting provides incredible atmosphere— rugged terrain softened by huge rhododendrons. This is America's Braemar. This is the Games to attend to see everybody who is anybody in the Scottish world. Space precludes band competitions and almost precludes walking as well. Arrive early to park on the mountain; shuttlebuses transport visitors to MacRae Meadow. The two-day Games stretches out to four days if one comes for the Thursday picnic and torch procession and for the Friday night ceilidh or Scottish country dance gala.

Red Springs—Flora Macdonald Highland Games; two days; first weekend in October. Established 1977. Heavy events (s): professional and amateur; stone, two hammers, 28d, 56d, 56h, caber. Dancing (s). Solo piping (s) and drumming (s). Bands (s): Carolina Pipe Band Championships. Other events: children's games; tug-of-war; foot races; sheepdog demonstration; Revolutionary War battle reenactment. Clans. Vendors. Tartan ball. Contact: Flora Macdonald Highland Games, Inc., P.O. Box 547, Red Springs, NC 28377. Member ASGF.

There is something about this Games that makes it special to many participants and spectators alike, but it is difficult to pinpoint what that is. Perhaps it is the rural setting—the welcoming morning glories clinging to the crops edging the dirt lane, the huge open field encircled by thick pine forests. Perhaps it is the down-home feeling evidenced by the folks there or being able to buy homemade apple cider and bread. Perhaps it is the crispness in the air on a lazy fall day in the South. Perhaps it is knowing that the Games are named for Scotland's dear heroine, Flora Macdonald (two of her sons are buried in the area). Perhaps it is a combination of all of these things. Whatever it is, a feeling of closeness unites the crowd, making this Games an eagerly anticipated event for many.

Waxhaw—Gathering of the Clans and Scottish Games; one day; last Saturday in October. Established 1980. Held in Waxhaw Amphitheater. Heavy events: amateur; stone, caber, sheaf, hammer, 28d. Dancing (s). Solo piping (s) and drumming (s); quartet (s). Pipe bands for performance. Other events: foot races; bonniest knees; tug-of-war; parade of clans for a challenge cup. Clans. Vendors. Ceilidh. Contact: The Scottish Society of the Waxhaws, Ltd., Robert Burns Station, P.O. Box 143, Waxhaw, NC 28173. Member ASGF.

Waxhaw is a sketch of a town, not big or busy enough for a stoplight, but full of antique shops. Its active Scottish society sponsors the Games. The society received quite a bit of publicity in 1981 for holding a mock Royal Wedding at the amphitheater (which is a large, natural outdoor theater) and inviting the Lord

Chamberlain in England to attend. He sent his regrets, but even this response generated a lot of excitement and media coverage. The Waxhaw gathering is small, but spirited; when I attended in 1981, it happened to be Halloween, and the bandsmen wore Halloween masks. The Games day ends with a Scottish barbecue at the site.

OHIO

Oberlin—Ohio Scottish Games; one day; fourth Saturday in June. Established 1978. Heavy events (s): professional heptathlon (North American Heptathlon Championship); amateur. Dancing (s): Ohio Open Dancing Championships. Hosted 1983 U.S. Inter-Regional Highland Dancing Championships. Solo piping (s): awarding of MacCrimmon Quaich. Drumming (s). Bands (s): Grades II–IV. Clarsach. Other events: kilted mile. Demonstrations: Scottish country dancing; sheepdogs; Highland cattle. Clans. Vendors. Ceilidh (at Games site, Friday evening). Contact: Ohio Scottish Games, P.O. Box 21169, Cleveland, OH 44121. Member ASGF.

When I attended the Ohio Games in 1981, they were held at Wooster College, another school that offers courses in the Scottish arts. The Games' new site is Oberlin College. This is one of the most ambitious Games I have encountered; they want to grow and are planning to offer major competitions in all areas. For example, to attract major athletes, they have instituted the North American Heptathlon Championship. The Ohio Scottish Arts School is held at Oberlin College the week after the Games.

OKLAHOMA

Tulsa—Tulsa Scottish Games and Gathering; one day; fall date, usually October. Established 1980. Heavy events: open and amateur; heptathlon (28h replaces 56h). Dancing (s). Solo piping. Guest band for performance. Other events: tug-of-war; beer keg toss; children's games; parade of tartans; Scottish culinary contest; kirking of tartans. Clans. Vendors. Ceilidh. Contact: Tulsa Scottish Games, Inc., 1733 S. Fulton, Tulsa, OK 74112. Member ASGF.

OREGON

Athena—Athena Caledonian Games; one day; second Saturday in July. Established 1899; revived 1976. Heavy events: professional; stone, hammer, 56d, 56h, sheaf, caber. Dancing (s). Solo piping under direction of British Columbia Pipers' Association. Other events: tug-of-war; fun run; women's caber and rolling pin toss; children's games; tattoo. Clans and Scottish organizations. Vendors. Barbecue. Ceilidh (street dance). Contact: Donald R. Duncan, P.O. Box 600, Athena, OR 97813.

This Games was originally held in 1899 under the auspices of the Umstella County Caledonian Society. The gathering was held until World War I. In 1976 it was revived by the Athena Chamber of Commerce. This is not a large Games; admission is free, except for the evening tattoo. Trailer and motor home accommodations are available, as is free beer for all spectators wearing the kilt. Every effort is made to make the Games convenient for the competitors, who are drawn from Oregon, Washington, California, British Columbia, Alberta and, often, Scotland. Piping and dancing events are held under the shade of trees in the city park; the heavy events are contested at the high school athletic field. A swimming pool is available for all competitors and spectators.

Portland—Portland Highland Games; one day; third Saturday in July. Established 1952. Held at David Douglas High School. Heavy events: amateur; stone, hammer, 28d, sheaf, caber. Dancing (s): special Oregon-only competition, baby through adult; Inverness Challenge Shield awarded to best open dancer under 16. Hosted 1982 U.S. Inter-Regional Highland Dancing Championships. Solo piping (s): professional piobaireachd held Friday evening. Drumming: novice through professional. Bands (s). Other events: ladies' frying pan toss; pillow fight; hop-step and jump; tug-of-war. Demonstrations: Scottish country dancing; sheepdogs. Clans and Scottish organizations. Vendors. Ceilidh. Contact: Dixie McKendrick, president, 4242 S.W. South Shore Blvd., Lake Oswego, OR 97034.

PENNSYLVANIA

Devon—Delco Scottish Games; one day; third Saturday in June. Established 1967. Held at Devon Show Grounds. Workshop weekend held in February. Heavy events (s): professional heptathlon. Dancing (s). Solo piping (s) and drumming (s): amateur snare, open tenor and snare; drum major; drum corps. Bands (s): Grades II–IV. Friday evening piobaireachd competition sponsored by the St. Andrew's Society of Philadelphia. Other events: puppet show and games for children. Demonstrations: fiddling; Scottish country dancing; crafts. Clans and Scottish organizations. Vendors. Contact: 181 Foxcatcher Ln., Media, PA 19063. Member ASGF.

The Devon Show Grounds offers plenty of grandstand seating on both sides, and as I have been told is the case at many Games in Scotland, most of the events take place in the center arena for all to see. This creates a crowd involvement not often felt at Games. The athletes are not fond of throwing from the sandy surface, but the electricity in the air keeps them moving! The vendors are located in a shaded area that is crowded throughout the day. The "mushroom capital of the world," Kennett Square, PA, is nearby, and one may try French fried mushrooms at this Games. This is another good Games to attend if one wants to see many (usually more than 20) pipe bands. On three occasions I have had the pleasure of witnessing the renowned Pipes and Drums and Military Brass Band of the 48th Highlanders of Canada. The annual weekend workshop sponsored by the Games in February is one of the largest and most popular workshops in the country.

Ligonier—Ligonier Highland Games; one day; first Saturday after Labor Day. Established 1959. Heavy events (s): professional heptathlon. Dancing (s). Solo piping (s) and drumming (s): Eastern U.S. Amateur Solo Piping and Drumming Championships; drum major; drum corps. Bands (s): Grades II–IV. Fiddling (s): Allegheny Mountain Championship. Other events: tug-of-war. Demonstrations: sheepdogs; Scottish weaving and dyeing.

Clans and Scottish organizations. Vendors. Ceilidh. Contact: 1208 24th Ave., Altoona, PA 16601. Member ASGF.

The Games site is Idlewild Park, a family amusement park situated in a heavily wooded area. Though the Games date is past the park's season, Idlewild opens its concessions and rides for the weekend, much to the delight of the children.

Pipersville—Bucks County Scottish Country Fair; one day; third Saturday in September. Established 1974. Held on 22 acres of countryside. Heavy events: caber, hammer, stone, sheaf. Dancing demonstrations. Piping: bands for performance by invitation. Clans and Scottish organizations. Vendors. Ceilidh. Contact: P.O. Box 157, Warrington, PA 18976.

This fair is sponsored by the First Highland Watch of Pennsylvania as an educational and entertainment affair. It has an average attendance of 8,000.

SOUTH CAROLINA

Charleston—Charleston Scottish Games and Highland Gathering; one day; third Saturday in September. Established 1972. Heavy events (s): professional heptathlon; six amateur events. Dancing (s). Solo piping (s) and drumming (s). Bands (s): Grades III and IV. Other events: Highland wrestling; tug-of-war; tam o'shanter run; children's games; sheepdog demonstration; kirking of tartans Sunday morning in historic First Scots Presbyterian Church. Clans and Scottish organizations. Vendors. Tartan ball. Contact: President, Scottish Society of Charleston, P.O. Box 10932, Charleston, SC 29411. Member ASGF.

A National Historic Landmark, Middleton Place on the Ashley River is the other stately home Games site (see Old Westbury, NY). Middleton Place Gardens, begun in 1741, contains the oldest landscaped gardens in the United States. Three of the first four camellia plants brought to this country from France still bloom in the gardens. The main portion of the house was burned during the Civil War (also referred to in that part of the country as the War of Northern Aggression), but the large and lovely original guest wing still stands and is furnished with period furniture. The vast open lawn in front of the house serves as the athletics area and is surrounded by the tents of the clans and other organizations. Giant live oaks with fluffy droopings of Spanish moss shade the dancing platform. There is plenty of space to picnic and bask in the late summer sun. In the stables area are horses, goats, ducks, and chickens, which delight children of all ages. Charleston, full of lovely historic homes and sites, is the home of the first St. Andrew's Society in this country (1729). It is also the home of The Citadel, a military college that has its own tartan and its own pipe band, now under the direction of Pipe Major Sandy Jones.

TENNESSEE

Gatlinburg—Great Smoky Mountains-Gatlinburg Highland Games; two days; third weekend in May. Established 1982. Heavy events: amateur heptathlon. Dancing (s). Solo piping (s) and drumming (s). Bands (s): Grades II–IV. Other events: Highland wrestling; tug-of-war; kilted mile; women's kilted mile; clan competitions; children's games; haggis hurling; bonniest knees contest (with blindfolded judges); sheepdog demonstrations. Clans and Scottish organizations. Vendors. Ceilidh. Tartan ball. Scottish country dance. Contact: P.O. Box 750, Gatlinburg, TN 37738. Member ASGF.

In the active resort town of Gatlinburg, one can easily be distracted from the grandeur of the surrounding mountains. To fully appreciate that Gatlinburg is called "the gateway to the Smoky Mountains," just ride the 344 feet to the top of the Space Needle at night; the deep darkness of the mountains completely engulfs and silences the hub below. Mills Park, the Games site, is at the bottom of a hill, which allows natural and easy viewing of the entire area.

Before this gathering, Scottish Highland Games in this area were an unfamiliar phenomenon. Billie Bethel and her committee worked long and hard to make the first Games an affair to remember. The inaugural Games opened with a parade through the town. Thirteen professional athletes, including two from Canada and one from California, gathered. Competitions were held in all events, and the clans rallied in large numbers to help launch the premiere Games. Colin Grant-Adams of Oban was (and continues to be) the official Games vocalist. Sunday morning worship services and kirking of the tartans were followed by children's games and amateur athletics.

Since Gatlinburg is only about 35 miles from Knoxville, some of the competitors from the first Games provided a demonstration at the 1982 World's Fair on the following Monday. The Chimney Rock Highlanders, headed by Drum Major Joe Bailey and six Highland dancers, led eight professional athletes and one brave amateur (Bill Schmidt, director of sports for the fair and winner of a bronze medal in the javelin in the 1972 Olympics, who had never worn a kilt or tried any of the heavy events before) to a designated area. Thousands of visitors were treated to the Highland fling, seann triubhas, sword dance, sheaf toss, stone throw, and caber as I, serving as announcer, explained to the puzzled spectators what was happening. It was a great day for the Games and for the tartan!

TEXAS

Dallas—Dallas Scottish Highland Games; one day; third Saturday in September. Established 1972. Unsanctioned competitions in athletics, dancing, piping and drumming, and bands. Clans and Scottish organizations. Ceilidh. Contact: Robert C. Forbes, 8523 San Leandro Dr., Dallas, TX 75218.

Houston—Houston Highland Games; one day; second Saturday in May. Established 1967. Heavy events (s): professional—heavy stone, 28d, 56d, 56h, caber; amateur—heavy stone, sheaf, caber. Dancing (s): Southwestern Regional Championships; Southwestern United States Championships; Texas-Oklahoma Closed Championships. Solo piping (s): Southwestern Championship Solo Piping (open). Drumming (s): Southwestern Championship Solo Drumming (open). Bands (s): Grades II–IV; Southwestern Pipe Band Championship. Other events: children's games; baking contest; Irish dance competition. Demonstrations: Scottish country dancing; Morris dancers; court dancers; clog hoppers; sheepdogs; reenactment of Viking raid on Scottish Highlands. Clans and Scottish organizations. Vendors. Contact: Houston

Highland Games Association, 4210 Sable Ct., Houston, TX 77014. Member ASGF.

The Games site is St. Thomas Episcopal School, a private school with an enrollment of approximately 700 students, kindergarten through twelfth grade. The school is unique in that Highland dancing is a requirement for all students through seventh grade. The late Stewart Smith, a former Scottish champion who taught in this country for many years, was a teacher here. The school also has its own pipe band. The Games' open piping competition is held indoors on Friday night; the drumming, band, and amateur solo piping events are held outdoors on Saturday. Highland dancing is held in an enclosed courtyard.

Lubbock—West Texas Highland Games; two days; third weekend in June. Established 1982. Small, local Games with demonstrations in all events. Scottish activities are relatively new to this area but have drawn interest rapidly. Clan involvement is growing; Scottish heritage clubs have been formed in Lubbock and nearby Amarillo. The Games is expected to grow, too. There is a golf tournament Friday afternoon, a dinner and ceilidh Friday evening, and a kirking of tartans on Sunday. Contact: P.O. Box 2081, Lubbock, TX 79408.

Plano—Plano Highland Games/Cityfest; one day; last Saturday in September. Established 1984. Festival including Highland and Scottish country dancing, pipe bands, fiddlers, Scottish harp, folk singers, Scottish terrier contest; other nationalities represented. Clans and Scottish organizations. Tartan ball. Contact: Box 304, Plano, TX 75074.

Salado—Texas Scottish Gathering and Highland Games; two days; second full weekend in November. Established 1961. Heavy events. Dancing (s). Solo piping (s) and drumming; drum major (s). Bands (s). Other events: Texas Heritage Sheepdog Trials; Sunday morning worship service with kirking of tartans; parade of tartans; kilted mile. Clans. Vendors, including museum-owned bagpipe shop at Games. Two ceilidhs. Contact: Central Texas Area Museum, Inc., Salado, TX 76571.

When this Games started over 20 years ago, there was not one bagpipe known in Texas. The organizers were able to get two pipers and one dancer for their program. Now there is much Scottish interest in the area, and the Games attract large numbers of competitors. America's only gold medalist, Michael Cusack, is the piping chairman. The Games are held on the village green in this former stagecoach town. On Sunday morning, a pipe band parades through the town, collecting people (a la the Pied Piper) who follow the band back to the green for the church service. The Games' sponsor, the Central Texas Area Museum, has a Scottish research library. Salado, which was founded by Scots, was featured in a recent 24-part Scottish television series called "Scotland's Story."

UTAH

Payson—Payson Scottish Festival; one day; last Saturday in August. Established 1984. Heavy events: caber, hammer, sheaf. Dancing: Payson Sword of Scotland presented to most promising dancer. Solo piping. Bands. Other events: women's frypan toss and rolling pin throw; children's games (three-legged race, sack race, wheelbarrow race, caber, tug-of-war); Friday golf tournament. Clans and Scottish organizations. Vendors. Contact: 545 E. 300 South, Payson, UT 84651.

This Games is held in the city park. At the bandstand during the day, entertainment is presented to acquaint spectators with all phases of the Games. The day opens with a parade up Main Street and ends with a pot-luck barbecue. All participants are given passes to the city pool, located at the Games site.

Salt Lake City—Utah Scottish Festival and Highland Games; one day; mid-June. Established 1974. Highland dancing, piping, and drumming school held week prior to Games. Heavy events: amateur; stone, caber, hammer, 28d, 56h, sheaf. Dancing (s). Solo piping (s) and drumming (s); drum major (s). Trios (s). Bands (s). Fiddling. Other events: races; women's stone; tug-of-war; haggis hurling; children's games; Scottish baking contest. Clans and Scottish organizations. Vendors. Contact: Utah Scottish Association, 483 8th Ave., Salt Lake City, UT 84103.

VERMONT

Essex Junction—Vermont International Highland Games; one day; third Saturday in June. Established 1984. Heavy events: amateur. Dancing. Solo piping (s). Bands (s). Vermont International Fiddling Competition. Clarsach. Clans. Vendors. Contact: P.O. Box 692, Essex Junction, VT 05452. Member ASGF.

Quechee—Quechee Scottish Festival; one day; third Saturday in August. Established 1972. Heavy events: amateur; caber, sheaf, stone, hammer. Piping and drumming. Bands for performance. Other events: kilted mile; ladies' rolling pin toss; egg/spoon race; children's games; rugby; New England Area Invitational Sheepdog Trials; Scottish deerhound coursing. Demonstrations: Highland and Scottish country dancing; fiddling. Clans and Scottish organizations. Vendors. Contact: Scotland-by-the-Yard, Quechee, VT 05059.

I have not been to Quechee when the Games were going on, but I have visited the site. It is lovely! Quechee is a very small town bisected by a river. Nearby is 163-foot Quechee Gorge, called "Vermont's Little Grand Canyon." The Games site is Quechee Polo Field, which is flanked by woods and located across the road from the river.

VIRGINIA

Alexandria—Virginia Scottish Games; two days; fourth weekend in July. Established 1974. Heavy events (s): professional and amateur heptathlon. U.S. Highland Heptathlon Championship. Dancing (s): hosted the first U.S. Inter-Regional Highland Dancing Championships in 1981. Solo piping (s): Eastern U.S. Open Individual Piping Championship. Drumming (s); drum major; drum salute. Bands (s): Grades II-IV. Fiddling (s): Potomac Valley Championship; U.S. National Scottish Fiddling Championship. Clarsach: U.S. National Scottish Harp Competition. Other events: celebrity haggis hurl; children's games; cairn terrier field trials; tug-of-war. Demonstrations: Scottish country dancing; sheepdogs; Scottish deerhound coursing. Clans and Scottish organizations. Vendors. Ceilidh. Highland ball. Contact: President, Virginia Scottish Games Association, Box 1338, Alexandria, VA 22313. Member ASGF.

Alexandria is a city founded by Scots and is sister city to Dundee. This Games has rapidly grown in stature to become one of the major Scottish Highland Games in this country. It offers championships in athletics, piping, and fiddling. In 1984 the organizers inaugurated the clarsach competition. The Games site, Episcopal High School, has sprawling grounds that well accommodate the varied activities.

Norfolk—Tidewater Scottish Festival and Clan Gathering; two days; fourth Saturday in June. Established 1979. Heavy events (s): professional heptathlon; amateur. Dancing (s). Solo piping (s) and drumming (s). Bands (s). Fiddling (s). Other events: children's games; clan games; invitational haggis hurl; cairn terrier trials; worship service at Games. Demonstrations: Scottish country dancing; Scottish dog breeds; Scottish deerhound coursing. Clans and Scottish organizations. Vendors. Ceilidh. Contact: Tidewater Scottish Festival, P.O. Box 2000, Virginia Beach, VA 23452. Member ASGF.

Until 1984, when the event was moved to its new date and location, this Games was held in Virginia Beach. The new site, Norfolk Gardens By the Sea, is famous for the annual International Festival of Roses attended by many foreign ambassadors and dignitaries from the Washington, D.C., area. The atmosphere of this gathering is relaxed and informal. This is the only Games I have attended at which I have heard the pipes drowned out—in Virginia Beach, the jets flying over from nearby Oceana Naval Air Station won every time!

Williamsburg—Williamsburg Scottish Festival; one day; fourth weekend in September. Established 1978. Heavy events: amateur. Dancing (s). Bands (s). Children's games. Demonstrations: Scottish country dancing; sheepdogs. Clans and Scottish organizations. Vendors. Ceilidh. Contact: Secretary, Williamsburg Scottish Festival, Inc., P.O. Box 866, Williamsburg, VA 23187. Member ASGF.

The Games are held on the lovely campus of the College of

William and Mary, the second oldest college in the United States (founded in 1693). The Games are popular with competitors, who enjoy visiting the beautiful and historic restored area of Williamsburg (within walking distance of the college) along with getting another chance to compete.

WASHINGTON

Bellingham—Bellingham Highland Games; one day; first Saturday in June. Established 1960. Heavy events: amateur. Dancing (s). Solo piping and drumming [(s), British Columbia Pipers Association]. Bands [(s), Western Pipe Band Association]. Clans. Vendors. Contact: Isla Paterson, 639 Hunters Point Dr., Bellingham, WA 98225.

Everett—Pacific Northwest Highland Games; one day; mid-August. Established 1945. Sponsors piping school in mid-summer. Heavy events: amateur; caber. Dancing (s). Solo piping (s): novice, intermediate, professional. Drumming (s). Bands (s): Grades I–IV; marching and deportment awards given. Other events: children's games; tug-of-war; hay bale toss. Clans. Vendors. Ceilidh. Contact: Walter R. Clark, president, Seattle Highland Games Association, 16820 8th St., S.W., Seattle, WA 98166.

Spokane—Spokane Scottish Festival; one day; last weekend in July. Established 1958. Heavy events: stone, hammer, caber, sheaf. Dancing (s). Solo piping: all classes. Bands for performance. Other events: tug-of-war; keg toss. Clans. Vendors. Ceilidh. Contact: Mary Alward, 418 E. 11th St., Spokane, WA 99202.

This gathering was originated by the grandfather of Sandy Jones, director of piping at The Citadel, as a Scottish picnic in Coeur d'Alene, Idaho. A summer school for piping is held every summer at North Idaho College on the shores of Coeur d'Alene Lake.

Tacoma—Tacoma Highland Games; one day; mid-June. Established 1968. (Competitions open only to residents of or bands from Washington, Oregon, and Idaho.) Heavy events: stone, hammer, caber, sheaf. Dancing: all classes. Solo piping and drumming. Bands. Clans. Vendors. Contact: Joyce Denton, 241 E. 63rd St., Tacoma, WA 98404.

Vashon—Vashon Island Strawberry Festival and Highland Games; one day; second Saturday in July. Established 1984. Heavy events: heptathlon. Dancing. Solo piping. Bands. Fiddling demonstration. Other events: foot races. Clans. Vendors. Ceilidh. Contact: Dr. Sterling Hill, 10450 15th Ave., S.W., Seattle, WA 98146.

Vashon Island is a small farming community that has celebrated its annual Strawberry Festival for several years. In 1984 the Scottish element on the island decided to see how a Highland Games would go over in conjunction with this festivity. It was highly successful, and plans were made to build it into a major event. The first Games began with a march of clan leaders through the village to the Games site, a large open field (according to the founder, "a site like you would find in Scotland"). Although none of the events were sanctioned the first year, the events were run according to specifications. A highlight of the day was the presentation of a special award to the 80-year-old competitor who won the sheaf event with a toss of 20 feet.

Appendix
PRONUNCIATION GUIDE

(Note: *ch* is pronounced as in the German *Bach*)

Aboyne	a-boy´-yen
arasaid	ar´-a-sade
Boreraig	borr´-er-aig
canntaireachd	kan´-trock
ceilidh	kay´-lee
Ceol Beag	kell beck
Ceol Mor	kell more
clachneart	klack-nert´
clarsach	klar-sack´
crunluath	kroon-loo´-uh
gillie chalium	gillie kal´-um
piobaireachd	pee´-brock
quaich	kwayck
seann triubhas	shawn trues´
Sleat	slate
strathspey	strath-spay´
Tamnavulin	tam-nuh-voo´-lin
urlar	oolr´-lar

Select Bibliography

Allan, Charlie. *The Games: A Guide to Scotland's Highland Games.* Gartocharn, Alexandria, Scotland: Famedram Publishers Ltd., 1974.

Berthoff, Rowland. *British Immigrants in Industrial America, 1790–1950.* New York: Russell & Russell, 1968.

———. "Under the Kilt: Variations on the Scottish-American Ground." *Journal of American Ethnic History* 1:5–34.

Collinson, Francis. *The Traditional and National Music of Scotland.* London: Routledge & Kegan Paul Ltd., 1966.

Colquhoun, Sir Iain, and Machell, Hugh. *Highland Gatherings.* London: Heath Cranton Limited, 1927.

Halsall, Eric. *Sheepdogs: My Faithful Friends.* Cambridge, England: Patrick Stephens, 1980.

Highland Dancing: The Official Textbook of The Scottish Official Board of Highland Dancing. 3d ed. Edinburgh: Holmes McDougall Limited.

Hood, Evelyn M. *The Story of Scottish Country Dancing: The Darling Diversion.* London: William Collins Sons and Company, Ltd., 1980.

Keller, Phillip. *Lessons from a Sheepdog.* Waco, Texas: Word Books, 1983.

MacLellan, John. *The Pipers' Handbook.* London: Paterson's Publications Ltd., 1964.

MacNeill, Seumas. *Piobaireachd: Classical Music of the Highland*

Bagpipe. Edinburgh: British Broadcasting Corporation, 1968.

Morton, H. V. *In Search of Scotland.* London: Methuen & Company Ltd., 1932.

Redmond, Gerald. *The Caledonian Games of Nineteenth-Century America.* Rutherford, N.J. : Fairleigh Dickinson University Press, 1971.

———. *The Sporting Scots of Nineteenth-Century Canada.* Rutherford, N.J. : Fairleigh Dickinson University Press, 1982.

Vining, Elizabeth Gray. *Flora: A Biography.* New York: J. B. Lippincott Company, 1966.

Webster, David. *Scottish Highland Games.* Edinburgh: Reprographia, 1973.

Index

249